HPBooks

Simply Sensational
DESSERTS

Sharon Tyler Herbst

Sharon Tyler Herbst

Sharon Tyler Herbst attributes her natural enthusiasm for food to the day on which she was born—Thanksgiving! She grew up in a creative kitchen environment where innovation and experimentation was encouraged. Her mother is an excellent cook and her father has always been an appreciative audience. Together they helped instill and expand Sharon's flair for food. "It seems," says Sharon, "that all of my best memories are somehow involved with food!" She even met her husband Ron while apprenticing in the kitchens of a popular Denver restaurant.

Although she has been a culinary professional for over ten years, Sharon began as a short-story writer. Whenever she had writer's block, she found herself in the kitchen, whipping up something delicious and, hopefully, inspirational. It was a natural step to combine her two loves—cooking and writing! Sharon's first cookbook, *Breads*, was an immediate success and was honored with the prestigious Tastemaker Award, the Oscar of the cookbook world.

A popular cooking teacher, Sharon shares her talent and expertise through classes, television demonstrations and magazine articles. She has appeared on dozens of TV and radio shows across the country, and can frequently be seen on the nationally syndicated *Hour Magazine*, hosted by Gary Collins. Sharon is also on the Board of Directors of the International Association of Cooking Professionals, a worldwide organization with over 1,300 members in food-related professions.

Sharon and her husband Ron live near San Francisco—just across the Golden Gate Bridge in beautiful Marin County. Sharon credits Ron as her source of continual inspiration, support and encouragement, and relies on him as her number one "taster" when testing her recipes. They love to travel and always plan their itinerary around a region's restaurants.

A spontaneous and talented cook, Sharon enjoys sharing her enthusiasm, creativity and knowledge with others. In this book, she brings you a celebration of sweets—a spectacular array of desserts, both simple and elaborate. Dessert lovers everywhere will delight in the taste-tempting recipes, not to mention the raves they'll receive whenever they serve these luscious creations!

Acknowledgments

A heartfelt thanks to all my friends and relatives for their interest, support and eagerness to taste my recipes during the two years it took to create this book. And a special thanks to:

—my mother and father, Kay and Wayne Tyler, who had the style to have me on Thanksgiving Day at noon, and who instilled in me a love and zest for fine food;

—my editor, Roni Durie, who generously shared her talent, expertise and friendship, and whose continual patience and sense of humor were a constant source of strength;

—and, above all, my husband and best friend Ron for his unending support, patience and love. And for his always being there with his wonderful warm smile, words of inspiration and enthusiastic encouragement to *"go for it."*

Contents

ANOTHER BEST-SELLING VOLUME FROM HPBooks®

Publisher: Rick Bailey; Executive Editor: Randy Summerlin;
Editorial Director: Elaine R. Woodard; Editor: Veronica Durie;
Art Director: Don Burton; Book Design: Kathleen Koopman;
Production Coordinator: Cindy Coatsworth; Typography: Michelle Carter;
Director of Manufacturing: Anthony B. Narducci; Food Stylist: Carol Flood Peterson;
Assistant Food Stylist: Susan Draudt; Photography: Teri Sandison, Lightra Inc.

Published by HPBooks
A division of HPBooks, Inc.
P.O. Box 5367, Tucson, AZ 85703 602/888-2150
ISBN 0-89586-237-9
Library of Congress Catalog Card Number 86-80358
© 1986 HPBooks, Inc. Printed in the U.S.A
1st Printing

The author wishes to thank the following stores for providing accessories for use in the photography: Geary's, Beverly Hills, California; Bullock's, Beverly Center, Los Angeles, California; By Design, Beverly Center, Los Angeles, California and Le Kookery, Sherman Oaks, California.

For cover identification, see caption on page 6.

PERFECT ENDINGS

Was there ever a dish so completely designed to give pure pleasure as dessert? It teases, it contents, it soothes, it delights. It gives a meal a satisfying sense of completion. A fine dessert hints at luxury and indulgence as few other courses can. It's one of the richest gastronomical experiences possible.

For centuries, desserts were luxuries only the affluent could afford. This was because sugar, sometimes referred to as *white gold*, was scarce, and therefore expensive. Although Persia and ancient Arabia were cultivating sugar in the fourth century B.C., the Western world didn't know of it until the ninth century when the Moors conquered the Iberian peninsula.

Early sugar wasn't the granulated, alabaster substance we know today. Instead, it came in the form of large, solid loaves or blocks, ranging from off-white to light brown in color. Chunks of the rock-hard sucrose had to be chiseled off and ground to a powder with a mortar and pestle. Thankfully, sugar is no longer scarce or expensive, and those of us with a sweet tooth may indulge in desserts whenever we wish.

The actual word *dessert* comes from the French *desservir*, meaning *to clear the table*. Indeed, the table is usually cleared to make way for the grand finale of the meal. Dessert is an integral part of a menu and should be planned so its flavors both complement and harmonize with the other dishes served. It can be a simple, country ending like Peach-Berry Clafouti, page 106, baked and served in the same dish. Or, it can be a showstopping extravaganza, like the Tunnel-of-Fudge Cheesecake, page 54.

Any dessert, from simple to smashing, should have a degree of inherent elegance and be presented with pride. For this reason, it's especially important to buy the very best ingredients for your desserts. Cheap substitutions and imitation products always betray their value in the final result.

Various desserts intrigue and appeal to me at different times for different reasons. And this book records over 200 of my favorites. Each recipe has been personally tested and tasted—again and again—until it produced a perfect result. Some are quick and easy and can be made in a flash for last-minute company. Others require more elaborate preparation, but are worth the extra time because the results are so spectacular!

Shown on the preceding pages, starting at top right: Strawberry-Champagne Silk, page 121; Champagne-Mousse Pie, page 43; Paris-Brest with Praline Cream, page 140; Chocolate Truffles, page 125; Mocha Creams, page 134; Mousse-Filled Chocolate Cups, pages 130 and 131, with Caramel Crowns, page 148; Mosaic Fruit Tart, page 34; Raspberry-Ripple Cheese Mold, page 50; and Gâteau Noir, page 25.

Caramel Crown, page 148.

Celestial Cream, page 84.

I've included many recipes which can be made ahead. Frozen and refrigerated desserts are among my favorites because they're a cook's culinary security. Like money in the bank, they're always available when needed in times of entertaining emergency.

None of the following recipes are difficult, nor do they require special skills to re-create. The key, as with any type of cooking, is to read the recipe thoroughly before beginning, to be sure you have the necessary equipment and ingredients on hand. Usually, it's impossible to substitute one size pan for another, skim milk for cream, or cocoa powder for chocolate and expect the dessert to turn out as it should. It's equally important to follow a recipe's instructions. If a cheesecake recipe calls for overnight refrigeration, don't try to get by with a three-hour chill. The results may be passable, but the cheesecake won't have the proper creamy texture and may fall apart when you try to cut it!

The axiom, "you eat with your eyes first" was never truer than with dessert. The little eye-pleasing finishing touches you give your finales can be the simple difference between a good dessert and a spectacular one. A garnish doesn't have to be time-consuming or elaborate, but it should reflect the flavor of the dessert it adorns. It can be as simple as a single fresh raspberry set on top of an individual raspberry mousse, or as sensationally showy as Chocolate Leaves, page 126, or a Caramel Crown, page 148, and shown above.

One of my favorite ways to entertain a large group is to serve a simple, single-course meal—perhaps a wonderful bouillabaisse with warm loaves of homemade bread—and follow it with an elaborate dessert buffet; see the photo on pages 4 and 5. The groans of ecstasy when guests first see the spectacular array of scrumptious sweets is music to my ears! I try to include something for everyone and the desserts can range from little goodies, like White-Chocolate Swirls, page 68, and Kahlúa-Pecan Tartlets, page 40, to large spectaculars like Gâteau Noir, page 25, or Marvelous Mandarin Torte, page 23. For friends who like their desserts less sweet, I might offer Lemon-Cheese Torte, page 57, and Apple-Brie Tart, page 36. Pie aficionados could choose from the Champagne-Mousse Pie, page 43, Fudge-Truffle Pie, page 39, or Piña-Colada Pie, page 37. The list of possibilities is endless but, as you can see, there's no way anyone will leave our house unhappy.

A dessert should be an event—a celebration—a personal statement! It should end a meal with style and grace. A truly wonderful dessert—whether simple or elaborate—should dazzle the eye, excite the mind and delight the palate. It should be the quintessential pièce de résistance! I *love* dessert and have given whatever magic I possess to the following recipes. May you enjoy them—both in the preparation and in the plaudits you receive when you serve them.

CAKES & TORTES

One of my earliest and fondest childhood memories is that of standing on tiptoes, eyes level with the kitchen tabletop, gazing in awed and silent fascination as my mother formed magical swirls in a frosting as white and fluffy as a summer cloud. With the tip of a teaspoon and a flick of her graceful wrist, she would casually create wondrous peaks and valleys in the frosting, making sure none of her famous Lane Cake showed through. My tiny taste buds tingled with anticipation. The thought of waiting until after dinner for such a creation was made bearable only by the bribe of licking the bowl.

Little did I know at the time that I was not alone in my reverence for cake. From the earliest days of civilization, cake has played a pivotal role in symbolic and religious celebrations. In ancient times, Greeks and Egyptians considered it food for the gods. It was said that those who ate consecrated cake would be blessed with its magical benefits. Northern Europeans believed sanctified honey cakes offered at the winter solstice would please the gods and ensure a fruitful new year. And, of course, for centuries mankind has been using cakes in personal celebrations such as birthdays, weddings and anniversaries.

There are few experiences more satisfying than creating a perfect cake. And anyone who can read, follow a recipe and has an oven can do just that. But remember, baking a cake is not like making meatloaf—one cannot simply add ingredients according to availability or whim. Like a chemical formula, cakemaking requires a precise balance of ingredients, plus careful direction-following. With this in mind, you might want to take a few moments to read *Hints For Successful Cakes*, opposite.

One of my personal favorites is the incredibly tender and moist Chocolate Angel Food Cake. There's a simple secret to making perfect angel food—the egg whites must be beaten until *almost* stiff. Not beating the whites to their full capacity allows room for their expansion from steam produced within the cake while baking. The result is a heavenly light cake "fit for the gods." Overbeaten whites often deflate when confronted with the onslaught of oven heat, producing dense, tough angel food.

A must for those of you who are dedicated chocolate-lovers is the wickedly delicious Gâteau Noir, literally translated as *black cake*. This dark chocolate-sour-cream sensation is enrobed in a velvety chocolate cream and crowned with a chocolate doily. I created Gâteau Noir for a special dessert tasting conducted by a group of fellow cooking professionals. It was voted the most decadently delicious dessert of the day!

On the opposite end of the spectrum is the refreshingly tart and tangy Lively Lemon Pound Cake. Crushed lemon-drop candies create moist pockets of flavor excitement in this beautiful Bundt cake. A creamy lemon-cheese frosting provides sweet contrast, and additional crushed lemon candies are sprinkled on top for a sparkling finish!

The Ginger-Apple Roll delivers pure, melt-in-your-mouth pleasure. A delicate sheet of ginger sponge cake enfolds a filling of Calvados-scented cream bursting with apples, walnuts and crystallized ginger. This elegant cake has all the attributes of a perfect dessert—it's beautiful, delicious, and can be made in advance for ultimate entertaining ease!

Remember, even with careful recipe-following and precise oven regulation, your cake can only be as good as the ingredients that go into it. Buy the best, freshest ingredients you can afford and you're sure to produce cakes that will establish your reputation as a blue-ribbon baker.

Hints for Successful Cakes

● Read the recipe carefully to make sure you have all the necessary equipment and ingredients on hand. *Do not* make any substitutions. Any change in the basic proportions of a cake recipe will drastically alter the finished product.

● Assemble ingredients in the order they will be used. Allow refrigerated products to reach room temperature before using.

● Use the appropriate measuring cups; nested cups for dry ingredients and glass cups for liquid ingredients.

● It is essential to use the size pan specified in the recipe. Pans should be generously, but not excessively, greased. If you use too little shortening, a cake may stick to the pan and be difficult to remove after baking.

● When a recipe requires that a pan is greased and floured, grease pan then add about 1 tablespoon flour. Rotate pan to distribute flour, then tap out excess.

● Position oven rack in center of oven. Preheat oven 15 minutes. Use an oven thermometer for accurate oven temperature. If using glass cake dishes, reduce oven heat by 25F.

● Unless otherwise directed, do not sift flour. Measure by lightly spooning flour into measuring cup; level top with the flat edge of a knife.

● Place cake pans in oven so they have at least 2 inches between each other and sides of oven. If cakes are baked on 2 shelves, position them so that 1 does not sit directly beneath another. Do not bake more than 3 cake layers at a time in 1 oven. For good results, oven heat must circulate freely and evenly.

● Have a timer on hand. To allow for variations in ovens, test cake for doneness 5 minutes before minimum time indicated in recipe.

● Do not open oven door during first 15 minutes of baking time. If it is necessary to open oven after this time, do so gently. Sudden movement or temperature changes can cause a cake to fall.

● Each cake recipe in this book gives a test for doneness for that particular cake. In general, a cake is done when a wooden pick inserted in the center comes out clean.

● Unless a recipe indicates otherwise, cool cakes in their pans 5 to 10 minutes before turning out. If necessary, run a thin knife between cake and pan to loosen edges. Place a cake rack over top of pan and gently invert cake onto rack; remove pan. Warm cakes are very delicate and should be handled with care. A cake should be completely cool before frosting.

● Cakes baked in ungreased pans, such as angel food, should be cooled in the pan. To do so, invert pan, positioning center tube opening over a narrow-necked bottle, page 11.

● Before frosting a cake, use a pastry brush to whisk any crumbs from surface of cake. If a cake is extremely soft, a *crumb coating* will prevent excess crumbs from marring the surface of the frosting. To apply a crumb coating, spread a *very* thin layer of frosting on cake to seal surface, set crumbs and fill in any imperfections. Allow this coating to dry before applying remaining frosting.

Sponge Cake

This delicate cake needs little adornment—fresh berries and whipped cream add the perfect touch.

6 eggs, separated, room temperature
2 tablespoons water, liqueur or fruit juice
1-1/2 teaspoons vanilla extract
1-1/4 cups sugar

1/4 teaspoon salt
1/2 teaspoon cream of tartar
1-1/4 cups cake flour, sifted

Preheat oven to 375F (190C). Grease bottom only of a 10-inch tube pan or 2 round 9-inch cake pans. Line bottom of pan(s) with waxed paper. Grease and flour waxed paper. In a small mixer bowl, beat egg yolks, water, liqueur or fruit juice, and vanilla until foamy. Beating constantly, gradually add 1/2 cup plus 2 tablespoons sugar, 2 tablespoons at a time. Beat 5 minutes or until mixture is thick, pale and ribbons form in bowl when beaters are lifted. Turn mixture into a large bowl; set aside. In a large mixer bowl, beat egg whites, salt and cream of tartar to soft-peak stage. Beating constantly, gradually add remaining 1/2 cup plus 2 tablespoons sugar, 2 tablespoons at a time. Continue beating until egg whites are glossy and firm. Fold into yolk mixture alternately with flour, 1/3 at a time. Turn into prepared pan(s); smooth tops. Bake 25 to 30 minutes for tube pan and 15 to 20 minutes for round cake pans, or until cake springs back when lightly pressed in center with your fingertips or until a wooden pick inserted in center comes out clean. Invert cake in tube pan over neck of a bottle; cool completely. Cool cakes in round pans on racks; cool completely. To loosen cake(s), run a thin knife around inside edges of pan(s). Turn out cake(s). Peel off waxed paper from bottom. Frost as desired or as suggested in specific recipes. Makes 1 (10-inch) tube cake or 2 round 9-inch cakes.

Variations
To halve Sponge-Cake recipe, use 3 eggs, 1 tablespoon water, liqueur or fruit juice, 3/4 teaspoon vanilla extract, 1/8 teaspoon salt, 1/4 teaspoon cream of tartar and 1/2 cup plus 2 tablespoons *each* sugar and cake flour. Use small mixer bowl instead of large for egg whites as well as egg yolks. Turn yolk mixture into large bowl before folding in beaten egg whites and flour.

Jelly Rolls: Preheat oven to 375F (190C). Grease bottoms only of 2 (17″ x 11″) jelly-roll pans. Line bottom of pans with waxed paper; grease and flour waxed paper. Divide cake batter evenly between pans, spreading evenly and into corners. Bake 5 to 8 minutes or until cakes test done, as above. Cool in pans on racks 5 minutes. Place 2 kitchen towels on work surface; cover with waxed paper. Sprinkle waxed paper with powdered sugar. To loosen cakes, run a thin knife around inside edges of pans. Carefully turn each cake out onto a waxed-paper-lined towel. Gently peel waxed paper off bottom of cakes. Roll up each cake with waxed paper and towel; set aside to cool, seam-side down. If necessary, trim brown edges from cake before completing as directed in specific recipe.

Ginger Sponge Cake: Omit 2 tablespoons water, liqueur or fruit juice. Add 7 tablespoons molasses to egg yolks. Beat until creamy before adding sugar. Stir 1 teaspoon *each* ground ginger and ground cinnamon, and 1/4 teaspoon *each* ground cloves and ground nutmeg into flour before folding into egg yolks.

To halve Ginger-Sponge-Cake recipe, use batter proportions given to halve Sponge-Cake recipe, above. For flavorings use 3-1/2 tablespoons molasses, 1/2 teaspoon *each* ground ginger and ground cinnamon, and 1/8 teaspoon *each* ground cloves and ground nutmeg.

Orange Sponge Cake: Substitute 1 tablespoon orange-flower water and 1 tablespoon orange juice for 2 tablespoons water, liqueur or fruit juice. Add finely grated zest of 1 medium orange to egg yolks before beating.

Cocoa Sponge Cake: Substitute 1/2 cup sifted unsweetened cocoa for 1/2 cup cake flour. Sift flour and cocoa together before folding into egg-yolk mixture.

How to Make Sponge Cake

1/Beat egg-yolk mixture 5 minutes or until thick, pale and ribbons form in bowl when beaters are lifted.

2/To cool baked cakes, invert cake in tube pan over neck of a bottle; set cakes in round pans on racks. Cool completely.

Buttermilk-Cocoa Cake

An old-fashioned dessert that brings back memories of grandmother's kitchen. Buttermilk creates a cake that's tender, moist and light as a feather!

Sifted unsweetened cocoa
1 cup butter, softened
2-1/2 cups sugar
1-1/2 teaspoons vanilla extract
2 eggs, room temperature
2-1/2 cups cake flour
3/4 cup sifted unsweetened cocoa

1 teaspoon baking soda
1/2 teaspoon baking powder
1/2 teaspoon salt
1 pint buttermilk (2 cups)
Fluffy Praline Frosting or
    Maple-Fluff Frosting, page 146

Preheat oven to 350F (175C). Grease 2 round 9- or 10-inch cake pans; lightly dust with unsweetened cocoa. In a large mixer bowl, beat butter, sugar and vanilla until light and fluffy. Add eggs, 1 at a time, beating well after each addition; set aside. In a medium bowl, combine flour, 3/4 cup cocoa, baking soda, baking powder and salt. Add to butter mixture alternately with buttermilk, 1/3 at a time, stirring well after each addition. Divide batter evenly between prepared pans; smooth tops. Bake 35 to 45 minutes or until a wooden pick inserted in center comes out clean. Cool in pans on racks 10 minutes. Carefully turn out cakes onto racks; cool completely. Prepare Fluffy Praline Frosting or Maple-Fluff Frosting. If desired, cut each cooled layer in 1/2 horizontally to make 4 layers or, use 2 regular-size layers. Fill and frost with your choice of frosting. Makes 8 to 10 servings.

Holiday Eggnog Cake

A small slice of this festive, ultra-rich dessert will send you to eggnog heaven!

2-1/4 cups all-purpose flour
1 cup sugar
1 tablespoon baking powder
1/2 teaspoon salt
1/2 teaspoon ground nutmeg
3/4 cup dairy eggnog, not canned,
   room temperature
1/2 cup butter, melted, cooled
1/4 cup light rum
4 egg yolks, room temperature,
   lightly beaten

2 teaspoons freshly grated orange zest
2 teaspoons vanilla extract
7 egg whites, room temperature
1/2 teaspoon cream of tartar
Eggnog Chiffon Pudding, page 79,
   using 1 egg white instead of 4
4-1/2 tablespoons light rum, if desired
Frosting, see below
Candied-cherry halves and
   green-pineapple wedges, if desired

Frosting:
1-1/2 cups whipping cream
3 tablespoons powdered sugar

1 teaspoon vanilla extract
1-1/2 tablespoons light rum, if desired

Preheat oven to 325F (165C). In a large bowl, combine flour, sugar, baking powder, salt and nutmeg. Make a well in center of dry ingredients. Add eggnog, butter, 1/4 cup rum, egg yolks, orange zest and vanilla. Beat with a spoon until dry ingredients are moistened and batter is smooth; set aside. In a large mixer bowl, beat egg whites and cream of tartar until stiff but not dry. Gently fold egg whites into batter. Turn batter into an ungreased 10-inch tube pan; smooth top. Bake 35 to 45 minutes or until a wooden pick inserted in center comes out clean. While cake is baking, prepare mixture for Eggnog Chiffon Pudding, as directed on page 79, through folding in whipped cream; cover and refrigerate. Invert cake in pan over neck of bottle, page 11, or on a rack. Cool 1 hour. To loosen cake, run a thin knife around inside edges of pan. Turn out cake onto a rack; cool completely. Prepare Frosting; refrigerate.

To complete Eggnog Chiffon Pudding, in a small bowl, beat 1 egg white and a pinch of cream of tartar until stiff but not dry; fold into eggnog-pudding mixture. Refrigerate 1 hour before using.

To complete cake, cut cooled cake into 3 even horizontal layers. If desired, sprinkle each layer with 1-1/2 tablespoons rum. Place bottom cake layer on a serving plate. Spread with 1/2 of Eggnog Chiffon Pudding. Place second layer on top; spread with remaining pudding. Cover with top layer of cake. Spread top and sides of cake with Frosting. If desired, decorate top with cherries and green pineapple. Refrigerate 3 hours before serving. Makes 10 to 12 servings.

Frosting:
In a small bowl, beat cream until soft mounds begin to form. Beating constantly, add powdered sugar, vanilla and 1-1/2 tablespoons rum, if desired; beat until stiff.

Variations
Add 1/3 cup finely chopped, thoroughly blotted dry, maraschino cherries to Eggnog Chiffon Pudding before spreading on cake layers.

For a chocolate-eggnog-flavored filling, add 2 ounces finely chopped semisweet chocolate to cooked pudding; stir until chocolate is melted. Garnish top of cake with 1 ounce Grated Chocolate, page 126.

Kay's Lane Cake

My mother's addition of lemon zest to both cake and filling brightens the flavor of this classic cake.

Lane-Cake Filling, see below
1-1/4 cups butter, softened
2 cups sugar
2 teaspoons vanilla extract
Freshly grated zest of 1 large lemon
3 cups all-purpose flour
4-1/2 teaspoons baking powder

1 teaspoon salt
1-1/4 cups milk, room temperature
8 egg whites, room temperature
Lane-Cake Frosting, page 146
8 pecan halves
8 maraschino-cherry halves,
   thoroughly blotted dry

Lane-Cake Filling:
1/2 cup butter
1/4 teaspoon salt
1 cup sugar
1/2 cup bourbon or brandy
Freshly grated zest of 1 large lemon
8 egg yolks, lightly beaten

1 teaspoon vanilla extract
1 cup chopped pecans
1 cup chopped raisins
1 cup chopped maraschino cherries,
   thoroughly blotted dry
1 cup shredded or flaked coconut

Grease and flour 3 round 8- or 9-inch cake pans. Preheat oven to 375F (190C). Prepare Lane-Cake Filling; cover and refrigerate until thoroughly chilled. In a large mixer bowl, beat butter, sugar, vanilla and lemon zest until light and fluffy; set aside. In a medium bowl, combine flour, baking powder and salt. Add to butter mixture alternately with milk, 1/3 at a time, beating only until smooth after each addition. In a large mixer bowl, beat egg whites until stiff but not dry. Stir about 1 cup beaten egg whites into batter to lighten mixture. Gently fold in remaining egg whites. Divide batter evenly between prepared cake pans; smooth tops. Bake 18 to 23 minutes or until cake springs back when lightly pressed in center with your fingertips or a wooden pick inserted in center comes out clean. Cool in pans on racks 10 minutes. Turn out cakes onto racks; cool completely. Prepare Lane-Cake Frosting; set aside.

To complete cake, using a pastry brush, brush excess crumbs from sides of cakes. Place 1 cake layer on a serving plate. Spread with 1/2 of chilled Lane-Cake Filling. Repeat with second cake layer and remaining filling. Place third layer on top. Frost sides and top with Lane-Cake Frosting. Alternate pecan halves and cherry halves around outside edge of top for decoration. Makes 8 to 10 servings.

Lane-Cake Filling:

In top of a double boiler, combine butter, salt, sugar, bourbon or brandy, lemon zest and egg yolks. Place top of double boiler over simmering water. Cook, stirring constantly, 5 minutes or until mixture thickly coats the back of a metal spoon. Remove from heat; stir in remaining ingredients. Refrigerate until thoroughly chilled and thickened.

TIP *A raisin is a dried grape. The word* raisin *comes from the Latin word* racemus, *which means a cluster of grapes or berries.*

Wayne's Strawberry Dream Cake

Two of my dad's favorite flavors combine in this fabulous creation. Strawberry-chocolate mousse inside and chocolate-dipped strawberries outside make a "dreamy" dessert!

1 (10-inch) tube Sponge Cake, page 10,
   or Plain Angel Food Cake, page 17,
   or purchased cake
1/4 cup orange-flavored liqueur,
   if desired
1 (1/4-oz.) envelope unflavored gelatin
   (scant 1 tablespoon)
1/3 cup orange-flavored liqueur,
   orange juice or water
1 cup strawberry puree, made from 1 pint
   fresh strawberries or 2 cups drained,
   thawed, frozen fruit

1/2 cup sugar
3 cups whipping cream
3 oz. Grated Chocolate, page 126,
   or 1/2 cup miniature semisweet
   chocolate pieces
1 cup finely chopped fresh strawberries
   (3/4 pint)
12 Chocolate-Dipped Whole Strawberries,
   page 98

Using a serrated knife, cut a 3/4- to 1-inch layer from top of cake; set aside. Cut around cake 1 inch from outer edge and 1 inch from center hole. Carefully remove cake from center with your fingers or a spoon, leaving a cavity with 1-inch walls and a 1-inch cake base. Freeze removed cake pieces for future use. Brush inside of reserved cake top, sides and bottom with 2 tablespoons orange-flavored liqueur, if desired; set aside. In a small saucepan, stir gelatin into 1/3 cup orange-flavored liqueur, orange juice or water; let stand 5 minutes to soften. Stir over medium heat just until gelatin dissolves. Remove from heat; cool until barely warm. In a small bowl, combine strawberry puree and 1/4 cup sugar; set aside. In a large bowl, beat whipping cream until soft mounds begin to form. Beating constantly, pour slightly warm gelatin mixture all at once into center of cream. Add remaining 1/4 cup sugar; beat until cream is stiff. Place 3 cups whipped-cream mixture in a medium bowl. Whisk in remaining 2 tablespoons orange-flavored liqueur, if desired; refrigerate. Prepare Grated Chocolate, if using; refrigerate. Fold sweetened strawberry puree, chopped strawberries and Grated Chocolate or miniature chocolate pieces into remaining whipped-cream mixture. Spoon strawberry mixture into cake cavity until even with top of cake. Replace reserved top cake slice, liqueur-side down. Refrigerate 8 hours or overnight. Frost entire cake with reserved whipped-cream mixture; refrigerate up to 6 hours before serving. Prepare Chocolate-Dipped Whole Strawberries. Garnish top of cake with Chocolate-Dipped Whole Strawberries up to 4 hours before serving. Makes about 12 servings.

Wayne's Strawberry Dream Cake

Strawberry Soirée

Airy meringue layers filled with chocolate, strawberries and whipped cream make a spectacular celebration—definitely worth the effort!

Meringue:

5 egg whites, room temperature
1/4 teaspoon cream of tartar

1/4 teaspoon salt
1-1/4 cups sugar

Filling & Topping:

Chocolate-Dipped Halved Strawberries,
  page 98, using 18 to 24 medium
  strawberries and 3 to 4 oz. semisweet
  chocolate melted with 1 teaspoon
  vegetable oil
4 oz. semisweet Grated Chocolate, page 126

3-1/2 cups whipping cream
2 teaspoons vanilla extract
1/3 cup powdered sugar
2 teaspoons finely grated orange zest
1 pint strawberries, hulled, sliced

Meringue:

Preheat oven to 250F (120C). Line 2 large baking sheets with waxed paper; lightly grease waxed paper. Leaving at least 1/2 inch between them, trace 2 (8-inch) circles on 1 waxed-paper-lined baking sheet; trace 1 (8-inch) circle on the other. In a large mixer bowl, beat egg whites, cream of tartar and salt to soft-peak stage. Beating constantly, gradually add sugar, 2 tablespoons at a time. Continue beating until whites are glossy and firm. Spread 1/3 of meringue mixture evenly over each traced circle. Make sure meringue is level and the same thickness all over. Bake 30 minutes, then rotate sheets on oven racks. Bake 30 minutes longer; turn off oven. Leave meringue layers in oven 30 to 45 minutes or until completely dry. Remove from oven; gently peel waxed paper from bottom of meringue. Cool meringue layers completely on racks.

Filling & Topping:

Prepare Chocolate-Dipped Halved Strawberries and Grated Chocolate; refrigerate. In a large mixer bowl, beat cream and vanilla until mixture begins to mound. Add powdered sugar; beat until stiff. Reserve 2-1/2 cups sweetened whipped cream. Fold orange zest and Grated Chocolate into remaining whipped cream. Place 1 meringue layer on a serving plate. Spread with 1/2 of chocolate whipped cream. Top with 1/2 of sliced strawberries, placing berries 1/2 inch from outer edge. Repeat with second meringue layer, remaining chocolate whipped cream and sliced strawberries. Top with third meringue layer. Frost top and sides with reserved whipped cream. Place concentric circles of Chocolate-Dipped Halved Strawberries, flat-side down and stems out, on top of torte. Refrigerate 3 hours before serving. Makes 8 to 10 servings.

 TIP *To freeze leftover egg whites: Place 1 egg white in each section of an ice-cube tray. Freeze until firm. Turn frozen egg-white cubes into a plastic bag. Seal tightly and return to freezer. Defrost at room temperature before using. Use leftover egg whites for meringues, angel food cakes or soufflés.*

Chocolate Angel Food Cake

A heavenly cake—moist, chocolatey, tender and light—the quintessential angel food!

3/4 cup cake flour
1/2 cup sifted unsweetened cocoa
1-1/2 cups sugar
1/2 teaspoon salt
10 egg whites, room temperature
1 tablespoon water mixed with
   1/4 teaspoon baking soda

1-1/2 teaspoons cream of tartar
1 teaspoon vanilla extract
Fluffy Chocolate Frosting or
   Fluffy Orange Frosting, page 146

Set oven rack 1/3 up from bottom of oven. Preheat oven to 350F (175C). Sift flour, cocoa, 3/4 cup sugar and salt through a fine sieve twice; set aside. In a large mixer bowl, beat egg whites and water-soda mixture on medium speed until frothy. While beating, add cream of tartar. Increase mixer speed to medium-high; gradually add 1/4 cup sugar, 2 tablespoons at a time. Continue beating until whites form medium-firm peaks which fold over slightly when beaters are lifted; whites should not be absolutely stiff. Gently fold in vanilla. Sprinkle 1/3 of remaining 1/2 cup sugar over egg whites. Gently fold into whites. Repeat with remaining sugar, 1/2 at a time. Using a large rubber spatula and a minimum of strokes helps retain body and prevents deflating egg whites. Sprinkle 1/5 of flour mixture over whites; gently fold in. Repeat with remaining flour mixture, 1/4 at a time. Fold in flour mixture just until it disappears; be careful not to overhandle mixture. Turn into an ungreased 10-inch tube pan. Gently cut through batter with a knife to deflate any large air bubbles; smooth top. Bake 35 to 40 minutes or until cake springs back when lightly pressed with your fingertips. Invert cake in pan over neck of a bottle until completely cool, page 11. To loosen cake, run a thin knife around inside edges of pan. Turn out cake onto a serving plate. Prepare Fluffy Chocolate Frosting or Fluffy Orange Frosting. If desired, cut cake in 1/2 horizontally and fill with frosting before frosting outside of cake. Makes 8 to 10 servings.

Variations

Plain Angel Food Cake: Substitute additional 1/2 cup cake flour for 1/2 cup cocoa and 1 tablespoon lemon juice for 1 tablespoon water and soda mixture. Decrease sugar by 1/4 cup.

Mocha Angel Food Cake: For water and soda mixture, dissolve 1-1/2 tablespoons instant coffee powder or granules and 1/4 teaspoon soda in 1 tablespoon hot water. Continue with Chocolate Angel Food Cake, as above.

Spiced Angel Food Cake: Sift 3/4 teaspoon ground cinnamon, 1/2 teaspoon ground nutmeg and 1/2 teaspoon ground allspice with flour.

TIP *If you don't have a sifter, rub cocoa or powdered sugar through a very fine strainer with the back of a spoon. Measure sifted powdered sugar or cocoa by lightly spooning it into a measuring cup; level top with the flat edge of a knife.*

Chocolate-Raspberry Shortcake

Deep-red raspberries, whipped cream and fudge sauce crown dark-chocolate shortcake—dedicated to our friend Gene Bain!

1-3/4 cups all-purpose flour
1/3 cup unsweetened cocoa
1 cup sugar
2 teaspoons baking powder
1/2 teaspoon baking soda
1/2 teaspoon salt
1/2 cup firm cold butter, cut in 8 pieces

1 egg, lightly beaten
1/2 cup whipping cream
5 cups fresh raspberries
Spirited or Plain Whipped Cream, page 156
Mint sprigs, if desired
Fudge Velvet Sauce, page 150, if desired

Preheat oven to 375F (190C). Grease a round 9-inch cake pan. In a medium bowl, combine flour, cocoa, 3/4 cup sugar, baking powder, baking soda and salt. Using a pastry blender or 2 knives, cut in butter until mixture resembles coarse crumbs. Add egg and cream. Stir just until dry ingredients are moistened. Pat or spread dough in an even layer over bottom of prepared pan. Bake 20 to 30 minutes or just until shortcake begins to pull away from side of pan. Cool in pan on a rack 15 minutes. Turn out shortcake onto rack; cool completely. Set aside about 20 attractive raspberries for garnish. In a large bowl, combine remaining berries and remaining 1/4 cup sugar. You may wish to use more sugar, depending on sweetness of berries; let stand 30 minutes. Prepare Spirited or Plain Whipped Cream; refrigerate.

To complete shortcake, using a serrated knife, cut shortcake in 1/2 horizontally. Place bottom shortcake layer on a serving plate. Spoon 1/2 of sweetened berries and their juice over shortcake; top with 1/2 of whipped cream. Place second shortcake layer on top. Repeat with remaining sweetened berries and whipped cream; swirl cream decoratively. Garnish with reserved raspberries and mint sprigs, if desired. Refrigerate up to 3 hours before serving. Prepare Fudge Velvet Sauce, if desired; cool to room temperature. Drizzle shortcake with sauce immediately before serving. Pass additional sauce, if desired. Makes 6 to 8 servings.

TIP *To use leftover whipped cream, place in a bowl. Tightly cover bowl of leftover whipped cream with plastic wrap; refrigerate. Use within 24 hours, rewhipping, if necessary. Or, place whipped cream in a plastic bag; seal and freeze up to 3 months. When ready to use, turn frozen cream into a small mixing bowl; thaw in refrigerator. Beat at high speed until it reaches desired stiffness. Or, line a baking sheet with plastic wrap, allowing ends to extend over ends of pan by 6 inches. Using a kitchen tablespoon, spoon dollops of whipped cream, 2 inches apart, over surface of prepared baking sheet. Freeze until solid. Fold ends of plastic wrap over frozen cream mounds; lift off baking sheet and place in a plastic bag. Seal and freeze up to 3 months. To use, fill a cup or mug 3/4 full with coffee or hot chocolate. Top with a mound of frozen whipped cream.*

How to Make Chocolate-Raspberry Shortcake

1/Pat or spread shortcake dough in an even layer over bottom of prepared pan.

2/Complete shortcake by layering with whipped cream and sweetened raspberries. Garnish with raspberries and mint sprigs, if desired.

Maple-Pecan Cake

Pure maple syrup, rather than maple-flavored syrup, infuses an authentic flavor that's not overly sweet. It's more expensive but quality always comes through in the final product.

1-1/4 cups butter, softened
1 cup sugar
1 teaspoon vanilla extract
4 eggs
3 cups all-purpose flour
1-1/2 teaspoons baking powder
1/2 teaspoon baking soda

1/2 teaspoon salt
1-1/2 cups pure maple syrup
1-1/2 cups toasted finely chopped pecans
Maple-Fluff Frosting, page 146
8 to 10 pecan halves or
   3 tablespoons toasted chopped pecans

Preheat oven to 350F (175C). Grease and flour 3 round 9-inch cake pans. In a large mixer bowl, beat butter, sugar and vanilla until light and fluffy. Add eggs, 1 at a time, beating well after each addition; set aside. In a medium bowl, combine flour, baking powder, baking soda and salt. Add to butter mixture alternately with maple syrup, 1/3 at a time, blending well after each addition. Fold in 1-1/2 cups toasted pecans. Divide batter evenly between prepared pans; smooth tops. Bake 20 to 30 minutes or until a wooden pick inserted in center comes out clean. Cool in pans on racks 10 minutes. Turn out cakes onto racks; cool completely. Prepare Maple-Fluff Frosting. Fill cooled cake and frost all over. Decorate top with pecan halves or chopped pecans. Makes 10 to 12 servings.

Coconut-Sour-Cream Cake

This cake is moist with sour cream and filled with a velvety chocolate frosting—scrumptious! For an entirely different flavor, try toasting the coconut before adding it to the batter.

1 cup butter, softened
2 cups sugar
1 tablespoon vanilla extract
5 eggs, separated, room temperature
2 cups all-purpose flour
1/2 teaspoon baking soda
1/4 teaspoon salt

1/2 pint dairy sour cream (1 cup),
　room temperature
2 cups shredded or flaked coconut
1-1/2 recipes Chocolate-Buttercream Frosting,
　page 147
1 cup chopped walnuts or pecans

Preheat oven to 325F (165C). Grease a 15″ x 10″ jelly-roll pan. Line bottom of pan with a 17-inch length of waxed paper; grease paper. In a large mixer bowl, beat butter and sugar until light and fluffy. Add vanilla, then egg yolks, 1 at a time, beating well after each addition; set aside. In a medium bowl, combine flour, baking soda and salt. Add to butter mixture alternately with sour cream, 1/3 at a time, stirring just to combine after each addition. In a large mixer bowl, beat egg whites until stiff but not dry. Stir 1/4 of egg whites into batter to lighten mixture. Fold in remaining whites and coconut. Turn into prepared pan; smooth top. Bake 25 to 30 minutes or until cake springs back when lightly pressed in center with your fingertips or a wooden pick inserted in center comes out clean. Cool 10 minutes in pan on a rack. Carefully turn out cake onto rack; gently peel off waxed paper. Cool completely. Prepare Chocolate-Buttercream Frosting.

To complete cake, trim brown edges from cake, if necessary. Cut cake crosswise into 3 equal pieces, each about 4-3/4 inches wide. Place 1 cake layer on a serving plate. Spread with 1 cup frosting, going all the way to cake edges. Repeat with second cake layer and another 1 cup frosting. Top with third cake layer; spread top and sides with remaining frosting. Sprinkle sides of cake with chopped nuts. Makes 8 to 10 servings.

Variation
Bake and cool cake as above. Make 1 recipe Chocolate-Buttercream Frosting. Set aside 1 cup frosting; stir 1 cup chopped walnuts or pecans into remaining frosting. Cut cake as above. Spread 1/2 of frosting-nut mixture on bottom cake layer. Repeat with second cake layer and remaining nut frosting. Spread top cake layer with reserved 1 cup frosting without nuts. Sprinkle top of cake with 3 to 4 tablespoons shredded or flaked coconut.

Coconut-Sour-Cream Cake

Cherry-Pecan Torte

Chocolate-dipped cherries crown this festive finale—created for an appearance on TV's Hour Magazine.

1/2 cup miniature semisweet chocolate pieces or 3 oz. Grated Chocolate, page 126
6 eggs, separated, room temperature
1-1/4 cups powdered sugar
1/2 cup butter, softened
3 tablespoons cornstarch
1 tablespoon vanilla extract
1-2/3 cups toasted finely ground pecans
1/2 cup toasted coarsely chopped pecans

1/2 cup coarsely chopped maraschino cherries, thoroughly blotted dry
1/4 teaspoon salt
1/4 teaspoon cream of tartar
8 Chocolate-Dipped Cherries with stems, page 98, using 1-1/2 oz. semisweet chocolate and 1/2 teaspoon vegetable oil
Bittersweet-Chocolate Glaze, page 147
8 pecan halves

Preheat oven to 375F (190C). Grease a 9-inch springform pan. Place a round of waxed paper in bottom of pan; grease waxed paper. Flour sides and bottom of pan. Prepare Grated Chocolate, if using; refrigerate. In a large mixer bowl, beat egg yolks and 1 cup powdered sugar until thick, pale and ribbons form in bowl when beaters are lifted. Add butter, cornstarch and vanilla. Beat 1 minute, until fluffy and smooth. Stir in ground pecans, chopped pecans, chopped cherries and Grated Chocolate or chocolate pieces; set aside. In a large mixer bowl, beat egg whites, salt and cream of tartar to soft-peak stage. Beating constantly, gradually add remaining 1/4 cup powdered sugar, 2 tablespoons at a time. Continue beating until whites are stiff but not dry. Stir 1/3 of egg-white mixture into batter to lighten mixture. Gently fold in remaining egg-white mixture. Turn batter into prepared pan; smooth top. Bake 30 to 40 minutes or until a wooden pick inserted in center comes out clean. Cool in pan on a rack 10 minutes. To loosen torte, run a thin knife around inside edge of pan; remove side of pan. Invert torte onto rack. Using knife, ease bottom of pan away from torte. Gently peel waxed paper from bottom of torte. Cool completely on rack. Prepare Chocolate-Dipped Cherries; refrigerate. Prepare Bittersweet-Chocolate Glaze; set aside.

To complete torte, using a pastry brush, brush off any excess crumbs from surface of torte. Pour 1/3 of Bittersweet-Chocolate Glaze on top of torte; spread evenly over top with a narrow, metal, spreading spatula. Refrigerate 10 minutes to set glaze. Pour remaining glaze onto top of torte; spread so a little glaze runs down sides. Smooth a thin layer of glaze over sides with spatula. Do not work glaze any more than necessary or it will lose its sheen. Place pecan halves and Chocolate-Dipped Cherries alternately around outside edge of top of torte; lightly press into surface. Torte can be made ahead and frozen unglazed. Package airtight to freeze. Bring to room temperature before glazing. May be glazed 6 to 8 hours before serving; store and serve at room temperature. Makes 12 servings.

How to Make a Decorator Cone

1/Fold a 10-inch square of waxed or parchment paper in half diagonally. Holding long side of triangle away from you, bring left corner to middle corner.

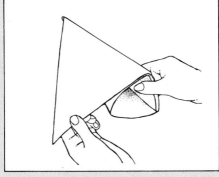

2/Bring other corner around cone, pulling it tight to form a sharp tip.

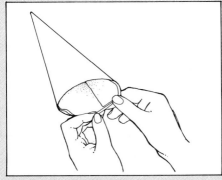

3/Fasten decorator cone by folding down corners; make a double fold.

Marvelous Mandarin Torte

This elegant, three-layered torte combines the magic of chocolate and mandarin oranges.

5 oz. Grated Chocolate, page 126
6 eggs, separated, room temperature
1 cup powdered sugar
1/4 cup cornstarch
1/4 teaspoon salt
1 teaspoon vanilla extract
1 cup toasted finely ground almonds

Freshly grated zest of 1 small orange
1/4 teaspoon cream of tartar
2 tablespoons orange-flavored liqueur,
   if desired
1 (11-oz.) can mandarin-orange segments
Fluffy Orange Frosting, page 146

Preheat oven to 375F (190C). Grease a 9-inch springform pan. Prepare Grated Chocolate, setting aside 1 ounce for garnish; refrigerate. In a large mixer bowl, beat egg yolks until lemon-colored. Beating constantly, gradually add powdered sugar. Beat 5 minutes or until mixture is thick, pale and ribbons form in bowl when beaters are lifted. Add cornstarch, salt and vanilla; beat until blended. Gently fold in almonds, orange zest and 4 ounces Grated Chocolate. In a large mixer bowl, beat egg whites and cream of tartar until stiff but not dry. Fold egg whites, 1/2 at a time, into batter; turn into prepared pan. Bake 25 to 35 minutes or until a wooden pick inserted in center comes out clean. Cool in pan on a rack. **To complete torte,** remove side of cake pan. Loosen cooled torte from bottom of pan. Using a serrated knife, carefully slice torte horizontally into 3 layers, each about 1/2 inch thick. If desired, sprinkle bottom and middle layer each with 1 tablespoon orange-flavored liqueur; set aside. Drain oranges; reserve 7 for garnish. Coarsely chop remaining oranges. Thoroughly blot on paper towels; set aside. Prepare Fluffy Orange Frosting. Transfer 2/3 of frosting to a medium bowl. Fold in chopped oranges; Place bottom torte layer on a serving plate. Spread with 1/2 of frosting-orange mixture, going all the way to torte edges. Top with second torte layer; spread with remaining frosting-orange mixture. Place third torte layer on top; spread top of torte with plain frosting, swirling decoratively. Do not frost sides of torte. Sprinkle reserved 1 ounce Grated Chocolate in a 1-1/2-inch border around top frosted edge of torte. Arrange reserved orange segments, pinwheel-fashion, in center. Makes 12 servings.

4/For ease in handling, set decorator cone in a medium glass. Spoon frosting into decorator cone.

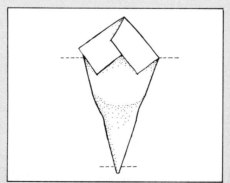

5/Fold 2 sides of filled cone in toward the middle. Fold down top to seal in frosting. Snip off tip of cone as directed in recipe.

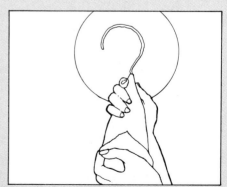

6/Holding cone with both hands and applying even pressure, pipe frosting as directed in recipe.

Ginger-Apple Roll

A delicate ginger cake filled with apples, ginger and raisins for a flavor that's pure pleasure.

1/2 recipe Ginger Sponge Cake, page 10, baked as 1 jelly roll
2 tablespoons butter
2-1/2 cups finely chopped tart apple, peeled or unpeeled (about 2 medium apples)
2 teaspoons freshly grated lemon zest
1/4 cup raisins
1/2 cup packed brown sugar

1/4 cup Calvados, regular brandy, or apple juice
1/4 teaspoon salt
1/2 cup toasted chopped walnuts or pecans
1 tablespoon minced crystallized ginger
2 (3-oz.) pkgs. cream cheese, softened
2/3 cup whipping cream, whipped
Powdered sugar

Prepare Ginger Sponge Cake as directed for jelly roll, page 10. Roll up cake; set aside to cool. In a large skillet, melt butter; add apples, lemon zest and raisins. Cook over medium-high heat until apples begin to soften. Stir in brown sugar and 2 tablespoons Calvados, regular brandy or apple juice; cook, stirring occasionally, until liquid is reduced to about 2 teaspoons. Remove from heat. Add salt, nuts and ginger; cool to room temperature. In a large bowl, beat cream cheese and remaining 2 tablespoons Calvados, regular brandy or apple juice. Stir in cooled apple mixture. Fold in whipped cream.
To complete cake, unroll cake roll. Spread evenly with apple mixture. Starting with narrow end, reroll cake, using waxed paper to help you roll. Wrap cake roll in plastic wrap; refrigerate at least 3 hours. Fold a 12″ x 5″ length of waxed paper in half lengthwise; cut out design of choice. Carefully position cut waxed paper down center of cake roll. If necessary, secure waxed paper to cake with wooden picks. Generously dust exposed cake area with powdered sugar. Carefully remove wooden picks and waxed paper without disturbing powdered-sugar design. Refrigerate until ready to serve. Cut cake roll using a serrated knife. Makes 10 to 12 servings.

Caramel-Apple Cake

The flavor of this easy cake evokes childhood memories of carnival caramel apples.

2 tablespoons vegetable oil
2 eggs, room temperature
2/3 cup packed brown sugar
1 teaspoon vanilla extract
1-1/4 cups all-purpose flour
1/2 teaspoon ground nutmeg
1/2 teaspoon ground cinnamon

1 teaspoon baking soda
1/4 teaspoon salt
2 cups finely chopped, peeled, tart apples
2 teaspoons freshly grated orange zest
3/4 cup chopped walnuts
3/4 to 1 cup Hot Caramel Sauce, page 155

Preheat oven to 325F (165C). Grease an 8-inch-square baking pan. In a large bowl, combine oil, eggs, brown sugar and vanilla. Add flour, nutmeg, cinnamon, baking soda, salt, apples, orange zest and 1/2 cup nuts. Stir only until dry ingredients are moistened. Turn into prepared pan. Bake 30 to 40 minutes or until a wooden pick inserted in center comes out clean. Cool in pan on a rack 20 minutes. Prepare Hot Caramel Sauce. Pour about 3/4 to 1 cup sauce over surface of cake; sprinkle with remaining 1/4 cup nuts. Let stand 10 to 15 minutes before serving warm. Or, serve at room temperature. Refrigerate leftover caramel sauce for another use. Makes 6 to 8 servings.

How to Make Ginger-Apple Roll

1/Unroll baked cake and spread evenly with apple mixture. Starting with narrow end, reroll cake, using waxed paper to help you roll.

2/Position paper cutout down center of filled cake roll. Generously dust exposed cake area with powdered sugar. Carefully remove waxed paper without disturbing powdered-sugar design.

Gâteau Noir
Photo on page 4.

A wickedly delicious chocolate cake enrobed in velvety chocolate cream—for dedicated chocophiles only!

Chocolate Doilies, Chocolate Leaves or Chocolate Triangles, page 126
Unsweetened cocoa
2-1/2 cups cake flour
2 teaspoons baking powder
1 teaspoon baking soda
1 teaspoon salt
3/4 cup butter, softened

1 cup packed brown sugar
1-1/2 cups granulated sugar
2 teaspoons vanilla extract
4 eggs, room temperature
6 oz. unsweetened chocolate, melted, cooled
1 pint dairy sour cream (2 cups)
Chocolate-Ganache Soufflé, page 147

Prepare chocolate decorations of choice; refrigerate. Preheat oven to 350F (175C). Generously grease 3 round 9- or 10-inch cake pans; lightly dust with unsweetened cocoa. In a medium bowl, combine flour, baking powder, baking soda and salt; set aside. In a large mixer bowl, beat butter, sugars and vanilla 2 minutes at medium speed. With mixer running, add eggs, 1 at a time, beating well after each addition. Scrape sides of bowl as necessary. Gradually beat in chocolate; beat 2 minutes at high speed. Beat in sour cream. Fold in flour mixture. Divide batter evenly between prepared pans; smooth tops. Bake 25 to 35 minutes or until a wooden pick inserted in center comes out clean. Cool cakes in pans on racks 10 minutes. Carefully turn out cakes onto racks; cool completely. Cake is very fragile. Prepare Chocolate-Ganache Soufflé; use to fill and frost cake. Decorate frosted cake with Chocolate Doilies, Chocolate Leaves or Chocolate Triangles. Refrigerate until serving time. Makes 8 to 10 servings.

Orange-Candy Cake

Use scissors to snip orange-slice candies into marble-sized pieces for this moist, confectionlike cake.

4 cups all-purpose flour
1 lb. orange-slice candy
1 teaspoon baking soda
1/2 teaspoon salt
3/4 teaspoon ground ginger
1-1/2 cups sugar
1 cup butter, softened
4 eggs, room temperature

1/4 cup thawed frozen orange-juice
   concentrate
1/4 cup orange-flavored liqueur or water
2 cups toasted chopped pecans
2 cups shredded or flaked coconut
Sunshine Glaze, see below
2 tablespoons toasted finely chopped pecans

Sunshine Glaze:
2-1/2 cups sifted powdered sugar
1/3 cup thawed frozen orange-juice
   concentrate

1/3 cup orange-flavored liqueur or water

Preheat oven to 250F (120C). Generously grease and flour a 10-inch tube pan. Place flour in a large bowl. Use scissors to snip orange slices into 1/2-inch pieces, letting pieces fall into bowl of flour. Toss mixture often to separate candy and coat with flour. Stir in baking soda, salt and ginger; set aside. In a large mixer bowl, beat sugar and butter until light and fluffy. Add eggs, 1 at a time, beating well after each addition. In a small bowl, combine orange-juice concentrate with orange-flavored liqueur or water. Add to butter mixture alternately with flour-candy mixture, 1/3 at a time, blending well after each addition. Stir in 2 cups chopped pecans and coconut. Spoon batter into prepared pan. Bake 2-1/4 hours or until a wooden pick inserted in center comes out clean. Prepare Sunshine Glaze. Remove cake from oven; leave in pan on a rack.

To complete cake, using an ice pick or thick skewer, poke holes all over hot cake almost all the way to bottom of pan. Pour 1/2 of Sunshine Glaze evenly over cake. Let stand 10 minutes or until cake absorbs glaze. Turn out cake onto rack placed over a sheet of waxed paper. Spoon 1/2 of remaining glaze over warm cake. Cool cake completely. Stir remaining glaze; spoon over top of cake, allowing excess to drizzle down sides and center hole. Sprinkle with 2 tablespoons chopped pecans. Let glaze set 20 minutes before serving. Makes 12 to 14 servings.

Sunshine Glaze:

In a medium bowl, combine all ingredients; stir until smooth and creamy.

TIP

To make stabilized whipped cream, in a small bowl, stir 1 teaspoon unflavored gelatin into 3 tablespoons cold water. Or, if making Spirited Whipped Cream, page 156, stir gelatin into liqueur; set aside 5 minutes to soften. Place bowl in a pan of hot water; stir until gelatin is completely dissolved. Cool to room temperature. Beating constantly, drizzle gelatin mixture into whipped cream just before cream reaches stiff-peak stage. Use immediately for frosting cakes; mixture sets up quickly and becomes difficult to spread.

Lively Lemon Pound Cake

Crushed lemon-drop candies create moist pockets of flavor excitement!

1 cup butter, softened
2-1/2 cups sugar
2 tablespoons lemon juice
6 eggs, separated, room temperature
3 cups all-purpose flour
1/2 teaspoon salt
1/4 teaspoon baking soda

1/2 pint dairy sour cream (1 cup)
1/4 teaspoon cream of tartar
1 cup coarsely crushed lemon-drop candies
Lemon-Cheese Frosting, see below
2 tablespoons finely crushed
   lemon-drop candies

Lemon-Cheese Frosting:
1 (3-oz.) pkg. cream cheese, softened
1 tablespoon lemon juice
1 teaspoon vanilla extract

Finely grated zest of 1 medium lemon
2 cups sifted powdered sugar

Preheat oven to 350F (175C). Generously grease and flour a 10-cup Bundt pan or 10-inch tube pan. In a large mixer bowl, beat butter and sugar until light and fluffy. Add lemon juice and egg yolks, 1 at a time, beating well after each addition. In a medium bowl, combine flour, salt and baking soda. Add to butter mixture alternately with sour cream, 1/3 at a time, stirring only until smooth after each addition; set aside. In a large mixer bowl, beat egg whites and cream of tartar until stiff but not dry. Fold egg whites and 1 cup crushed lemon candy into batter. Turn batter into prepared pan. Bake 1 hour or until a wooden pick inserted in center comes out clean. Cool in pan on a rack 10 minutes. Turn out cake onto rack; cool completely. Prepare Lemon-Cheese Frosting. Spoon frosting over cooled cake, smoothing top and allowing excess to drip down sides and center hole. Sprinkle top with 2 tablespoons crushed lemon candy. Makes 10 to 12 servings.

Lemon-Cheese Frosting:
In a small mixer bowl, beat cream cheese, lemon juice, vanilla and lemon zest until blended. Add powdered sugar; beat until mixture is creamy and smooth.

Note: Crush candies by sealing them in a medium plastic bag. Place bag on a solid surface; hit candies lightly with a hammer or rolling pin.

 TIP *Butter can be creamed when cold if first cut into small pieces, then beaten at low speed until smooth.*

PIES & TARTS

Bas-reliefs in the tombs of Egyptian pharaohs show that bakers were making pies at least 30 centuries ago. But it wasn't until the fourth century B.C. that some of the Middle Eastern countries began to cultivate sugar cane—and that was definitely the start of something *big!*

For some reason, however, most of us think of pies and tarts as English creations. Perhaps because nursery rhymes and fairy tales relate visions of quaint English piemen roaming cobbled streets, peddling their wares from creaking wooden carts. There's even an old English legend that says anyone who eats 12 mince pies, one a day from Christmas until the Twelfth Night, will enjoy great prosperity and happiness for the next 12 months of the year. Doubtless he will also have a waistline as great as his prosperity!

Though the pies of early England were generally savory, meat-filled pastries, the more common offerings today are for those of us with a sweet tooth. Almost any filling is appropriate—fresh fruits, satiny creams, toasted nuts, egg-rich custards or melt-in-your-mouth mousses.

Broadly defined, pies and tarts consist of an edible container and a filling. Unfortunately, the fact that some type of crust is mandatory turns many fearless cooks into insecure bakers who shun making pies simply to avoid making crusts! I have a friend who will only make a pie if the filling can be put into a storebought graham-cracker crust. In fact, with a few basic principles (see *Hints For Successful Pies,* opposite) and a little practice, even the most timid baker can achieve sensational success.

A perfect pie pastry depends greatly on its proportion of fat to flour. Fat's main contribution is that it tenderizes the flour and, therefore, the resultant crust. Because of its exquisite flavor, I prefer using unsalted butter in my pastry crusts. Lard, though bland, contains a higher percentage of fat and will produce a more crumbly crust. Pastry crusts in this chapter use all-purpose flour, which contains a blend of hard and soft wheats. This multi-purpose blend makes doughs resilient, yet tender.

Pie crusts can be as versatile as the imagination of the creator and should always complement the filling. The Sweet Cornmeal Crust, for example, provides a delightfully crunchy contrast to the creamy, bourbon-scented custard in Kentucky Pumpkin Pie. The same crust lends an early American flavor to Tyler Pie, which my grandmother told me was named after President Tyler because of his love of sweet desserts. Apple-Brie Tart, created especially for those who prefer light, fruit desserts, features a crust of crisp, golden-brown puff pastry. The Grecian Tart enfolds its filling in buttery filo dough. Last, but not least, are the many cookie-crumb crusts—so quick and easy for a complete beginner.

If elegance is your entertaining goal, try the Champagne-Mousse Pie. Heady with sparkling champagne and enlivened with lemon, this festive finale is the perfect way to toast the New Year! Or, you might choose the Brandied Walnut Tart, a delicious union of sugar, cream and walnuts. Melted chocolate is drizzled over the top for added panache. Thin wedges of this ultra-rich dessert will satisfy the most demanding sweet tooth!

A bevy of fresh fruits star in many of this chapter's recipes. Marlborough Peach Pie is my variation of the early American classic which was made with apples and cream. The non-traditional streusel topping adds a delightful crunch to every bite. Honey-Plum Pie derives its fulsome flavor and beautiful hue from sweet purple plums. Peaches may be substituted for plums with equally delicious results. Pureed blueberries combine with whole blueberries and orange juice in Blue-Angel Pie. The filling is piled cloud-high in an orange-flavored crumb crust for a beautiful summer dessert.

Few desserts are greeted with such resounding applause as pie. So take the plunge, practice and experiment with different crusts and fillings, and be prepared for the raves you deserve!

Hints for Successful Pies

- Read the recipe carefully to make sure you have all the necessary equipment and ingredients on hand. Be sure ingredients such as flour and nuts are fresh. Stale nuts can ruin the final flavor.
- Assemble ingredients in the order they will be used.
- Use the appropriate measuring cups; nested cups for dry ingredients and glass cups for liquid ingredients.
- Use correct size pie pans. Measure diameter of pans from inside edge of rim. On a "9-inch" pie pan, for example, this measurement may vary up to 1/2 inch, depending on the manufacturer.
- Lightweight foil pans are usually smaller than regular pie pans. Extra filling may be poured into individual muffin tins and baked, refrigerated or frozen, depending on the recipe.
- Glass, dark-metal and dull-metal pans absorb heat and produce a crisp, golden-brown crust. Shiny aluminum pans produce pale crusts. Reduce oven heat by 25F when using glass dishes. Unless otherwise indicated, pie pans do not need to be greased.
- Position oven rack in center of oven. Preheat oven 15 minutes. Use an oven thermometer for accurate oven temperature.
- When preparing pastry, cut butter into flour until mixture resembles coarse crumbs. Once the liquid has been added, blend *only* until dough begins to hold together. Add additional liquid only if necessary for dough to hold together. Overmixing will create a tough crust.
- Form dough into a flat disk; wrap and refrigerate 30 minutes. Chilled pastry dough rolls out more easily than room-temperature dough.
- Several pastry doughs in this chapter do not require rolling and may instead be pressed into the pan. If you choose this method, work quickly and lightly to prevent baked crust from being tough.
- To roll out dough, use a large pastry board and a heavy rolling pin. Marble and textured-acrylic boards are the easiest to work with. Both pin and board should be lightly floured.
- Place rolling pin in center of dough disk. Roll dough firmly and evenly away from you. Then roll from middle of disk toward you. Continue rolling from center outward until circle of dough is 3 inches larger than inside diameter of your pie pan.
- If necessary, use a pastry scraper or large metal spatula to loosen dough from pastry board. Fold dough circle in half. Gently lift dough, positioning it so fold is across center of pan. Unfold dough, easing it into pan. Or, lay dough over rolling pin. Position it over pie pan; remove rolling pin. Do not stretch dough when placing it in pan. Stretched dough shrinks as it bakes.
- Use a knife to trim outer edge of dough, creating a 3/4- to 1-inch overhang; fold under. Form raised edge by pressing dough gently between your thumbs and index fingers. Decoratively crimp or flute raised edge as desired, page 33.
- For baked pie shells, use a fork to prick bottom and sides of unbaked shell at 1/2-inch intervals. Refrigerate unbaked crust 30 minutes or freeze 15 minutes before baking.
- For filled, baked pies, do not prick dough. To prevent a soggy crust, refrigerate unbaked crust 15 minutes. You can also brush unbaked crust with egg white, then refrigerate 15 minutes. Pour filling into pie shell immediately prior to baking. Setting pie pan on a metal baking sheet during baking also helps to prevent a soggy crust.
- Place pie pans in oven so they have at least 2 inches between each other and sides of oven. If pies are baked on 2 shelves, position them so that 1 does not sit directly beneath another. For good results, oven heat must circulate freely and evenly.
- Have a timer on hand. To allow for variations in ovens, check pies 5 minutes before minimum time indicated in recipe.
- Cool pies in pans on a rack.

Sweet Pastry Crust

An easy cookie-style dough you can either roll out or press right into the pan.

1-1/4 cups all-purpose flour	1/2 cup firm cold butter, cut in 6 pieces
3 tablespoons sugar	1 egg yolk
1/4 teaspoon salt	1 teaspoon vanilla extract

In a food processor fitted with a metal blade or in a medium bowl, combine flour, sugar and salt; add butter. Process in food processor using quick on/off pulses until mixture resembles coarse crumbs. Or, using a pastry blender or 2 knives, cut butter into dry ingredients until mixture resembles coarse crumbs. Add egg yolk and vanilla; process with quick on/off pulses or stir only until dough begins to hold together. Turn out onto work surface; form dough into a 1/2-inch-thick flat disc. Wrap and refrigerate at least 30 minutes before using. May be refrigerated up to 1 week. If dough is refrigerated longer than 30 minutes, let it stand at room temperature until soft enough to handle. Break off large pieces of dough and press over bottom and up sides of an ungreased 9- or 10-inch pie pan. Form a 1/2-inch raised edge; flute, page 33, if desired. Or, lay 2 (14-inch) lengths of plastic wrap crosswise to each other on work surface. Place dough in center; cover with 2 more pieces of plastic wrap. Roll out dough, page 29, to a 12-inch circle for a 9-inch pie, a 13-inch circle for a 10-inch pie or as directed in specific recipe. Remove top sheets of plastic wrap. Invert pie pan over dough circle. Carefully turn dough and pan right-side up. Gently press dough into pan; remove plastic wrap. Trim and flute edge. Using a fork, prick shell at 1/2-inch intervals. Refrigerate 30 minutes or freeze 15 minutes. Preheat oven to 475F (245C). Bake 8 to 10 minutes or until crust is golden brown. Cool on a rack before filling. Makes 1 (9- to 10-inch) pie crust.

Variations
Citrus Pastry Crust: Add finely grated zest of 1 large lemon, 1 small orange or 1/2 small grapefruit to dry ingredients.
Nutty Sweet Pastry Crust: Lightly press 1/2 cup finely chopped walnuts or pecans into bottom and sides of unbaked crust.
Coconut Pastry Crust: Lightly press 1/2 cup shredded coconut into bottom and sides of unbaked crust.

Coco-Nutty Crust

Nuts add color and texture to this heavenly crust featuring coconut. It's an absolute winner in Piña-Colada Pie, page 37.

2 cups shredded or flaked coconut	1/3 cup butter, melted
3/4 cup ground almonds, pecans or walnuts	

Preheat oven to 325F (165C). Generously grease a 9-inch pie pan. In a medium bowl, combine all ingredients; let stand 10 minutes. Press mixture firmly over bottom and up sides of greased pan. Bake 20 to 25 minutes or until edges are browned and middle is deep golden brown. Cool on a rack before filling. Makes 1 (9-inch) pie crust.

Chocolate Pastry Crust

Add a little decadence to your favorite pie filling with this chocolatey crust!

Sifted unsweetened cocoa
1 cup plus 2 tablespoons all-purpose flour
1/3 cup sugar
3 tablespoons unsweetened cocoa

1/4 teaspoon salt
1/2 cup firm cold butter, cut in 6 pieces
1 teaspoon vanilla extract
1 to 3 tablespoons iced water

Lightly grease a 9-inch pie pan, including rim. Lightly dust with unsweetened cocoa. In a food processor fitted with a metal blade or in a medium bowl, combine flour, sugar, cocoa and salt; add butter. Process in food processor using quick on/off pulses until mixture resembles coarse crumbs. Or, using a pastry blender or 2 knives, cut butter into dry ingredients until mixture resembles coarse crumbs. Add vanilla and about 1-1/2 tablespoons iced water; process using quick on/off pulses or stir only until dough begins to hold together. Add more water only if necessary. Turn out dough onto work surface. Form dough into a 1/2-inch-thick flat disc; let rest 5 minutes. If dough is very soft, wrap and refrigerate 30 minutes. May be refrigerated up to 1 week. If dough is refrigerated longer than 30 minutes, let it stand at room temperature until soft enough to handle. Break off large pieces of dough and press over bottom and up sides of prepared pie pan. Form a 1/2-inch raised edge; flute, page 33, if desired. Or, on a lightly floured work surface, roll out dough, page 29, to a 12-inch circle. Fold circle in half. Gently lift folded dough; place in prepared pan with fold in center. Unfold dough to fit pan. Trim and flute edge. Using a fork, prick shell at 1/2-inch intervals. Refrigerate 30 minutes or freeze 15 minutes. Preheat oven to 425F (220C). Bake 10 minutes or until crisp. Cool on a rack before filling. Makes 1 (9-inch) pie crust.

Nut Pastry Crust

Toasted nuts produce a crunchy crust. Vary the nuts you use to complement the filling.

1 cup all-purpose flour
3/4 cup toasted ground pecans, almonds
   or walnuts
3 tablespoons brown sugar

1/4 teaspoon salt
1/2 cup firm cold butter, cut in 8 pieces
1 egg yolk

In a food processor fitted with a metal blade or in a medium bowl, combine flour, nuts, brown sugar and salt; add butter. Process in food processor using quick on/off pulses until mixture resembles coarse crumbs. Or, using a pastry blender or 2 knives, cut butter into dry ingredients until mixture resembles coarse crumbs. Add egg yolk; process with quick on/off pulses or stir only until dough begins to hold together. Turn out onto work surface; form dough into a 1/2-inch-thick flat disc. Wrap and refrigerate 30 minutes to 1 hour before using. If dough is refrigerated longer than 1 hour, let it stand at room temperature until soft enough to handle. Preheat oven to 400F (205C). Break off large pieces of dough and press over bottom and up sides of an ungreased 9- or 10-inch pie pan or 10- or 11-inch tart pan. Bake 10 minutes or until golden brown. Cool on a rack before filling. Makes 1 (9- to 11-inch) pie or tart crust.

Sweet Cornmeal Crust

A wonderfully crisp crust—omit the sugar and use crust for savory pies as a nice change of pace!

1-1/3 cups all-purpose flour
3/4 cup yellow cornmeal
1/4 cup packed brown sugar

1/4 teaspoon salt
3/4 cup firm cold butter, cut in 10 pieces
1 to 3 tablespoons iced water

In a food processor fitted with a metal blade or in a medium bowl, combine flour, cornmeal, brown sugar and salt; add butter. Process in food processor using quick on/off pulses until mixture resembles coarse crumbs. Or, using a pastry blender or 2 knives, cut butter into dry ingredients until mixture resembles coarse crumbs. Add 1 tablespoon iced water; process with quick on/off pulses or stir only until dough begins to hold together. Add more water only if necessary. Gather dough into a ball; let rest 5 minutes. Break off large pieces of dough and press over bottom and up sides of an ungreased 9- or 10-inch pie pan. If necessary, dampen your fingertips for easy handling. Form a 1/2-inch raised edge; flute, opposite, if desired. Refrigerate 30 minutes or freeze 15 minutes. Fill and bake as directed in specific recipe. Makes 1 (9- or 10-inch) pie crust.

Cookie-Crumb Crust

Use any crisp cookie to make crumbs for this easy and delicious crust. Adding nuts to the crumb mixture creates a delightful crunch.

1-1/2 cups crisp-cookie crumbs
1/4 cup sugar

5 tablespoons butter, melted

In a medium bowl, combine all ingredients. Follow directions in specific recipe or turn mixture into a lightly greased 9-inch pie pan. Using the back of a large spoon, press mixture firmly and evenly over bottom and up sides of greased pan. Bake at 350F (175C) 10 minutes. Cool on a rack before filling. Instead of baking, crust can be chilled 10 to 15 minutes in freezer. Baked crusts are crisper. Makes 1 (9-inch) pie crust.

Variations
Honey-Nut Crust: Substitute 1/2 cup finely chopped nuts for 1/2 cup cookie crumbs; substitute 2 tablespoons honey for 1/4 cup sugar. Reduce butter to 3 tablespoons.
Cream-Filled-Cookie Crust: Use cream-filled-chocolate-cookie crumbs, reduce butter to 3 tablespoons; omit sugar.
Spiced Crumb Crust: Use gingersnap crumbs; add 1/2 teaspoon *each* ground cinnamon and ground nutmeg.
Double-Chocolate Crumb Crust: Use chocolate-wafer-cookie crumbs; add 1 tablespoon unsweetened cocoa and additional 1 tablespoon sugar.
Citrus Crumb Crust: Add finely grated zest of 1 large lemon, 1 small orange or 1/2 small grapefruit.
Nutty Crumb Crust: Substitute 1/2 cup *finely* chopped walnuts or pecans for 1/4 cup cookie crumbs.

How to Make Sweet Cornmeal Crust & Meringue-Nut Tartlet Shells

For Sweet Cornmeal Crust, press dough over bottom and up sides of pie pan. Form a 1/2-inch raised edge and flute, if desired.

For Meringue-Nut Tartlet Shells, grease and flour muffin cups. Spread a heaping tablespoon of meringue over bottom and up sides of each muffin cup. Do not go over rim of cup.

Meringue-Nut Crust

Wonderful for custard, chiffon or cream pies; medium-ground nuts will give your crust more texture. Always make sure the nuts you use are fresh—stale nuts will ruin the flavor.

1-1/3 cups ground nuts of choice
2 tablespoons cornstarch
1/4 cup sugar

2 egg whites, room temperature
1/4 teaspoon salt

Preheat oven to 350F (175C). Grease and flour a 9-inch pie pan. In a medium bowl, combine nuts, cornstarch and 2 tablespoons sugar; set aside. In a small mixer bowl, beat egg whites and salt to soft-peak stage. Beating constantly, gradually add remaining 2 tablespoons sugar. Continue beating until whites are glossy and firm. Sprinkle 1/2 of nut mixture over egg whites; fold in. Repeat with remaining nut mixture. Spread over bottom and up sides of prepared pie pan but not over rim. Bake 15 to 20 minutes or until crust is an even golden brown. Cool on a rack before filling. Makes 1 (9-inch) pie crust.

Variation
Meringue-Nut Tartlet Shells: Grease and flour 12 (2-1/2-inch) muffin cups. Spread a heaping tablespoon meringue over bottom and up sides of each muffin cup. Do not go over rim of cup. Bake at 350F (175C) 15 minutes or until golden brown. To loosen tartlet shells, run a thin knife around inside edges of muffin cups. Carefully place shells on a rack. Cool before filling. Makes 12 tartlet shells.

Mosaic Fruit Tart

Photos opposite and page 4.

Choose the prettiest fresh fruit you can find to make a stunning tart of kaleidoscope colors.

1/2 recipe Celestial Cream, page 84,
   with changes noted below
1 Nut Pastry Crust, page 31, or
   Sweet Pastry Crust, page 30, made in
   an 11-inch tart pan

1 cup apricot jam or apple jelly
Selection of fresh fruits, peeled,
   sliced, if necessary

Prepare Celestial Cream, omitting Spirited Whipped Cream and orange slices or candied zest; cover and refrigerate as directed. Prepare pastry crust; bake and cool as directed. In a small saucepan, stir jam or jelly over medium heat until melted. Press jam through a fine sieve into a small bowl. Refrigerate jam or jelly 20 minutes or until cool. Spread chilled Celestial Cream in bottom of baked pastry crust. Arrange fruit of your choice in an attractive pattern over cream. Spoon apricot or apple glaze over fruit. Cover and refrigerate 6 to 8 hours until ready to serve. Makes 1 (11-inch) tart.

Variation
If using mostly red berries for fruit, use strawberry or red-currant jelly.

Blue-Angel Pie

Fresh are best, but frozen blueberries will still give this beautiful pie a "heavenly" taste.

1 (9-inch) Citrus Crumb Crust, page 32,
   using orange zest
1 (1/4-oz.) envelope unflavored gelatin
   (scant 1 tablespoon)
3/4 cup orange juice
6 egg yolks, room temperature
3/4 cup blueberry puree (about 1-1/2 cups
   whole blueberries)
3/4 cup sugar
1 tablespoon freshly grated orange zest

1/2 teaspoon ground cinnamon
2 egg whites, room temperature
1/2 teaspoon salt
1/2 pint whipping cream (1 cup), whipped
1 pint fresh or 2 cups drained, thawed,
   loosepack, frozen blueberries
Additional 1/4 to 1/2 cup whipping cream,
   if desired, whipped
Additional 1/4 cup fresh or drained, thawed,
   loosepack, frozen blueberries, if desired

Prepare Citrus Crumb Crust; bake and cool as directed. In a small bowl, stir gelatin into 1/4 cup orange juice; let stand 5 minutes to soften. In a medium saucepan, combine egg yolks, blueberry puree, 1/2 cup sugar, orange zest, cinnamon and remaining 1/2 cup orange juice. Cook over medium heat, stirring constantly, 3 to 5 minutes or until mixture thickly coats the back of a metal spoon. Remove from heat. Add gelatin mixture; stir 1 minute or until dissolved. Pour into a large bowl. Refrigerate, stirring occasionally, until mixture begins to mound when spooned on top of itself. If mixture sets too firmly, beat until smooth before continuing. In a small mixer bowl, beat egg whites and salt to soft-peak stage. Beating constantly, add remaining 1/4 cup sugar, 2 tablespoons at a time. Continue beating until egg whites are glossy and firm. Fold whipped cream, then egg-white mixture and 2 cups blueberries into chilled gelatin mixture. Spoon into prepared crust, mounding high in center. If desired, decorate with whipped-cream rosettes, placing 1 whole blueberry in center of each rosette. If using thawed frozen blueberries for garnish, place on pie no more than 5 to 10 minutes before serving. Refrigerate 3 to 4 hours before serving. Makes 1 (9-inch) pie.

Apple-Brie Tart

Sugar-glazed apples and creamy Brie cheese, crisply upholstered in puff pastry—created for Jeff!

12 oz. ripe Brie cheese, room temperature
1 egg
1 egg yolk
2 tablespoons brandy
1/3 cup butter
1/4 cup sugar

1 lb. crisp tart apples, peeled, cored,
   cut in 1/4-inch slices
1 (17-1/4-oz.) pkg. thawed
   frozen puff pastry
1 egg mixed with 1 teaspoon water
   for glaze

Remove rind from Brie. In a small bowl, combine Brie, egg, egg yolk and brandy. Beat until smooth; refrigerate. Cheese mixture must be thick enough not to run when spread. In a large skillet, melt butter. Add sugar; cook over high heat 1 minute. Reduce heat to medium-high. Add apples; cook until crisp-tender. Transfer apple mixture to a plate to cool. On a lightly floured work surface, roll out 1 puff-pastry sheet to a 10-inch square; cut out a 10-inch circle. Place in center of an ungreased baking sheet. Roll out remaining pastry sheet to an 11-inch square; cut out an 11-inch circle. Spread cheese mixture over 10-inch pastry circle to within 3/4 inch of edge. Spoon cooled apple mixture on top of cheese. Score 11-inch pastry circle into 8 equal wedges, cutting only halfway through pastry. Brush bottom pastry border with egg glaze. Gently lift scored pastry circle and place it on top of apples. Firmly press edges of pastry together with the tines of a fork to seal. Brush surface with egg glaze; do not let glaze drip onto baking sheet or cooked pastry will stick to sheet. Using a sharp pointed knife, make 1/2-inch-long cuts all the way through center of pastry in a star pattern, following scoring. Refrigerate at least 20 minutes. No more than 2 hours before serving, preheat oven to 450F (230C). Bake tart 10 minutes. Reduce oven temperature to 400F (205C); bake 25 to 35 minutes longer or until puffed and golden brown. Cool on a rack. Serve warm or at room temperature. Makes 1 (11-inch) tart.

Frozen Strawberry-Daiquiri Pie

Serve this heady delight year-round by substituting 10 to 12 ounces frozen loosepack strawberries for fresh.

1 (9-inch) Nutty Crumb Crust, page 32,
   using walnuts and
   shortbread-cookie crumbs
1 pint strawberries, hulled
3/4 cup sugar
1 (1-/4-oz.) envelope unflavored gelatin
   (scant 1 tablespoon)

1/3 cup lime juice
1/3 cup light rum
1/2 pint whipping cream (1 cup), whipped
5 large strawberries, leaves attached

Prepare Nutty Crumb Crust; bake and cool as directed. In a blender, combine hulled strawberries and sugar; process until berries are pureed. Set aside 15 minutes for mixture to soak and blend. In a small saucepan, stir gelatin into lime juice; let stand 5 minutes to soften. Stir over medium heat just until gelatin dissolves. With blender running at medium speed, add gelatin mixture to pureed strawberry mixture; process 30 seconds. Add rum; process until blended. Strain through a fine sieve into a large bowl. Refrigerate, stirring often, until mixture begins to mound when spooned on top of itself. Fold in whipped cream. Spoon into prepared crust; smooth top. Freeze 4 hours. Cut 4 of large strawberries in half. Immediately before serving, decorate top edge of pie with 8 strawberry halves; place remaining whole strawberry in center. Makes 1 (9-inch) pie.

How to Make Apple-Brie Tart

1/Using a sharp pointed knife, make 1/2-inch-long cuts all the way through center of pastry in a star pattern, following scoring. Refrigerate tart at least 20 minutes.

2/Bake tart until puffed and golden brown. Cool on a rack. Serve warm or at room temperature.

Piña-Colada Pie

One bite of this tropical-tasting pie will make you feel like you're on a Caribbean island! Cream of coconut can be found in the gourmet or liquor sections of most supermarkets.

1 (9-inch) Coco-Nutty Crust, page 30
1 (8-oz.) can crushed pineapple
   in its own juice
About 1 cup pineapple juice
1 (1/4-oz.) envelope plus 1 teaspoon
   unflavored gelatin
   (about 3-1/2 teaspoons)

1/3 cup sugar
1/2 cup cream of coconut
1/3 cup light rum, or 1/3 cup milk
   and 1/2 teaspoon imitation rum extract
Toasted Coconut, page 145
1/2 pint whipping cream (1 cup), whipped

Prepare Coco-Nutty Crust; bake and cool as directed. Using the back of a spoon, press pineapple in a sieve to drain juice thoroughly. Set fruit aside. Reserve juice, adding enough additional pineapple juice to equal 1-1/3 cups. Pour 1/3 cup pineapple juice into a small saucepan. Stir in gelatin; let stand 5 minutes to soften. Add sugar. Stir over low heat until gelatin and sugar dissolve. Remove from heat; set aside. In a large bowl, blend coconut cream, rum or milk and rum extract, and remaining 1 cup pineapple juice. Slowly whisk in gelatin mixture. Refrigerate, stirring occasionally, until mixture begins to mound when spooned on top of itself. Prepare Toasted Coconut; cool. Stir drained pineapple into gelatin mixture; fold in whipped cream. Spoon mixture into prepared crust. Garnish with coconut. Refrigerate 3 hours before serving. Makes 8 servings.

Marlborough Peach Pie

A variation on an early American recipe using peaches instead of apples and adding a streusel topping.

1 (9-inch) Sweet Pastry Crust, page 30

Filling:

1-1/3 cups peach puree
   (2 to 3 medium peaches)
1 tablespoon lemon juice
1/2 cup packed brown sugar
3 eggs
1/2 cup whipping cream
1/2 teaspoon salt

1/2 teaspoon ground nutmeg
1/4 teaspoon ground cinnamon
Streusel Topping, see below
1/2 recipe Spirited Whipped Cream, page 156,
   if desired, flavored with brandy
Additional ground nutmeg, if desired

Streusel Topping:

3 tablespoons all-purpose flour
3 tablespoons sugar
1/2 teaspoon ground nutmeg

2 tablespoons firm cold butter,
   cut in 4 pieces

Preheat oven to 450F (230C). Prepare Sweet Pastry Crust; bake 10 minutes. While crust is baking, place peach puree, lemon juice, brown sugar, eggs, 1/2 cup whipping cream, salt, 1/2 teaspoon nutmeg and cinnamon in a large bowl. Beat until blended, but do not allow mixture to foam. Pour into hot pie crust. Reduce oven temperature to 325F (165C); bake 30 minutes. Prepare Streusel Topping. Carefully remove pie from oven; sprinkle Streusel Topping evenly over surface. Bake 25 to 30 minutes longer or until a knife inserted in center comes out clean. Cool on a rack to room temperature; refrigerate. Prepare Spirited Whipped Cream, if desired. Garnish pie with dollops or rosettes of whipped cream; sprinkle with nutmeg, if desired. Makes 1 (9-inch) pie.

Streusel Topping:

In a small bowl, combine all ingredients. Using a pastry blender or 2 knives, cut in butter until mixture resembles coarse crumbs.

Tyler Pie

Grandmother said this pie was named for President Tyler (no relation) because of his love of sweets. Try using freshly grated nutmeg for added flavor excitement.

1 unbaked (9-inch) Sweet Cornmeal Crust,
   page 32, or Sweet Pastry Crust,
   page 30, do not prick dough
3 eggs, room temperature
1 cup packed brown sugar
1 tablespoon all-purpose flour
1/4 teaspoon ground nutmeg

1/4 teaspoon salt
1 cup half and half, room temperature
2 teaspoons vanilla extract
1/4 cup melted butter
1 cup whipping cream, whipped
Additional ground nutmeg

Prepare unbaked pie crust of your choice; refrigerate 30 minutes. Preheat oven to 425F (220C). In a medium bowl, beat eggs, brown sugar, flour, 1/4 teaspoon nutmeg and salt until light and creamy. Gradually stir in half and half, vanilla and butter; do not beat. Pour into unbaked crust. Bake 10 minutes. Reduce oven temperature to 325F (165C). Bake 20 to 25 minutes longer or until a knife inserted in center comes out clean. Cool in pan on a rack. Spread cooled pie with whipped cream. Lightly sprinkle with ground nutmeg. Refrigerate until ready to serve. Makes 1 (9-inch) pie.

How to Make Fudge-Truffle Pie

1/Drizzle filled pie with remaining Fudge Velvet Sauce.

2/Using the flat edge of a dinner knife, cut through mixture in a wide zigzag pattern to create a marbled effect.

Fudge-Truffle Pie

A dreamy chocolate-truffle filling marbled with fudge sauce—the ultimate chocolate fantasy!

1 (9-inch) Chocolate Pastry Crust,
  page 31
2 oz. semisweet chocolate
2 tablespoons butter
1 cup butter
6 oz. semisweet chocolate, coarsely chopped
1-1/4 cups sifted powdered sugar

5 eggs, lightly beaten
1/2 cup Fudge Velvet Sauce, page 150,
  room temperature
3/4 cup whipping cream, whipped
1/2 recipe Plain Whipped Cream,
  page 156, if desired

Prepare Chocolate Pastry Crust; bake and cool as directed. In a small saucepan, melt 2 ounces chocolate and 2 tablespoons butter over low heat; cool. Spread cooled chocolate mixture over bottom and halfway up sides of cooled crust. Refrigerate until chocolate is set. In a medium, heavy saucepan, melt 1 cup butter. Remove from heat. Add chopped chocolate; stir until melted. Whisk in powdered sugar and eggs, whisking until well-blended. Return to low heat. Cook 1 minute, stirring constantly. Turn into a large mixer bowl. Refrigerate, stirring occasionally, until cool. Prepare Fudge Velvet Sauce; cool until very thick. Beat cooled chocolate mixture at high speed 2 minutes. Fold in first amount of whipped cream. Spoon 1/2 of mixture into crust; smooth top. Using 1/4 cup Fudge Velvet Sauce, place teaspoonfuls randomly in 5 to 6 places, pressing fudge sauce into pie filling with the back of a spoon. Spoon remaining pie filling into crust; smooth top. Drizzle with remaining sauce. Using the flat edge of a dinner knife, cut through mixture in a wide zigzag pattern to create a marbled effect. Do not marble too much or colors will blend and not contrast. Do not smooth surface of pie. Refrigerate 3 hours before serving. If desired, prepare Plain Whipped Cream; pass with pie. Makes 1 (9-inch) pie.

Kahlúa-Pecan Tartlets

Kahlúa creates dark magic in these tiny tarts—perfect for holiday or special entertaining!

1 recipe dough for Sweet Pastry Crust,
  page 30
1 cup toasted chopped pecans
3 tablespoons butter, melted
1/3 cup packed brown sugar
3 eggs
1/4 teaspoon salt

1/3 cup light corn syrup
1/3 cup dark corn syrup
1/3 cup Kahlúa or other
  coffee-flavored liqueur
24 pecan halves
Spirited Whipped Cream, page 156,
  if desired, flavored with Kahlúa

Prepare dough for Sweet Pastry Crust. Form into a 12-inch-long log; wrap in plastic wrap. Place in refrigerator or freezer 30 to 45 minutes. Cut dough into 24 (1/2-inch) slices. Refrigerate 12 slices. Working with remaining 12 slices, place 1 dough slice in each of 12 (2- or 3-inch) tartlet tins; press dough over bottom and up sides. Dough layer should be even and thin without any bare spots. Repeat with refrigerated dough slices and 12 more tartlet tins. Spoon a heaping 1/2 tablespoon chopped pecans into each tartlet shell. Place tart tins on 1 large or 2 medium baking sheets. Refrigerate 30 minutes. Preheat oven to 375F (190C). In a blender or food processor fitted with a metal blade, process butter, brown sugar, eggs, salt, light and dark corn syrups, and coffee-flavored liqueur 45 seconds or until well-blended. Spoon about 2 tablespoons egg mixture into each unbaked tartlet shell; top with a pecan half. Bake 15 minutes or until filling is set. Cool 5 minutes in tins. Carefully slip tartlets out of tins onto racks; cool to room temperature. Prepare Spirited Whipped Cream, if desired, to serve with tartlets. Makes 24 tartlets.

Brandied Walnut Tart

Thin wedges of this decadently rich tart will satisfy the most demanding sweet tooth!

1 recipe dough for Sweet Pastry Crust,
  page 30
2 cups sugar
1/2 pint whipping cream (1 cup)
1/4 teaspoon salt

1/4 cup brandy or Cognac
1/2 teaspoon vanilla extract
2 cups coarsely chopped walnuts
1 oz. semisweet chocolate, melted, cooled
Unsweetened whipped cream, if desired

Prepare dough for Sweet Pastry Crust; wrap and refrigerate 30 minutes. Place sugar in a large skillet over medium-high heat. Cook, stirring occasionally with a long-handled wooden spoon, until sugar melts and turns a deep-golden color. Sugar may not dissolve completely. Quickly add cream, stirring rapidly with wooden spoon. Mixture will bubble and steam, and sugar will clump. Continue stirring 2 to 3 minutes or until mixture is smooth. Remove from heat. Add salt, brandy and vanilla; stir until blended. Stir in nuts. Cool in pan on a rack, stirring occasionally, until barely warm. Preheat oven to 350F (175C). Break off pieces of refrigerated dough and press over bottom and 1-1/4 inches up side of an ungreased 9-inch springform pan. Make sure top edge of crust is straight and even. Refrigerate 15 minutes. Turn cooled filling into crust. Bake 40 minutes or until edges of pastry are golden. Cool in pan on rack. To loosen tart, run a thin knife around inside edge of pan. Remove side of pan. Loosen tart from pan bottom; place on serving plate. Make a decorator cone out of waxed or parchment paper, page 22; cut an 1/8-inch-wide tip. Fill halfway with melted chocolate. Or, use a pastry bag fitted with a small plain tip; or, use a kitchen teaspoon. Drizzle chocolate over top of tart in a lacy pattern. Let chocolate set before serving. Serve at room temperature with unsweetened whipped cream, if desired. Makes 1 (9-inch) tart.

How to Make Grecian Tart

1/Spoon refrigerated cream-cheese mixture over nuts; spread to within 3/4 inch of edge.

2/Repeat layering with filo circles and nuts. Using your fingertips, firmly press down on edges of tart. Sprinkle top with 1/4 cup nuts.

Grecian Tart

The trick to handling filo is to work quickly, keeping unused portions covered with a damp cloth.

1 (8-oz.) pkg. cream cheese, softened
1 egg yolk
1/4 cup honey
Freshly grated zest of 1 medium orange
1/4 teaspoon ground cinnamon
1/4 teaspoon ground nutmeg

8 sheets filo dough
About 1/4 cup butter, melted
About 1-1/4 cups toasted finely
  chopped walnuts
Honey Whipped Cream or Orange Whipped
  Cream, page 156

Preheat oven to 350F (175C). Butter sides only of a 9-inch springform pan. In a small bowl, beat cream cheese, egg yolk, honey, orange zest, cinnamon and nutmeg until creamy; refrigerate. Place 8 filo sheets in a single stack. Using a sharp pair of scissors, cut through all 8 layers to form 8 (9-inch) circles. Cover circles with a slightly dampened towel; refrigerate or freeze remaining filo dough for another use. Place 1 filo circle in bottom of prepared pan. Brush with melted butter; sprinkle with 2 tablespoons nuts. Repeat process with 3 more filo circles. Spoon refrigerated filling mixture into center; spread to within 3/4 inch of edge. Place a filo circle over filling. Brush with melted butter; sprinkle with 2 tablespoons nuts. Repeat process with remaining 3 filo circles. Using your fingertips, firmly press down on edges of tart. Sprinkle top with 1/4 cup nuts. Bake 50 minutes or until crisp and golden brown. If necessary, loosen side of tart with a knife before removing side of pan. Cool on a rack 20 minutes. Prepare Honey Whipped Cream or Orange Whipped Cream; refrigerate. Ease tart away from pan bottom; transfer to a serving plate. Serve warm with cream. Makes 8 servings.

Kentucky Pumpkin Pie

This bourbon-scented pie boasts a crisp cornmeal crust and a delicious praline topping!

**1 unbaked (10-inch) Sweet Cornmeal Crust,
    page 32**

Filling:

1 (1-lb.) can pumpkin (2 cups)
1 cup packed brown sugar
3/4 teaspoon ground cinnamon
1/2 teaspoon ground nutmeg
1/2 teaspoon ground ginger
1/2 teaspoon salt

3 eggs
1 cup half and half
1/3 cup bourbon or half and half
**Spirited Whipped Cream, page 156,
    flavored with bourbon**

Praline Topping:

3/4 cup packed brown sugar
1/4 teaspoon ground nutmeg

1/4 cup butter, melted
2/3 cup chopped pecans

Prepare unbaked Sweet Cornmeal Crust; refrigerate 30 minutes. Preheat oven to 350F (175C). In a large bowl, beat pumpkin, brown sugar, cinnamon, nutmeg, ginger, salt and eggs just until blended. Stir in half and half and bourbon or extra half and half. Turn into prepared pie shell. Bake 45 to 55 minutes or until a knife inserted in center comes out clean. If crust begins to brown too quickly, cover edges lightly with foil. Cool pie on a rack to room temperature. Prepare Spirited Whipped Cream; refrigerate. Prepare Praline Topping; spoon evenly over pie filling. Preheat broiler. Watching carefully, broil pie 6 inches from heat, just until surface begins to bubble. Serve pie warm or at room temperature with Spirited Whipped Cream. Makes 1 (10-inch) pie.

Praline Topping:

In a medium bowl, combine all ingredients.

Lime-Yogurt Tartlets

Tiny meringue-nut crusts with a luscious, low-fat filling—perfect for summer alfresco dining!

12 Meringue-Nut Tartlet Shells, page 33
2 teaspoons unflavored gelatin
1/3 cup fresh lime juice
1 (8-oz.) pkg. Neufchâtel cheese, softened
1 cup sugar

8 oz. plain yogurt (1 cup)
3 to 5 drops green food coloring
2 or 3 drops yellow food coloring
3 thin lime slices, quartered

Prepare Meringue-Nut Tartlet Shells; bake and cool as directed. In a small bowl, stir gelatin into lime juice; let stand 5 minutes to soften. Place bowl in a larger bowl of very hot water. Stir until gelatin dissolves; set aside. In large mixer bowl, beat cheese and sugar until perfectly smooth. Add yogurt and gelatin mixture; beat 1 minute at medium speed. Beat in green and yellow food coloring. Refrigerate, stirring frequently, until mixture begins to mound when spooned on top of itself. Spoon into prepared tartlet shells, mounding high in center. Serve immediately or refrigerate up to 6 hours. Or, wrap and freeze tartlets 3 hours; remove from freezer 20 minutes before serving. Garnish each serving with a quartered lime slice. Makes 12 servings.

Honey-Plum Pie

Full-flavored purple plums give this honey-sweetened pie its luscious flavor and beautiful hue.

1 (9-inch) Honey-Nut Crust, page 32,
    using walnuts
1 (1/4-oz.) envelope unflavored gelatin
    (scant 1 tablespoon)
1/4 cup water
5 egg yolks
1 cup ripe-purple-plum puree,
    do not peel plums (4 to 5 plums)
1/3 cup honey

1-1/4 cups whipping cream
1/2 teaspoon salt
1/4 teaspoon ground ginger
1/4 teaspoon ground cinnamon
1/2 teaspoon vanilla extract
1-1/2 cups chopped ripe purple plums
    (3 to 5 plums)
1/2 recipe Honey Whipped Cream, page 156
Plum slices

Prepare Honey-Nut Crust; bake and cool as directed. In a small bowl, stir gelatin into water; let stand 5 minutes to soften. In a medium saucepan, combine egg yolks, plum puree, honey, 1/2 cup cream, salt, ginger and cinnamon. Cook over medium heat, stirring constantly, until mixture thickly coats the back of a metal spoon. Remove from heat. Add gelatin mixture; stir 1 minute or until dissolved. Pour into a large bowl. Place in refrigerator or freezer, stirring frequently, until mixture is almost set. In a small mixer bowl, beat remaining 3/4 cup cream and vanilla until stiff. Using a whisk, beat plum mixture to remove any lumps. Fold in chopped plums, then whipped cream. Spoon into cooled crust, mounding high in center. Refrigerate 2 to 3 hours or until set. Prepare Honey Whipped Cream. Garnish chilled pie with rosettes of cream around outer edge; arrange a pinwheel of plum slices in center. Makes 1 (9-inch) pie.

Champagne-Mousse Pie   *Photo on page 5.*

What better way to toast a special occasion—perfect for New Year's Eve!

1 (9-inch) Nut Pastry Crust, page 31,
    using almonds
1 (1/4-oz.) envelope unflavored gelatin
    (scant 1 tablespoon)
1-1/4 cups extra-dry champagne
3 eggs, separated, room temperature
Freshly grated zest of 1 medium lemon

2 teaspoons lemon juice
1 cup sugar
1/8 teaspoon salt
1/2 pint whipping cream (1 cup), whipped
1/2 recipe Spirited Whipped Cream,
    page 156, if desired, flavored
    with champagne
Red and green seedless-grape halves

Prepare Nut Pastry Crust; bake and cool as directed. In a small bowl, stir gelatin into 1/4 cup champagne; let stand 5 minutes to soften. In top of a double boiler, combine egg yolks, lemon zest, lemon juice, sugar and 1/2 cup champagne. Place top of double boiler over simmering water. Cook, stirring constantly, until mixture thickly coats the back of a metal spoon. Remove from heat. Add gelatin mixture; stir 1 minute or until dissolved. Stir in remaining 1/2 cup champagne. Strain through a fine sieve into a large bowl. Refrigerate, stirring occasionally, until mixture begins to mound when spooned on top of itself. In a small mixer bowl, beat egg whites and salt until stiff but not dry. Gently fold beaten egg whites, then whipped cream into champagne mixture. Spoon into prepared crust, mounding high in center. Refrigerate 3 hours or until set. Prepare Spirited Whipped Cream, if desired. Pipe rosettes of cream around outside edge of pie, if desired. Garnish pie with grape halves. Refrigerate up to 4 hours before serving. Makes 1 (9-inch) pie.

CHEESECAKES & OTHER CHEESE DESSERTS

For most of us, the first bite of cheesecake's cool, creamy excess transports our taste buds to a place where only angels dare to tread. The seductively smooth texture is undeniably enticing and has been known to arouse strong passions in the most gentle soul. No matter that every bite threatens to add instant inches to one's physical form. Some things in life are simply worth the price!

As with so many of mankind's treasures, the Greeks are rumored to have created the first cheese desserts. One can only guess whether they were actually in the form we know today as *cheesecake*. In the eighteenth century, Mrs. Hannah Glasse's *The Art of Cookery Made Plain and Easy* was one of the earliest cookbooks to discuss cheesecake. Since then, countless cheesecake recipes have been published, each with advocates who swear their favorite is the best.

It wasn't until 1872, thanks to American ingenuity, that cheesecake's most popular ingredient was discovered. Called *cream cheese* because of its smooth texture, this spreadable cheese has a delicate, slightly tangy flavor. It's made from cow's milk and, by law, must contain at least 33 percent butterfat. Other cheeses such as cottage, ricotta, Neufchâtel and even Swiss and Cheddar are also used to create a multitude of cheese desserts. In fact, one of the many pleasures of this popular finale is that the flavors and combinations are limited only by the imagination of the cook!

One reason cheesecakes are so popular is that they can be made well ahead, leaving the cook plenty of time for other last-minute details. Unfortunately, many cooks think this dessert is beyond their culinary skill. In fact, creating delicious, beautiful cheesecakes is not at all difficult. Like most things worthwhile, it simply takes care, patience and a little practice. For guaranteed success, be sure and scan *Hints For Successful Cheesecakes*, opposite, and you'll soon be a master of the art!

To crust or not to crust—that is the *first* question. Purists insist a crust has no place on cheesecake and only detracts from the dessert's purity. Others claim cheesecake requires at least a dusting of cookie or bread crumbs if for nothing more than eye appeal. Then there are those of us who feel a crisp or crunchy crust makes the perfect foil for most creamy-smooth fillings. Crusts can range from a delicate buttery pastry to a crisp cookie-crumb crust—the decision is yours!

Today's cheese dessert choices are limitless. There are large, showstopping spectaculars such as the Tunnel-of-Fudge Cheesecake, featuring a rich vanilla filling with a thick, fudgy core. Or, Pastiera, a fabulous dessert taught to me by my friends Carmen and Rae. This Italian masterpiece is studded with plump whole wheat berries and scented with orange-flower water.

Then there are small, individual cheese pleasers like Amaretto-Cheesecake Squares, flecked with toasted almonds. Devotees of soft cheese desserts will adore Cheese-Custard Suzette, baked in a water bath and enrobed in a heady orange sauce.

Unbaked cheese desserts are many and varied. For instance, cool and creamy Raspberry-Ripple Cheese Mold, which is delicately laced with Chambord liqueur and provocatively ribboned with sparkling Raspberry Jewel Sauce. Those who fancy lightly sweet desserts will enjoy the airy Suisse Torte which gets its nutlike nuance from Swiss cheese. For summer celebrations, try the frozen Red, White & Blueberry Cheese Torte, highlighting layers of pureed fresh blueberries and strawberries, for a stand-up-and-shout grand finale!

It has been said that cheese is *"milk's leap toward immortality."* That statement receives no argument from me, especially when cheese is incorporated into the most sensuous of desserts—the wonderfully tempting, often decadent and always alluring *cheesecake.*

Hints for Successful Cheesecakes

- Read the recipe carefully to make sure you have all the necessary equipment and ingredients on hand. *Do not* make any substitutions or the finished product can be drastically altered.
- Assemble ingredients in the order they will be used.
- Use the appropriate measuring cups; nested cups for dry ingredients and glass cups for liquid ingredients.
- It is essential to use the size pan specified in the recipe.
- Position oven rack in center of oven. Preheat oven 15 minutes. Use an oven thermometer for accurate oven temperature.
- To help prevent a pastry crust from becoming soggy, brush it lightly with egg white. Refrigerate 15 minutes before filling and baking.
- When making a crumb crust for cheesecake, form a "skirt" of foil around bottom of springform pan to prevent any butter from leaking out into oven, page 59.
- Cheese being used *must* be at room temperature. This makes it easier to blend with other ingredients creating a smooth, homogeneous mixture.
- Ricotta- and cottage-cheese-style cheeses should be processed in a blender until *perfectly* smooth before being added to other ingredients.
- Add and blend cheesecake ingredients in the precise order given in each recipe.
- Beat all ingredients together until very smooth before folding in whipped cream or stiffly beaten egg whites. Fold gently to retain as much air as possible.
- Have a timer on hand. To allow for variations in ovens, test cheesecake for doneness 5 minutes before minimum time indicated in recipe.
- Some delicate, custard-style cheesecakes are baked in a *water bath*. This means that the cheesecake pan is halfway immersed in hot water. The water acts as insulation and diffuses oven heat so mixture will set without separating. Although solid pans are suggested for use with water baths, springform pans may be used if foil is firmly pressed around outside of pan to prevent leakage.
- Cheesecakes require even heat in order to rise properly. For this reason, it is important not to open oven door during first 30 minutes of baking time. Drafts can cause a cheesecake to fall or crack.
- Each recipe in this chapter gives a precise baking time and it should be followed for the success of each cheesecake. Don't worry about a soft center. It will firm as cheesecake cools.
- Partially cooling a cheesecake in oven, with oven door propped open 1 to 3 inches, helps prevent cracks in top of cheesecake.
- Cracks are a common problem for which there are several causes. As a cheesecake bakes, its moisture evaporates. If it loses too much moisture, or if the moisture evaporates too quickly, cracking will occur. This problem can be alleviated by increasing humidity in the oven. To do so, place a shallow pan of hot water on bottom shelf.
- Concentric cracking and an overbrowned top indicate either oven heat was too high or cheesecake was baked too long.
- Cracks do not ruin a cheesecake! Most cheesecakes have toppings which cover cracks.
- Set baked cheesecake on a rack until completely cool. Cover and refrigerate as directed in recipe. If a cheesecake recipe calls for overnight refrigeration, try to allow for that time. If you refrigerate it for less time, the results may be passable, but the cheesecake won't have the proper creamy texture and may fall apart when you try to cut it!

Pastiera

Wheat berries add an intriguing touch to this old-country cheesecake from Naples. Traditionally served at Easter, it is wonderful any time at all!

1/3 cup whole wheat berries
  (whole-wheat kernels)
2 cinnamon sticks, each broken in 2 pieces
2 oz. Grated Chocolate, page 126, or
  1/3 cup miniature semisweet
  chocolate pieces
1 recipe dough for Citrus Pastry Crust,
  page 30
1 egg white, lightly beaten

2 lbs. ricotta cheese (4 cups),
  room temperature, drained if necessary
1 cup granulated sugar
1/4 cup cornstarch, sifted
1-1/2 tablespoons orange-flower water
6 eggs, separated, room temperature
1/4 cup finely chopped citron
1/2 teaspoon salt
Powdered sugar

In a medium saucepan, combine wheat berries and enough warm water to cover; soften overnight. Drain berries. Add cinnamon sticks and 3 cups fresh water; bring to a boil. Reduce heat; cover and simmer 2 hours or until berries are tender and some are split open. Drain berries. Rinse with cold water; drain again. Line a baking sheet with paper towel. Turn berries out onto baking sheet; set aside. Wheat berries may be prepared in advance, covered and refrigerated up to 1 week. Before using, blot excess moisture from berries with paper towel. Prepare Grated Chocolate, if using; refrigerate. Lightly grease a 9-inch springform pan. Prepare dough for Citrus Pastry. Pinch off 1/4 of dough. Between 2 sheets of plastic wrap, roll dough into a 9-1/2" x 4" rectangle, 1/4 inch thick. Remove top piece of plastic wrap. Trim ragged edges of dough. Return scraps to remaining dough and form into a ball. Cut rectangle into 8 (9-1/2" x 1/2") strips. Cover with plastic wrap; set aside. Position rack in center of oven and preheat to 350F (175C). Between sheets of plastic wrap, roll out remaining dough to a 14-inch circle. Remove top sheet of plastic wrap; gently flip dough into prepared pan. Firmly press dough into pan; remove plastic wrap. Trim dough around top edge, leaving enough to form a 1/2-inch raised edge. Patch any bare spots with dough scraps. Brush bottom and sides of dough with egg white. Place in freezer 10 minutes. Bake 5 minutes; cool on a rack. In a large bowl, beat ricotta cheese, granulated sugar, cornstarch, orange-flower water and egg yolks only until combined. Stir in wheat berries, citron and Grated Chocolate or chocolate pieces. In a large mixer bowl, beat egg whites and salt until stiff but not dry. Stir 1/4 of beaten egg whites into cheese mixture to lighten. Gently fold in remaining whites. Turn into cooled crust; smooth top. Arrange dough strips in a lattice pattern on top of cheese mixture. Trim strips to fit. Securely pinch ends of strips to raised dough edge. Bake 60 to 75 minutes or until center is soft but set. Turn off oven. Let cheesecake cool in oven 2 hours with oven door propped open 1 to 3 inches. Lightly dust cooled cheesecake with powdered sugar. Cool in pan on a rack to room temperature. Refrigerate at least 8 hours before serving. To serve, remove side of pan. Using 2 large metal spatulas, carefully slide cheesecake off pan bottom onto a serving plate. Makes 8 to 10 servings.

TIP *Orange-flower water is a delightfully aromatic flavoring, heady with the scent of orange blossoms. It adds a dash of intrigue to cakes, cheesecakes, custards—almost any dessert! You can find orange-flower water in the gourmet section of most supermarkets.*

Amaretto-Cheesecake Squares

Two-bite, finger-food cheesecakes studded with toasted almonds—they'll be the hit of your party!

6 (8-oz.) pkgs. cream cheese, softened
1/2 cup butter, softened
3/4 cup packed brown sugar
1/2 cup granulated sugar
1/4 teaspoon salt
6 eggs

1/2 cup dairy sour cream
1 teaspoon vanilla extract
1/2 teaspoon almond extract
1/3 cup amaretto liqueur
1 cup toasted finely chopped almonds

Caramelized Almonds:
3/4 cup granulated sugar

54 toasted blanched whole almonds

Amaretto Glaze:
1/4 cup butter
1/2 cup packed brown sugar
1/8 teaspoon salt
1/3 cup amaretto liqueur

2 cups sifted powdered sugar
Additional 1 to 2 tablespoons amaretto
    liqueur or whipping cream

Position rack in center of oven and preheat to 350F (175C). Grease a 13" x 9" baking pan. In a large mixer bowl, beat cream cheese, butter, sugars and salt until perfectly smooth and creamy, scraping bowl as necessary. Add eggs, 1 at a time, beating well after each addition. Beat in sour cream, vanilla, almond extract and amaretto. Stir in almonds. Pour into prepared pan; smooth top. Bake 45 minutes or until top is light golden. Cool on a rack to room temperature. To loosen cheesecake, run a thin knife around inside edges of pan. Place a large baking sheet over cheesecake; invert. Remove pan. Cover cheesecake with plastic wrap; refrigerate overnight. Prepare Caramelized Almonds and Amaretto Glaze; set aside.

To complete cheesecake, score top of chilled cheesecake into 54 squares, scoring into 6 strips 1 way and 9 strips the other way. Using a long knife with a narrow blade, trim edges of cheesecake to square off. Following scoring pattern, cut cheesecake all the way through into squares. Rinse knife under hot running water after each cut. Place squares, 1 inch apart, on a rack over waxed paper. Spoon about 1 teaspoon Amaretto Glaze over each square. Glaze should completely cover top and drizzle down sides. Place 1 Caramelized Almond in center of each square, pressing down slightly to attach. Let stand 10 to 15 minutes or until glaze is set. Cover lightly; refrigerate until ready to serve. Makes 54 cheesecake squares.

Caramelized Almonds:

Butter a large baking sheet. Place sugar in a small heavy saucepan. Cook over low heat, stirring occasionally, 10 to 15 minutes or until sugar is melted and caramelized to a golden brown. Remove from heat. Drop 5 or 6 almonds at a time into caramel syrup, coating each one thoroughly. Remove almonds with a fork, draining excess syrup. Place coated almonds, 1 inch apart, on prepared baking sheet. Let stand until hardened. Store in an airtight container up to 1 week until ready to use.

Amaretto Glaze:

In a medium saucepan, combine butter, brown sugar, salt and 1/3 cup amaretto over low heat. Cook just until sugar melts and mixture is smooth. Remove from heat; cool 5 minutes. Gradually add powdered sugar, beating until mixture is smooth. Beat in enough additional amaretto or cream to make a smooth and creamy glaze of drizzling consistency.

TIP

To soften cream cheese quickly, place unwrapped cheese on a dish in the microwave oven at 50% power for 30 to 60 seconds.

Rae's Frozen Cassata

An old Sicilian classic, this updated frozen version is ideal for special parties and celebrations.

Cake Lining:
1 Jelly-Roll recipe (making 2 sheets),
  page 10
1/3 cup sugar

1/3 cup water
1/3 cup rum

Cassata Filling:
2 lbs. ricotta cheese (4 cups),
  room temperature, drained if necessary
1-1/2 cups sugar
1 teaspoon almond extract
1/3 cup orange-flavored liqueur
1/2 cup chopped candied cherries

3 oz. semisweet chocolate, finely chopped, or
  1/2 cup miniature semisweet
  chocolate pieces
1/2 cup toasted chopped almonds or
  natural unsalted pistachios, if desired

Bittersweet-Chocolate Glaze, page 147
Candied-cherry halves, thoroughly blotted
  dry maraschino-cherry halves, whole
  blanched almonds or natural unsalted
  pistachios

Cake Lining:
Prepare 2 sheets of Jelly-Roll Cake; do not roll. Cool as directed. In a small saucepan, bring sugar and water to a boil over high heat; boil 3 minutes without stirring. Remove from heat; stir in rum. Cool to room temperature. Trim crisp edges from cake. Remove bottom of a 9-inch springform pan; use as a pattern to cut out a circle of cake from 1 end of each sheet. Cut a total of 3 (1-1/2-inch-wide) cake strips crosswise from remaining cake. Generously brush darker side of strips and circles with cooled rum syrup. Use all syrup, allowing it to soak in between brushings. Line a 9-inch springform pan with 2 (30-inch) lengths of plastic wrap placed crosswise to each other, allowing excess to hang over edges. Place a circle of cake, rum-side up, on bottom of pan. Line sides of pan with 3 cake strips, rum-side in, cutting where necessary to fit edges snugly; set aside.

To fill cassata, prepare Cassata Filling. Spoon into cake-lined pan; smooth top. Trim any vertical ragged cake edges even with cheese mixture. Place second cake circle, rum-side down, on top. Cover top completely with overlapping lengths of plastic wrap. Place a 9-inch plate, cake pan, or bottom of another springform pan directly on top of cassata. Weight with 2 (1-pound) cans. Refrigerate 24 hours. Remove weights, then wrap and place in freezer 24 hours or up to 2 months. Prepare Bittersweet-Chocolate Glaze; cool to room temperature.

To complete cassata, remove pan side and bottom, then plastic wrap from frozen cassata. Place cassata on a rack over waxed paper. Pour 1/2 of glaze over cassata. Working quickly, use a narrow, metal, spreading spatula to smooth top, allowing glaze to drizzle liberally down sides. Let glaze set. Repeat with remaining 1/2 of glaze. Before second layer of glaze sets, decorate top with candied- or maraschino-cherry halves and almonds or pistachios, pressing lightly into surface. Using 2 large metal spatulas, carefully slide cassata off rack onto a serving plate. Return cassata to freezer until ready to serve. Cassata can be wrapped airtight and frozen 3 months. Let stand at room temperature 30 minutes to 1 hour before serving. Makes 12 servings.

Cassata Filling:
In a large mixer bowl, beat ricotta cheese and sugar until perfectly smooth and fluffy. Add almond extract and orange-flavored liqueur; beat until blended. Stir in chopped cherries, chocolate and toasted almonds or pistachios, if desired.

How to Make Rae's Frozen Cassata

1/Place a circle of cake, rum-side up, over plastic wrap on bottom of pan. Line sides of pan with 3 cake strips, rum-side in, cutting where necessary to fit edges snugly.

2/Spoon Cassata Filling into cake-lined pan; smooth top. Trim any vertical ragged cake edges even with cheese mixture. Place second cake circle, rum-side down, on top.

3/Pour 1/2 of Bittersweet-Chocolate Glaze over cassata. Working quickly, use a narrow, metal, spreading spatula to smooth top, allowing glaze to drizzle liberally down sides. Let glaze set, then repeat with remaining glaze.

4/Before second layer of glaze sets, decorate top with cherry halves and nuts, pressing lightly into surface.

Raspberry-Ripple Cheese Mold *Photo on page 4.*

I use the delicate black-raspberry-flavored Chambord liqueur—a strong raspberry brandy will ruin your dessert!

2 recipes Raspberry Jewel Sauce, page 150,
   with changes noted below
1 (1/4-oz.) envelope unflavored gelatin
   (scant 1 tablespoon)
1/4 cup raspberry-flavored liqueur
   (do not use raspberry-flavored brandy)

3 (8-oz.) pkgs. cream cheese, softened
1 cup powdered sugar
3 egg whites, room temperature
1/4 teaspoon cream of tartar
1/2 cup whipping cream, whipped
Fresh raspberries, if desired

Prepare 2 recipes Raspberry Jewel Sauce; set aside 3/4 cup sauce *before* adding liqueur or reserved whole raspberries called for in recipe. Stir reserved berries into remaining sauce; set aside 1/2 cup sauce with berries. Add 2 tablespoons raspberry-flavored liqueur to remaining sauce with berries; refrigerate until ready to use. Lightly oil a 6- to 8-cup decorative mold. In a small bowl, stir gelatin into 1/4 cup raspberry-flavored liqueur; let stand 5 minutes to soften. Place bowl in a larger bowl of very hot water. Stir until gelatin dissolves; set aside. In a large mixer bowl, beat cream cheese and 2/3 cup powdered sugar until perfectly smooth and fluffy. Beat in gelatin mixture and reserved 3/4 cup raspberry sauce without berries; set aside. In a small mixer bowl, beat egg whites and cream of tartar to soft-peak stage. Beating constantly, gradually add remaining 1/3 cup powdered sugar. Continue beating until whites are stiff but not dry. Fold egg-white mixture and whipped cream into gelatin mixture. Spoon 1/3 of mixture into prepared mold. Dollop with 6 teaspoons, randomly spaced, of 1/2 cup reserved sauce with berries. Keep sauce mixture 1 inch from edge of mold. Repeat second and third layers using remaining raspberry-cheese mixture and sauce. Using the flat edge of a dinner knife, cut through mixture in a wide zigzag pattern to create a marbled effect. Do not go to edge of pan or marble too much or colors will blend and not contrast. Cover and refrigerate at least 4 hours. Dip mold into a large container of very hot water 30 to 60 seconds. Invert and unmold dessert onto a serving plate. Refrigerate until ready to serve. Before serving, pour about 1/2 cup Raspberry Jewel Sauce around base of mold. Drizzle mold with about 1/3 cup Raspberry Jewel Sauce or garnish with fresh raspberries; pass remaining sauce. Makes about 8 servings.

Coeur à la Crème

The traditional mold for this is a heart-shaped basket or ceramic dish with a perforated bottom.

1-1/2 lbs. cream cheese, softened
1/3 cup powdered sugar
1/8 teaspoon salt

1/2 pint whipping cream (1 cup), whipped
About 2 pints fresh whole strawberries,
   blueberries or raspberries

Cut 2 (20-inch) lengths of cheesecloth, 2 layers thick. Moisten with cold water; wring out thoroughly. Line a coeur-à-la-crème mold, wicker basket or large fine-mesh sieve with cheesecloth, placing lengths crosswise and allowing excess to hang over edges. In a large bowl, beat cream cheese, powdered sugar and salt until perfectly smooth and fluffy. Stir in 1/4 of whipped cream to lighten mixture. Gently fold in remaining whipped cream. Turn into prepared mold; smooth top. Bring edges of cheesecloth up over top of cream-cheese mixture. Place mold in a medium bowl so bottom of mold does not touch bottom of bowl. Refrigerate to drain 8 hours or overnight. Discard any liquid in bottom of bowl. To serve Coeur à la Crème, remove cheesecloth from top. Invert mold onto center of a large serving plate. Carefully remove cheesecloth. Garnish top of mold with fresh berries, if desired. Arrange fresh berries on plate around mold. Makes 6 to 8 servings.

Black & White-Chocolate Cheesecake

A dessert spectacular featuring white and dark chocolate—elegant enough for a black-tie evening! Using white crème de cacao intensifies the chocolate flavor.

1 recipe mixture for Double-Chocolate
    Crumb Crust, page 32
3 (8-oz.) pkgs. cream cheese, softened
1/3 cup sugar
5 eggs
2/3 cup white crème de cacao or
    half and half
2 teaspoons vanilla extract
1 lb. white chocolate, melted,
    cooled to room temperature

1-1/2 cups miniature semisweet
    chocolate pieces
Chocolate Leaves, page 126,
    using 2 to 3 oz. cooled melted white
    chocolate to make 1 large, 1 medium and
    1 small leaf
Bittersweet-Chocolate Glaze, page 147

Grease sides only of a 9-inch springform pan. Prepare mixture for Double-Chocolate Crumb Crust. Firmly press over bottom of pan. Bake and cool as directed. Line outside of pan with a skirt of foil, page 59, to prevent butter in crust from leaking. Position rack in center of oven and preheat to 325F (165C). In a large mixer bowl, beat cream cheese and sugar until perfectly smooth. Add eggs, crème de cacao or half and half, and vanilla. Beat until smooth, scraping bowl often. Slowly beat in 1 pound melted white chocolate. Fold in semisweet chocolate pieces. Turn into cooled crust; smooth top. Bake 60 to 70 minutes or until barely set. Cheesecake should jiggle slightly in center. Cool in pan on a rack to room temperature. Cover and refrigerate at least 4 hours. Prepare Chocolate Leaves; refrigerate. Prepare Bittersweet-Chocolate Glaze; cool to room temperature before using.
To complete cheesecake, loosen by running a thin knife around inside edge of pan; remove side of pan. Place cheesecake on a rack over a baking sheet lined with waxed paper. Level top of cheesecake with a serrated knife. Pour 1/2 of Bittersweet-Chocolate Glaze over cheesecake, allowing excess to drizzle down sides. Smooth top with a narrow, metal, spreading spatula. Refrigerate 5 minutes or until set. Repeat with remaining glaze. Refrigerate until almost set. Arrange Chocolate Leaves, pinwheel-fashion, in center of cheesecake. Using 2 large metal spatulas, carefully slide cheesecake off pan bottom onto a serving plate. Refrigerate until serving time. Makes 10 to 12 servings.

TIP *White chocolate, also called* summer coating, *cannot be classified as* real *chocolate because it doesn't contain chocolate liquor. Chocolate liquor is the thick, dark paste left after cocoa butter is extracted from the cocoa nibs. White chocolate has just a whisper of chocolate flavor and is* extremely *sweet. It is generally a mixture of cocoa butter, sugar, milk, lecithin and vanillin. Because it has a tendency to scorch and clump when overheated, it must be melted very slowly.*

Banana-Rum Cheesecake

This creamy Caribbean-inspired cheesecake is crowned with apricot-glazed banana slices.

1/3 cup gingersnap or almond-cookie crumbs
3 (8-oz.) pkgs. cream cheese, softened
3/4 cup sugar
1/4 teaspoon ground cinnamon
1/4 teaspoon ground nutmeg
4 eggs
1 tablespoon lemon juice

1-1/2 cups very-ripe-banana puree
  (2-1/2 to 3 medium bananas)
1/2 cup light rum
1 teaspoon imitation rum extract
1 cup apricot jam
2 to 3 medium, firm bananas,
  cut in 1/4-inch spears

Position rack in center of oven and preheat to 300F (150C). Generously grease a 9- or 8-inch springform pan. Sprinkle bottom and sides with cookie crumbs. In a large mixer bowl, beat cream cheese, sugar, cinnamon and nutmeg until perfectly smooth and fluffy. Gradually add eggs, lemon juice, banana puree, rum and rum extract. Beat, scraping bowl as necessary, until mixture is creamy. Turn into prepared pan. Bake 1 hour. Turn off oven. Let cheesecake cool in oven 1 hour with oven door propped open 1 to 3 inches. Cool completely on a rack. Cover and refrigerate overnight.

To complete cheesecake, in a small saucepan, stir apricot jam over medium heat until melted. Press through a fine sieve into a small bowl. Refrigerate 20 minutes or until cool. Remove side of springform pan. Using 2 large metal spatulas, carefully slide cheesecake off pan bottom onto a serving plate. Arrange banana spears on top of cheesecake. Spoon apricot glaze over bananas, making sure each spear is completely covered. Allow excess glaze to drizzle down sides of cheesecake. Refrigerate until ready to serve. Makes 10 to 12 servings.

Black Forest Cheesecake

One bite of this cherry-crowned cheesecake and you'll be in chocolate-lover's heaven!

1 recipe mixture for Double-Chocolate
  Crumb Crust, page 32
3 (8-oz.) pkgs. cream cheese, softened
1 cup packed brown sugar
2 tablespoons unsweetened cocoa
1 tablespoon cornstarch
3 eggs
8 oz. semisweet chocolate, melted, cooled

1-1/2 pints dairy sour cream (3 cups)
2 teaspoons vanilla extract
1 (15-1/2-oz.) can pitted, dark, sweet
  cherries, well-drained
Sweet-Cherry Cheesecake Topping, page 154
1 oz. Grated Chocolate, page 126
3/4 cup whipping cream, whipped

Position rack in center of oven and preheat to 350F (175C). Grease sides only of a 10-inch springform pan. Prepare mixture for Double-Chocolate Crumb Crust; firmly press over bottom of pan. Bake and cool as directed. In a large mixer bowl, beat cream cheese, brown sugar, cocoa and cornstarch until perfectly smooth. Add eggs, 1 at a time, beating well after each addition, then beat in melted chocolate. Beat in sour cream and vanilla; stir in cherries. Turn into cooled crust; smooth top. Bake 1 hour; turn off oven. Let cheesecake cool in oven 30 minutes with oven door propped open 1 to 3 inches. Cool in pan on a rack to room temperature. Cover and refrigerate overnight. Prepare Sweet-Cherry Cheesecake Topping and Grated Chocolate; refrigerate. To loosen cheesecake, run a thin knife around inside edge of pan; remove side of pan. Using 2 large metal spatulas, carefully slide cheesecake off pan bottom onto a serving plate. Spoon cherry sauce in an even layer over top of cheesecake, spreading to within 1/2 inch of edge. Pipe whipped cream around outer edge of top. Sprinkle whipped cream with Grated Chocolate. Refrigerate until ready to serve. Makes 12 to 14 servings.

Tunnel-of-Fudge Cheesecake

Created for a special cheesecake class, this novel dessert has a chunky chocolate tunnel running through its core.

Crust:
**1 recipe dough for Nut Pastry Crust,
  page 31**

**2 oz. semisweet chocolate, if desired,
  melted, cooled**

Filling:
5 (8-oz.) pkgs. cream cheese, softened
1-1/2 cups sugar
5 eggs
1/4 cup all-purpose flour
1/2 teaspoon salt
1/4 cup whipping cream
3 oz. semisweet chocolate, melted, cooled

1/2 cup semisweet chocolate pieces
1 tablespoon vanilla extract
**2 oz. Grated Chocolate, Chocolate Triangles
  or Chocolate Leaves, page 126**
Chocolate-Clay Strips, page 132, if desired
Chocolate-Sour-Cream Topping, page 152
Caramel Crown, page 148, if desired

Crust:
Position rack in center of oven and preheat to 400F (205C). Grease sides only of a 9-inch springform pan. Prepare dough for Nut Pastry Crust; press firmly over bottom of prepared pan. Bake 10 to 15 minutes or until golden. Cool on a rack 10 minutes. If desired, brush melted chocolate over crust to within 1/2 inch of edge. Refrigerate 10 to 15 minutes or until chocolate is set before filling.

Filling:
Leave oven at 400F (205C) setting. In a large mixer bowl, beat cream cheese and sugar until perfectly smooth and fluffy. Add eggs, 1 at a time, beating well after each addition. Beat in flour, salt and cream. Place 2 cups cream-cheese mixture in a medium bowl. Gradually add melted chocolate, beating constantly until thoroughly blended. Stir in chocolate pieces; set aside. Stir vanilla into remaining cream-cheese mixture. Pour all but 1-1/2 cups light cheese mixture into prepared crust. Spoon chocolate-cheese filling in a 2-inch-wide ring over light cheese mixture, about 1-1/2 inches from edge of pan. Be careful not to get any in center of light mixture. Using the back of a spoon, carefully press chocolate mixture down into light mixture until top is level. Spoon reserved light cheese mixture evenly over all; smooth top. Place in center of middle oven rack. Place a 2-cup container of hot water on lower shelf. Bake 15 minutes. Reduce oven temperature to 300F (150C); bake 50 minutes longer. Turn off oven. Let cheesecake cool in oven 1 hour with oven door propped open 1 to 3 inches. Remove to a rack; cool completely. Cover and refrigerate overnight. Prepare Grated Chocolate, Chocolate Triangles or Chocolate Leaves, if desired; refrigerate. Prepare Chocolate-Clay Strips or Caramel Crown, if desired.

To complete cheesecake, run a thin knife around inside edge of pan; remove side of pan. Using 2 large metal spatulas, carefully slide cheesecake off pan bottom onto a serving plate. Prepare Chocolate-Sour-Cream Topping; spread over top of cheesecake. If desired, wrap sides of cheesecake in Chocolate-Clay Strips. Sprinkle Grated Chocolate in a 2-inch band around outer edge of top. Or, decorate top with Chocolate Triangles or Chocolate Leaves. Refrigerate at least 1 hour before serving. If using a Caramel Crown, add immediately before serving. Makes 12 to 16 servings.

TIP *Store chocolate in a cool (68-78F, 20-25C), dry place. Chocolate stored at warmer temperatures can develop a grayish "bloom." This is caused by cocoa butter which has separated and risen to the surface.*

How to Make Tunnel-of-Fudge Cheesecake

1/If desired, brush melted chocolate over cooled baked crust to within 1/2 inch of edge. Refrigerate until chocolate is set. Pour all but 1-1/2 cups light cheese mixture into prepared crust.

2/Spoon chocolate-cheese filling in a 2-inch-wide ring over light cheese mixture, about 1-1/2 inches from edge of pan. Using the back of a spoon, carefully press chocolate mixture down into light mixture until top is level.

Swirled Roquefort Torta

A cheese mold decorated with fruit—the perfect dessert for those who don't like sweet endings to a meal.

8 oz. Roquefort or other blue cheese,
  crumbled
1 cup toasted chopped walnuts or pecans
1-1/2 (8-oz.) pkgs. cream cheese, softened
1/2 cup butter, softened
1/4 teaspoon ground nutmeg

1/4 teaspoon salt
1/2 cup dairy sour cream
1/3 cup port wine
About 70 seedless red or black grapes, halved
Crisp unsalted crackers
Additional seedless grapes

Generously oil a 5-cup mold or bowl with a rounded base, such as a small electric-mixer bowl. In a medium bowl, toss together blue cheese and nuts; set aside. In a large mixer bowl, beat cream cheese, butter, nutmeg and salt until creamy and smooth. Add sour cream and port; beat until blended. Turn 1/3 of cream-cheese mixture into prepared mold. Sprinkle with 1/2 of Roquefort-nut mixture to within 1/2-inch of edges. Using the tip of a kitchen spoon, swirl Roquefort and nuts through cream-cheese mixture. Spoon another 1/3 of cream-cheese mixture over top. Sprinkle with remaining Roquefort mixture; swirl as before. Top with remaining cream-cheese mixture; smooth top. Cover mold with foil or plastic wrap. Refrigerate overnight. Up to 6 hours before serving, dip mold into a large container of very hot water 30 to 60 seconds. Invert onto a serving plate. If necessary, insert a blunt knife between mold and cheese to release suction. Smooth surface of mold with the back of a kitchen teaspoon. Press grape halves, cut-side in, over surface of cheese mold in concentric circles. Cover and refrigerate at least 3 hours. Let stand 30 minutes at room temperature before serving. Serve with unsalted crackers and additional grapes. Makes 10 to 12 servings.

Red, White & Blueberry Cheese Torte

Summer berries are highlighted in this carefree frozen dessert—use frozen berries in the winter!

1 recipe mixture for Nutty Crumb Crust,
   page 32
4 egg whites, room temperature
1/4 teaspoon cream of tartar
1-1/2 cups sugar
3 (8-oz.) pkgs. cream cheese, softened
1/2 pint dairy sour cream (1 cup)
2 teaspoons vanilla extract
1 to 2 drops blue food coloring, if desired

1/2 cup blueberry puree
   (1/2 pint blueberries)
1/2 cup strawberry puree (1 to 1-1/2 cups
   whole strawberries) or sieved raspberry
   puree (1/2 pint raspberries)
1/2 recipe Plain Whipped Cream, page 156,
   if desired
Whole blueberries and strawberries or
   raspberries, if desired

Lightly oil a 9-inch springform pan. Prepare mixture for Nutty Crumb Crust; firmly press over bottom of prepared pan. Freeze until ready to fill. In a small mixer bowl, beat egg whites and cream of tartar to soft-peak stage. Beating constantly, gradually add 3/4 cup sugar, 2 tablespoons at a time. Continue beating until whites are glossy and firm; set aside. In a large mixer bowl, beat cream cheese with remaining 3/4 cup sugar until perfectly smooth and fluffy. Add sour cream and vanilla; beat until blended. Stir 1/4 of egg-white mixture into cream-cheese mixture to lighten. Gently fold in remaining egg-white mixture, 1/3 at a time. Spoon 1/3 of mixture into prepared crust; smooth top. If desired, stir 1 to 2 drops blue food coloring into blueberry puree. Spoon 3 scant tablespoons each blueberry puree and strawberry or raspberry puree in dollops over top of cheese layer. Using the back of a spoon, lightly press puree into cheese mixture. Repeat with 2 more layers of cheese mixture and dollops of berry puree. Using the flat edge of a dinner knife, cut through cheese mixture in a wide zigzag pattern to create a marbled effect. Do not marble too much or colors will blend and not contrast. Cover and freeze overnight or until firm. Prepare Plain Whipped Cream, if desired; refrigerate. To loosen torte, run a thin knife around inside edge of pan; remove side of pan. Using 2 large metal spatulas, carefully slide cheesecake off pan bottom onto a serving plate. Garnish with whipped cream and berries, if desired. Serve frozen. Makes 8 to 10 servings.

Note: If using loosepack frozen berries, thaw and drain before pureeing.

 TIP *The final flavor of a fruit dessert reflects the quality of the fruit used. Make sure berries, peaches, plums and other fruit are unblemished and perfectly ripe for the fullest flavor.*

Lemon-Cheese Torte

This tart and tangy no-bake dessert is the ideal ending for a rich meal.

1 (1/4-oz.) envelope unflavored gelatin
  (scant 1 tablespoon)
1/3 cup lemon juice
1/2 cup butter
1 cup sugar
3 eggs, separated, room temperature
1/4 teaspoon salt
1 cup half and half

2 (8-oz.) pkgs. cream cheese, softened
1/2 teaspoon almond extract
Finely grated zest of 1 medium lemon
About 1/2 cup toasted sliced almonds
About 1/3 cup almond-macaroon or
  lemon-cookie crumbs
1/4 teaspoon cream of tartar
1 thin lemon slice, if desired

In a small bowl, stir gelatin into lemon juice; let stand 5 minutes to soften. In a medium saucepan, melt butter over medium heat. Whisk in sugar, egg yolks, salt and 1/2 cup half and half. Cook over low heat, stirring constantly, 5 minutes or until mixture coats the back of a metal spoon. Remove from heat. Add gelatin mixture; stir 1 minute or until dissolved. Set aside. In a large mixer bowl, beat cream cheese until perfectly smooth. Slowly beat in almond extract and remaining 1/2 cup half and half. Strain hot gelatin mixture through a fine sieve into cream-cheese mixture. Add lemon zest; beat until smooth and creamy. Refrigerate until mixture begins to mound when spooned on top of itself; set aside. Generously grease a 9-inch springform pan. Sprinkle about 1/3 cup almonds over bottom and sides of pan; reserve any almonds that do not stick to pan. Sprinkle any uncovered spaces on pan with some of cookie crumbs. In a small mixer bowl, beat egg whites and cream of tartar until stiff but not dry. Fold, 1/3 at a time, into chilled lemon mixture. Turn into prepared pan. Sprinkle top first with remaining cookie crumbs, then remaining almonds. Cover and refrigerate 4 hours or until set. To serve, remove side of pan. Using 2 large metal spatulas, carefully slide torte off pan bottom onto a serving plate. If desired, cut lemon slice once from outer edge to center. Twist slice to form an **S;** place in center of torte. Makes 8 to 10 servings.

TIP

To speed the setting of gelatin mixtures, place bowl containing mixture in a larger bowl of iced water. Stir constantly until mixture is cool and has reached syrupy consistency.

Pumpkin-Praline Cheesecake

A crunchy praline topping crowns this creamy-rich cheesecake—super for holiday parties!

1 recipe mixture for Cookie-Crumb Crust,
   page 32, with changes noted below
4 (8-oz.) pkgs. cream cheese, softened
1-1/3 cups packed brown sugar
1/4 cup all-purpose flour
5 eggs
1 (l-lb.) can pumpkin (2 cups)
1 teaspoon ground cinnamon

1/2 teaspoon ground ginger
1/2 teaspoon ground nutmeg
1/2 teaspoon ground allspice
1/2 teaspoon salt
Praline Topping, see below
Sweetened whipped cream, if desired
Pecan halves, if desired

Praline Topping:
1 cup packed brown sugar
1/2 teaspoon ground cinnamon

5 tablespoons butter, melted
1 cup chopped pecans

Grease a 10-inch springform pan. Prepare mixture for Cookie-Crumb Crust using 1-1/4 cups ginger-snap crumbs, 1/2 cup finely chopped pecans, 5 tablespoons butter and 1/4 cup brown sugar. Firmly press mixture over bottom of prepared pan. Bake and cool as directed. Line outside of pan with a skirt of foil to prevent butter in crust from leaking. Position rack in center of oven and preheat to 350F (175C). In a large mixer bowl, beat cream cheese, brown sugar and flour until perfectly smooth and fluffy. Add eggs, pumpkin, spices and salt; beat until blended. Turn into cooled crust. Bake 1 hour. While cheesecake is baking, prepare Praline Topping. Remove cheesecake from oven. Gently sprinkle Praline Topping evenly over surface. Return to oven; bake 15 to 30 minutes longer or until cheesecake is set. Cool on a rack to room temperature. Cover and refrigerate overnight. To loosen cheesecake, run a thin knife around inside edge of pan; remove side of pan. Using 2 large metal spatulas, carefully slide cheesecake off pan bottom onto a serving plate. Garnish with sweetened whipped cream and pecan halves, if desired. Makes 12 to 14 servings.

Praline Topping:

In a food processor fitted with a metal blade or in a medium bowl, combine brown sugar, cinnamon and butter. Process in food processor using quick on/off pulses until mixture resembles coarse crumbs. Or, using a pastry blender or 2 knives, cut butter into dry ingredients until mixture resembles coarse crumbs. Stir in nuts.

 TIP

Spices should be as fresh as possible to deliver their full flavor potential. Freshly grated nutmeg is almost twice as pungent as processed ground nutmeg, so use it with finesse!

How to Make Pumpkin-Praline Cheesecake

1/Line outside of pan with a skirt of foil to prevent butter in crust from leaking.

2/Garnish cooled baked cheesecake with sweetened whipped cream and pecan halves, if desired.

Cheese-Custard Suzette

Baked like a custard, this exquisite creamy-smooth cheesecake is crowned with a heady orange sauce.

2 (8-oz.) pkgs. cream cheese, softened	4 eggs
3/4 cup sugar	1/2 cup orange-flavored liqueur
Finely grated zest of 1/2 small orange	2-1/2 cups dairy sour cream
Pinch of salt	Suzette Sauce, page 150

Position rack in center of oven and preheat to 325F (165C). Grease a 1-1/2- to 2-quart soufflé dish. In a large mixer bowl, beat cream cheese, sugar, orange zest and salt until creamy. Add eggs, 1 at a time, beating well after each addition. Add liqueur and sour cream; beat until blended. Turn into prepared dish. Set dish in a large shallow baking pan; place in oven. Pour hot water into pan so it reaches halfway up side of dish. Bake 1-1/4 hours. Turn off oven. Let cheesecake stand in oven 30 minutes with oven door closed. Place on a rack to cool. After 1 hour, run a thin knife between dish and cheesecake. Cool to room temperature. Cover and refrigerate overnight. Prepare Suzette Sauce. To serve, invert chilled custard and unmold onto a serving plate. Spoon 1/2 to 3/4 cup Suzette Sauce over top, allowing excess to drizzle down sides and form a pool around base of cheesecake. Pass additional Suzette Sauce with cheesecake. Makes 8 servings.

Black-Bottom Cheesecake

Like the famous pie, this cheesecake boasts a chocolate layer topped with a creamy rum layer.

1 recipe mixture for Cream-Filled-Cookie
   Crust, page 32
4 (8-oz.) pkgs. cream cheese, softened
1/2 cup butter, softened
1 cup sugar
4 eggs
3/4 cup dairy sour cream

2 oz. semisweet chocolate, melted, cooled
1 tablespoon cornstarch
1/4 cup rum
2 teaspoons imitation rum extract
Chocolate-Clay Fettuccine, page 133, or
   1-1/2 oz. Grated Chocolate, page 126

Rum-Cream Topping:
1/2 pint whipping cream (1 cup)
2 tablespoons powdered sugar

3 tablespoons rum

Grease sides only of a 9-inch springform pan. Prepare mixture for Cream-Filled-Cookie Crust; press over bottom and halfway up side of pan. Bake and cool as directed. Line outside of pan with a skirt of foil, page 59, to prevent butter in crust from leaking. Position rack in center of oven and preheat to 325F (165C). In a large mixer bowl, beat cream cheese, butter and sugar until perfectly smooth and fluffy. Add eggs, 1 at a time, beating well after each addition. Beat in sour cream until blended. Remove 2-1/2 cups cream-cheese mixture; stir in melted chocolate. Pour into prepared crust; smooth top. Add cornstarch, rum and rum extract to remaining light cream-cheese mixture; beat until blended. Gently spoon rum-cheese mixture over chocolate mixture; smooth top. Bake 1 hour 15 minutes. Turn off oven. Without opening oven door, let cheesecake cool in oven 30 minutes. Leave cheesecake in oven 30 minutes longer with oven door propped open 1 to 3 inches. Cool in pan on a rack to room temperature. Cover and refrigerate overnight. Prepare Chocolate-Clay Fettuccine or Grated Chocolate; set aside. To loosen cheesecake, run a thin knife around inside edge of pan; remove side of pan. Using 2 large metal spatulas, carefully slide cheesecake off pan bottom onto a serving plate. Prepare Rum-Cream Topping; spread over top of cheesecake. Decorate a 2-inch band on outer edge of top with Chocolate-Clay Fettuccine or Grated Chocolate. Makes 10 to 12 servings.

Rum-Cream Topping:
In a small bowl, beat whipping cream to soft-peak stage. Add powdered sugar; gradually drizzle in rum, beating until mixture is stiff.

TIP   *Be sure not to let any moisture come in contact with melted chocolate. A few drops of water or other liquid will cause chocolate to seize (clump and harden). To correct this problem, add 1 to 2 tablespoons vegetable shortening for each 6 ounces chocolate. Slowly remelt and stir until smooth.*

Suisse Torte

Imagine yourself in the Swiss Alps when you taste this lightly sweet, orange-scented torte made with Swiss cheese.

2 (1/4-oz.) pkgs. unflavored gelatin
  (about 5 teaspoons)
1/2 cup orange juice
1 pint dairy sour cream (2 cups)
1-1/4 cups sugar
3 eggs, separated, room temperature
1 tablespoon finely grated orange zest

1/8 teaspoon salt
2-1/2 cups shredded Gruyère or other
  Swiss cheese (10 oz.), room temperature
1/2 cup toasted, sliced, unblanched almonds
1/2 pint whipping cream (1 cup), whipped
1/3 cup toasted, sliced, unblanched almonds
Suzette Sauce, page 150, if desired

In a small bowl, stir gelatin into orange juice; let stand 5 minutes to soften. In a medium, heavy saucepan, combine sour cream, 1 cup sugar, egg yolks, orange zest and salt. Cook over low heat, stirring constantly, until mixture is smooth and very warm. Do not allow mixture to boil. Stir in grated cheese. Stir vigorously with a rubber spatula until cheese melts; about 5 minutes. Add gelatin mixture; stir 1 minute or until dissolved. Pour mixture into a blender. Beginning at low speed and gradually increasing to high speed, process 2 minutes. Turn into a large bowl. Refrigerate, stirring occasionally, until mixture begins to mound when spooned on top of itself. Generously grease a 9-inch springform pan. Sprinkle 1/2 cup almonds over bottom and up sides of pan. In a small mixer bowl, beat egg whites to soft-peak stage. Beating constantly, gradually add remaining 1/4 cup sugar, 2 tablespoons at a time. Continue beating until whites are glossy and firm. Fold egg-white mixture, then whipped cream into cheese mixture. Spoon into prepared pan; smooth top. Sprinkle top with 1/3 cup almonds. Cover and refrigerate overnight. Prepare Suzette Sauce, if desired. To loosen cheesecake, run a thin knife around inside edge of pan; remove side of pan. Using 2 large metal spatulas, carefully slide cheesecake off pan bottom onto a serving plate. Refrigerate until ready to serve. Serve with sauce, if desired. Makes 10 to 12 servings.

Note: If using a food processor to shred cheese, use shredding disc instead of metal blade.

 TIP *Orange zest refers to the outer colored portion of the peel. Freshly grated lemon or orange zest packs a flavor wallop no dried zest can match.*

COOKIES & SMALL CAKES

Ever since I was a little girl, one of my favorite times of year has been autumn. To this day, the very word stirs a sense of anticipation deep within me. It's a season of change—of excitement—and, when I was young, the season when earnest cookie baking began.

On bright Colorado days, when the autumn air was enticingly crisp, my sister Tia and I would scurry around the family kitchen gathering the necessary components for our Saturday bake-fest, lovingly supervised by mom. Within an hour or two the fragrance of freshly baked goodness would permeate the house with the heady promise of sweet delights. Soon Tia and I would be sitting at the kitchen table, little hands clutching giant glasses of icy-cold milk, mouths full of warm, oven-fresh cookies and hearts humming with satisfaction.

Cookies have been satisfying people for ages. The first cookie-style cakes are said to date back to seventh-century Persia, though the word *cookie* is derived from the Dutch *koekje*, meaning *little cake*. Because of the multitude of different flavor, shape, texture and size possibilities, there are more varieties of cookies than any other single baked product! With this extraordinary diversity, is it any wonder that cookies have such universal appeal?

Cookies are ideal for gift giving, and perfect for countless occasions from casual nibbles, picnics and box lunches to elegant tea accompaniments and dinner finales. But, like any other form of oven-art, successful cookie baking requires knowledge of a few basics. For assured success, take a minute to read *Hints For Successful Cookies*, opposite, before you begin your next batch!

Whether you like your cookies gooey, chewy, buttery-crisp, moistly soft, large, small, simple or exotic, you're bound to find a favorite in the following pages. Bar-cookie fans will love White-Chocolate Swirls, flavored with delicious white chocolate and ribboned with a rich fudge filling.

Chocolate-Cherry Chews are tailored to tempt "moistly soft-cookie" lovers. Each fudgy, chocolate-frosted cookie hides a juicy cherry in the center!

For those who like their cookies crisp, Mama's Sugar Snaps are the answer. These huge, ultra-thin crisps are enticingly flavored with vanilla and so buttery they melt in your mouth. If you're feeling extravagant, try Tia's Macadamia Butterfingers. I created these for my sister, who fell in love with macadamia nuts while touring Hawaii when she was Miss Colorado. Buttery-rich, these nutmeg-scented crisps are elegant enough for your most important dinner parties!

Kids of all ages love the giant Cookie Monsters because they get to choose their own topping. Eight inches in diameter, these fun-filled cookies are bursting with oats, coconut and spices. Before baking, each cookie muncher can personalize their cookie with a topping of candy-coated chocolate pieces, raisins, malted-milk balls, nuts, gum drops—whatever their hearts desire!

In the small-cake category are chocolatey Princess Cupcakes, complete with a surprise pocket of fluffy cream filling—just like the famous store-bought brand! Lemon lovers will enjoy the Lemon-Poppy-Seed Cakes which feature tiny, poppy seed-studded cookie cups filled with tart lemon cream.

Traditionalists will recognize several age-old recipes with the non-traditional Herbst touch. The Butterballs, for example, boast seven delicious variations ranging from Double-Chocolate Balls to Jam Pockets. And Almond-Orange Shortbread gilds the shortbread lily with toasted almonds and orange zest. The cookies are then dipped into melted chocolate for an ultra-elegant finish!

Whether the cookie jar is half full or half empty generally depends on whether one asks the cookie baker or the cookie muncher. But there's one thing on which we all can agree—sugar and spice, and everything nice, *that's* what cookies are made of!

62

Hints for Successful Cookies

- Read the recipe carefully to make sure you have all the necessary equipment and ingredients on hand.
- Assemble ingredients in the order they will be used. Any change in the basic proportions of a cookie recipe will drastically alter the finished product.
- Use the appropriate measuring cups; nested cups for dry ingredients and glass cups for liquid ingredients.
- Measure flour by lightly spooning it into measuring cup; level top with the flat edge of a knife.
- Unless a recipe states otherwise, grease baking sheets or pans with vegetable shortening. Buttered pans can cause delicate cookie doughs to burn while baking.
- Preheat oven 15 minutes. Use an oven thermometer for accurate oven temperature. To ensure even browning when baking 2 sheets of cookies at a time, rotate sheets from top to bottom and from front to back of oven halfway through baking time.
- To allow for variations in ovens, check cookies 3 to 4 minutes before minimum baking time indicated in recipe to prevent overbaking.
- When baking consecutive batches of cookies, allow baking sheets to cool and regrease before placing new dough on them. Hot baking sheets cause bottom of dough to melt, creating changes in a texture and shape of cookies.

Coconut Chews

A childhood favorite, these bars have a gooey-good filling, similar to a pecan pie—yum-m-m-m!

1 cup butter, softened	2 tablespoons cornstarch
3 cups packed brown sugar	1/2 teaspoon salt
1/4 teaspoon ground nutmeg	1/4 teaspoon ground cinnamon
2 cups all-purpose flour	2 cups shredded or flaked coconut
4 eggs	2 cups toasted chopped pecans
1 tablespoon vanilla extract	Powdered sugar

Preheat oven to 325F (165C). Grease a 13″ x 9″ baking pan. In a large mixer bowl, beat butter, 1 cup brown sugar and nutmeg until light and fluffy. Add flour; beat at lowest speed until mixture is crumbly. Press firmly and evenly over bottom of prepared pan. Bake 20 minutes. Cool in pan on a rack 20 minutes. In a large mixer bowl, beat remaining 2 cups brown sugar, eggs, vanilla, cornstarch, salt and cinnamon until blended. Stir in coconut and pecans. Spread on baked layer. Bake 35 to 45 minutes or until firm. Loosen around edges while warm. Cool completely in pan on a rack. Cut into 32 bars, cutting 4 strips 1 way and 8 strips the other way. Lightly sprinkle cooled cookies with powdered sugar. Makes about 32 cookies.

Biscotti
Photo on page 69.

Created for Carmen, these crunchy Italian favorites are often served with a dessert wine for dunking.

1/2 cup butter, softened	3 eggs
1-1/3 cups sugar	3 cups all-purpose flour
1/2 teaspoon salt	2-1/2 teaspoons baking powder
Finely grated zest of 1 medium orange	1/2 teaspoon baking soda
Finely grated zest of 1 medium lemon	2 cups toasted sliced almonds,
1 tablespoon anise seeds	coarsely chopped

Preheat oven to 325F (165C). Generously grease 2 large baking sheets. In a large mixer bowl, beat butter, sugar, salt, orange and lemon zest, and anise seeds until light and fluffy. Add eggs, 1 at a time, beating well after each addition. Add flour, baking powder and baking soda; stir until blended. Stir in nuts. Divide dough into thirds. With buttered fingers, shape each portion of dough into a log, 12 inches long and about 1-1/2 inches in diameter. Place 2 logs 4 inches apart on 1 prepared baking sheet; place third log on remaining baking sheet. Slightly flatten logs until about 1 inch thick. Bake 25 minutes, rotating baking sheets top to bottom in oven midway through baking. Remove from oven; reduce heat to 275F (135C). Using a knife with a thin blade, cut logs at a 45-degree angle into 3/4-inch slices. Lay slices, cut-side down, 1-1/2 inches apart on baking sheets. Return to oven. Bake 40 minutes longer or until very dry. Cool completely on racks. Store in an airtight container. Makes about 48 cookies.

Variation
Chocolate-Dipped Biscotti: Melt 4 ounces semisweet chocolate. Place in a small bowl. Line 2 large baking sheets with waxed paper. Dip about 3/4 inch of both ends of cooled baked cookies into chocolate; place on prepared baking sheets. Refrigerate until chocolate is set.

Mama's Sugar Snaps

Ultra-thin and rich, these big butter-crisp cookies are bound to become family favorites!

1 cup butter, softened	2 cups all-purpose flour
1-1/2 cups sugar	1 egg white mixed with 1 teaspoon vanilla
1/4 teaspoon salt	extract for glaze
1-1/2 teaspoons vanilla extract	About 1/3 cup sugar
1/2 cup dairy sour cream	

In a large mixer bowl, beat butter, sugar, salt and vanilla until light and fluffy. Add sour cream and flour alternately in 2 additions, blending well after each addition. Spoon dough onto the center of a 12-inch length of plastic wrap. Fold long sides of plastic wrap over dough. With your palms, roll wrapped dough into a log, 8 inches long and 2-1/2 inches in diameter. Twist ends of plastic wrap to seal. Freeze or refrigerate until firm, 1 to 4 hours. Preheat oven to 350F (175C). Grease 4 large baking sheets. If only using 2 baking sheets, cool and regrease before using to bake additional cookies. Cut chilled dough into 1/8-inch-thick slices. Place slices 2 inches apart on prepared baking sheets. Brush with egg-white glaze; sprinkle generously with sugar, being careful not to get any on baking sheet. Bake 11 to 15 minutes or until edges are golden brown. Let stand 30 seconds before carefully removing from baking sheets. Cool completely on racks. Store in an airtight container. Makes about 54 cookies.

Butterballs

My husband Ron's very favorite cookie—with enough variations to please the most jaded palate.

1 cup butter, softened
2/3 cup powdered sugar
1/4 teaspoon salt
1 teaspoon vanilla extract

2 cups all-purpose flour
2 cups toasted finely chopped pecans
About 1 cup sifted powdered sugar

In a large mixer bowl, beat butter, 2/3 cup powdered sugar, salt and vanilla until light and fluffy. Gradually stir in flour and pecans. Cover with plastic wrap; refrigerate 2 to 3 hours or until firm enough to handle. Preheat oven to 325F (165C). Taking 1 teaspoonful at a time, roll dough into 1-inch balls. Place 2 inches apart on ungreased baking sheets. Bake 15 to 20 minutes or until golden. Using a metal spatula, gently loosen cookies from baking sheets. Place 1 cup powdered sugar in a shallow bowl. Roll warm cookies in powdered sugar. Place on racks to cool. Roll cookies in powdered sugar again when cool. Store in an airtight container. Makes about 60 cookies.

Variations

Toffee Butterballs: Substitute 1/2 cup packed brown sugar for 2/3 cup powdered sugar, and 1 cup finely crushed toffee candy or toffee bits for 1 cup pecans. Roll baked cookies in granulated sugar.

Jam Pockets: Photo on page 69.

Make an indentation with the tip your little finger halfway into each dough ball. Spoon 1/2 teaspoon of your favorite jam or jelly into indentation. Do not roll baked cookies in powdered sugar.

Chocolate-Chipper Butterballs: Substitute 1 cup miniature semisweet chocolate pieces for 1 cup pecans. Roll baked cookies in granulated sugar.

Almond Butterballs: Substitute 1/2 teaspoon almond extract for 1 teaspoon vanilla extract, and 2 cups toasted finely chopped almonds for pecans. Roll baked cookies in powdered sugar.

Spirited Hazelnut Butterballs: Substitute 2 tablespoons Frangelico or other hazelnut-flavored liqueur for vanilla extract, and 1 cup toasted finely chopped hazelnuts for 2 cups pecans. Roll baked cookies in powdered sugar.

Double-Chocolate Butterballs: Increase 2/3 cup powdered sugar to 1 cup. Substitute 1/2 cup sifted unsweetened cocoa for 1/2 cup flour, and 1 cup miniature semisweet chocolate pieces for 1 cup pecans. Roll baked cookies in granulated sugar.

Peanut-Butter Balls: Add 1/2 cup crunchy peanut butter to butter mixture before beating. Omit pecans. If desired, add 1 cup finely chopped unsalted peanuts. Roll baked cookies in granulated sugar.

 TIP *Cookies not removed from baking sheets while warm may stick because shortening used to grease sheets has cooled and hardened. Return baking sheet to oven for 2 minutes to remelt shortening; remove cookies immediately.*

Cookie Monsters

Kids of all ages will love choosing their favorite toppings for these chewy plate-sized treats. Omit the toppings and you'll have great old-fashioned oatmeal cookies.

1 cup butter, softened
1 cup packed brown sugar
1/2 cup granulated sugar
2 eggs
1-1/2 teaspoons vanilla extract
1 teaspoon ground cinnamon
1/2 teaspoon ground nutmeg
1/2 teaspoon salt
1-1/2 cups all-purpose flour
1 teaspoon baking soda

2 cups rolled oats, regular or
   quick-cooking
1 cup shredded or flaked coconut
About 1-1/4 cups multi-colored plain or
   peanut-candy-covered chocolate pieces,
   raisins, chocolate-covered raisins,
   semisweet chocolate pieces,
   malted-milk balls, chopped nuts,
   gum drops, jelly beans or candy corn

Preheat oven to 350F (175C). Generously grease 5 round 8-inch foil or regular pie pans. Place a round of waxed paper on bottom of each pie pan; grease waxed paper. In a large mixer bowl, beat butter and sugars until light and fluffy. Add eggs, vanilla, cinnamon, nutmeg and salt; beat until blended. Stir in flour, baking soda, oats and coconut. Divide dough evenly between prepared pans. With the back of a large spoon, spread dough evenly over bottom of pans. Sprinkle about 1/4 cup of your favorite topping over each cookie. If desired, write a name or a message with connecting pieces of chosen topping. Bake 15 to 20 minutes or until browned. Cool in pans. Turn cooled cookies out of pans; remove waxed-paper rounds. To serve, cut each cookie into 8 wedges. Makes 5 giant cookies (40 pieces).

Variations
Spicy Oat Cookies: Prepare dough as directed above. Spoon dough onto the center of an 18-inch length of plastic wrap. Fold long sides of plastic wrap over dough. With your palms, roll wrapped dough into a log, 13 inches long and 2-1/2 inches in diameter. Twist ends of plastic wrap to seal. Freeze or refrigerate until firm, 1 to 4 hours. Cut chilled dough into 1/4-inch-thick slices. Place slices 2 inches apart on greased baking sheets. Bake in a preheated 350F (175C) oven 15 minutes or until golden brown. Let stand 3 minutes before carefully removing from baking sheets. Cool on racks. Makes about 36 cookies.

Chocolate-Raisin Drop Cookies: Stir 1/2 cup semisweet chocolate pieces and 1/2 cup raisins into dough. Drop by rounded teaspoons 1-1/2 inches apart on greased baking sheets. Bake in a preheated 375F (175C) oven 8 to 10 minutes or until golden brown. Let stand 3 minutes before carefully removing from baking sheets. Cool on racks. Makes about 72 (2-inch) cookies.

TIP *Cut gumdrops, dates, marshmallows, candied fruits and other sticky foods with scissors. Dip scissors into hot water occasionally to make cutting easier.*

How to Make Cookie Monsters

1/Bake decorated cookie rounds until browned. Cool in pans, then turn out.

2/Cut each cookie into 8 wedges to serve.

Cocoa-Kahlúa Bon Bons

Created for my friend Natalie, a true chocoholic. These bon bons are best served the second day and doubly delicious when dipped in chocolate.

2 cups cream-filled-chocolate-cookie crumbs
  (about 22 cookies)
1/2 cup powdered sugar
2 tablespoons unsweetened cocoa
2 tablespoons light corn syrup
1/3 cup Kahlúa or other
  coffee-flavored liqueur

1 cup finely chopped pecans
About 1/4 cup granulated sugar
6 to 8 oz. semisweet or white chocolate,
  if desired, melted

In a medium bowl, combine cookie crumbs, powdered sugar, cocoa, corn syrup, liqueur and pecans. Cover and refrigerate 30 minutes. Shape dough into about 36 (1-inch) balls, dampening hands occasionally for ease in handling. Roll in granulated sugar, coating each ball generously. Store 24 hours in an airtight container at room temperature before serving or dipping in chocolate. If desired, dip 1/2 of each bon bon in melted chocolate. Place on a waxed-paper-lined baking sheet. Refrigerate until chocolate is set. Bon bons can be made 3 weeks ahead and refrigerated. Remove from refrigerator 30 minutes before serving. Makes about 36 bon bons.

White-Chocolate Swirls

This chewy white-chocolate bar has a rich fudge swirl for twice the chocolate taste!

3/4 cup butter, softened
1-1/4 cups sugar
4 eggs
1/2 teaspoon salt
1-1/2 teaspoons vanilla extract
1 cup all-purpose flour

2 oz. semisweet chocolate, melted, cooled
4 oz. white chocolate, melted, cooled
3/4 cup toasted chopped almonds
Chocolate Glaze, see below
1/3 cup toasted sliced almonds

Chocolate Glaze:
4 oz. semisweet or white chocolate

3 tablespoons whipping cream

Preheat oven to 350F (175C). Grease a 13″ x 9″ baking pan. In a large mixer bowl, beat butter and sugar until light and fluffy. Add eggs, 1 at a time, beating well after each addition. Add salt, vanilla and flour; beat just until combined. Transfer 1 cup batter to a medium bowl. Stir in melted semisweet chocolate; set aside. Stir melted white chocolate and chopped almonds into remaining batter. Turn into prepared pan; smooth surface. Drop heaping tablespoons of chocolate batter into light batter in 8 or 9 randomly spaced places. Using the back of a large spoon, press chocolate batter down into light batter. Using the flat edge of a dinner knife, cut through batters in a wide zigzag pattern to create a marbled effect. Do not marble too much or colors will blend and not contrast; smooth top. Surface will appear messy but interior of cookies will be marbled. Bake 20 to 25 minutes or until a wooden pick inserted in center comes out *almost* clean. Do not overbake. Cool completely on a rack. Prepare Chocolate Glaze. Spread over top of cooled cookies; sprinkle with sliced almonds. Refrigerate 15 minutes or until glaze is set. Using a sharp pointed knife, cut into 32 bars, cutting 4 strips 1 way and 8 strips the other way. Makes 32 cookies.

Chocolate Glaze:
In top of a double boiler over simmering water, melt chocolate and cream, stirring until blended and smooth.

Tia's Macadamia Butterfingers

I always make these for my sister Tia—my favorite macadamia nut!

1 cup butter, softened
1/2 cup packed brown sugar
1/2 cup granulated sugar
1 egg, separated
1/2 teaspoon ground nutmeg

2 cups all-purpose flour
1 teaspoon vanilla extract
1 tablespoon granulated sugar
1 cup macadamia nuts, finely chopped

Preheat oven to 275F (135C). Lightly grease a 15″ x 10″ jelly-roll pan. In a large mixer bowl, beat butter, brown sugar, 1/2 cup granulated sugar, egg yolk and nutmeg until light and fluffy. Add flour; stir to combine. Pat dough over bottom of prepared pan. In a small bowl, whisk egg white, vanilla and 1 tablespoon granulated sugar until frothy. Pour over dough; spread evenly with the back of a large tablespoon. Sprinkle nuts over dough; press lightly into surface. Bake 1 hour or until golden brown. Using a sharp pointed knife, cut pan of warm cookies into 40 bars, cutting 5 strips 1 way and 8 strips the other way. Loosen around edges while warm. Cool in pan on a rack. Makes 40 cookies.

Shown clockwise, starting at top right: Biscotti, page 64; Chocolate-Cherry Chews, page 75; Tia's Macadamia Butterfingers, above; Jam Pockets, page 65; and White-Chocolate Swirls, above.

Princess Cupcakes

Chocolatey cupcakes with a surprise pocket of cream filling—just like the famous store-bought brand!

1/3 cup butter, softened
1 cup packed brown sugar
1 teaspoon vanilla extract
2 eggs
2 oz. unsweetened chocolate, melted, cooled
1-1/4 cups all-purpose flour

3/4 teaspoon baking soda
1/4 teaspoon baking powder
1/4 teaspoon salt
3/4 cup milk
Cream Filling, see below
Bittersweet-Chocolate Glaze, page 147

Cream Filling:
1/2 cup vegetable shortening
3 tablespoons light corn syrup

1 tablespoon vanilla extract
1-1/2 cups powdered sugar

Decorator Icing:
1/3 cup powdered sugar

1 teaspoon water

Preheat oven to 375F (190C). Line 18 muffin cups with paper liners. In a large mixer bowl, beat butter, brown sugar and vanilla until blended. Add eggs, 1 at a time, beating well after each addition. Beat in cooled chocolate; set aside. In a medium bowl, combine flour, baking soda, baking powder and salt. Add to butter mixture alternately with milk in 3 additions, stirring only until smooth after each addition. Spoon batter into prepared muffin cups, filling each half full. Bake 15 to 20 minutes or until a wooden pick inserted in center comes out clean. Remove cupcakes from muffin tins. Cool completely on a rack. Prepare Cream Filling and Bittersweet-Chocolate Glaze; set aside.

To complete cupcakes, gently remove paper liners from cooled cupcakes. Using a serrated knife, cut 1/8 to 1/4 inch off each cupcake top. Keep cupcakes and matching tops together. Use a grapefruit spoon or small knife to remove center of each cupcake, leaving a 3/8- to 1/2-inch shell on sides and bottom of cake. Freeze cake crumbs for another use. Fill cake cavities with 1 heaping teaspoon Cream Filling. Filling should extend just above top of cupcake so it will spread when top is replaced and help hold top and bottom together. Replace tops of cupcakes, press down firmly. Set filled cupcakes on a waxed-paper-lined baking sheet. Spoon Bittersweet-Chocolate Glaze over each cupcake; spread down sides enough to cover and seal seam. Let stand until glaze sets. Prepare Decorator Icing. Make a decorator cone out of waxed or parchment paper, page 22; cut an 1/8-inch-wide tip. Fill cone halfway with icing. Pipe a decorative pattern across middle of each cupcake. Store in an airtight container at room temperature. Makes 18 cupcakes.

Cream Filling:
In a small mixer bowl, beat shortening, corn syrup, vanilla and 1/2 cup powdered sugar until smooth. Gradually add remaining powdered sugar; beat 2 minutes or until light and fluffy.

Decorator Icing:
In a small bowl, combine ingredients; stir until smooth.

A quick decorator cone can be made by spooning icing into a small plastic bag; press icing to one corner. Snip a tiny piece off corner of bag for your writing tip.

How to Make Princess Cupcakes

1/Use a grapefruit spoon or small knife to remove center of each cupcake, leaving a 3/8- to 1/2-inch shell on sides and bottom of cake. Fill cake cavities with 1 heaping teaspoon Cream Filling.

2/Spoon Bittersweet-Chocolate Glaze over each cupcake; spread down sides enough to cover and seal seam. Let stand until glaze sets. Using Decorator Icing, pipe a decorative pattern across middle of each cupcake.

Cappuccino Wafers

Wonderful Kahlúa-kissed wafers—perfect with after-dinner liqueurs or coffee.

1/3 cup Kahlúa or other
  coffee-flavored liqueur
1 tablespoon instant coffee powder or
  granules
3/4 cup plus 1 tablespoon butter,
  softened
1-1/4 cups sugar
1/2 teaspoon salt

2-1/3 cups all-purpose flour
1/4 teaspoon baking powder
About 2 tablespoons Kahlúa or other coffee-
  flavored liqueur for glaze, if desired
3 tablespoons sugar mixed with
  1 teaspoon instant coffee powder
  or granules and 1/8 teaspoon
  ground cinnamon

In a small bowl, combine 1/3 cup liqueur and 1 tablespoon instant coffee powder or granules. Set aside 5 minutes; stir to dissolve. In a large bowl, beat butter, 1-1/4 cups sugar and salt until light and fluffy. Gradually add liqueur mixture, beating well until blended. Stir in flour and baking powder until blended. Spoon dough onto the center of a 16-inch length of plastic wrap. Fold long sides of plastic wrap over dough. With your palms, roll wrapped dough into a log, 2 inches in diameter. Twist ends of plastic wrap to seal. Freeze or refrigerate until firm, 1 to 4 hours. Preheat oven to 375F (190C). Grease 3 large baking sheets. Cut chilled dough into 1/8-inch-thick slices. Place 1-1/2 inches apart on prepared baking sheets. Brush tops of cookies with additional liqueur, if desired. Sprinkle with sugar-coffee-cinnamon mixture. Bake 6 to 9 minutes or until edges are lightly browned. Cool on racks. Store in an airtight container. Makes about 72 cookies.

Almond-Orange Shortbread

Buttery, orange-scented cookies dipped in melted chocolate, then almonds—party-pretty and double-delicious!

1 cup butter, softened
1/2 cup powdered sugar
1 teaspoon vanilla extract
1/4 teaspoon salt
1 teaspoon freshly grated orange zest
1-2/3 cups all-purpose flour

1/3 cup cornstarch
3/4 cup toasted ground almonds
6 oz. semisweet chocolate
2 teaspoons vegetable oil
About 1-1/4 cups toasted sliced almonds,
    coarsely chopped

In a large mixer bowl, beat butter, powdered sugar, vanilla, salt and orange zest until light and fluffy. Add flour, cornstarch and ground almonds; stir until blended. Dough will be extremely soft. Spoon dough onto the center of a 20-inch length of plastic wrap. Fold long sides of plastic wrap over dough. With your palms, roll wrapped dough into a log, 15 inches long and 1-1/2 inches in diameter. Twist ends of plastic wrap to seal. Freeze or refrigerate until firm, 1 to 4 hours. Preheat oven to 300F (150C). Cut chilled dough into 1/4-inch-thick slices. Place 1 inch apart on ungreased baking sheets. Bake 15 to 20 minutes or until golden. Using a metal spatula, carefully remove from baking sheets; cool completely on racks. In top of a double boiler over simmering water, melt chocolate and oil together, stirring until smooth. Cool to room temperature. Line 2 or 3 large baking sheets with waxed paper. Place melted chocolate in a small bowl and chopped almonds in another. Dip each cookie halfway into chocolate, then into nuts. Allow excess chocolate to drain off cookie before dipping into nuts. Gentle handling is necessary as shortbread is very delicate. If chocolate begins to harden before you have completed dipping, gently reheat in double boiler. Place cookies on lined baking sheets; refrigerate until chocolate is set. Store in an airtight container in a cool place. Makes about 60 cookies.

Variations
Shortbread Sandwiches: Spread 1/2 teaspoon seedless raspberry jam or your favorite jam, on bottom of 1 shortbread cookie. Top with second cookie. Dip cookie sandwiches halfway into melted chocolate; do not coat chocolate with almonds.
Mexican-Chocolate Shortbread: Omit ground almonds. Substitute 1/3 cup unsweetened cocoa, preferably Dutch process, for 1/3 cup flour. Add 1/2 teaspoon *each* ground cinnamon and ground nutmeg. If desired, dip cooled cookies halfway into melted white or dark chocolate, then into chopped almonds.
Spicy Shortbread: Omit orange zest, if desired. Add 1 teaspoon ground cinnamon, 1/2 teaspoon *each* ground nutmeg and ground allspice with flour. Do not dip in chocolate.
Poppy-Lemon Shortbread: Substitute 2 teaspoons freshly grated lemon zest for 1 teaspoon orange zest. Add 1/4 cup poppy seeds with flour. Do not dip in chocolate.

TIP *Toast nuts and seeds in an ungreased skillet over medium heat, stirring frequently until golden brown. Or, oven-toast at 350F (175C), stirring occasionally, 15 minutes or until golden brown.*

Mocha-Chocolate-Chunk Cookies

Large chunks of chocolate replace the usual chocolate chips—for serious chocolate lovers only!

1 cup butter, softened
1 cup granulated sugar
1/2 cup packed brown sugar
3/4 teaspoon salt
1 teaspoon vanilla extract
2 eggs
1-1/2 tablespoons instant coffee powder
  or granules dissolved in
  2 teaspoons very hot water

2-1/3 cups all-purpose flour
1 teaspoon baking powder
1/2 teaspoon baking soda
16 oz. semisweet chocolate,
  cut in 3/8-inch chunks
1 cup coarsely chopped walnuts,
  if desired
6 to 8 oz. semisweet chocolate,
  if desired, melted

In a large mixer bowl, beat butter, sugars, salt and vanilla until light and fluffy. Add eggs and coffee liquid; beat until thoroughly combined. Add flour, baking powder, baking soda, chocolate chunks and walnuts, if desired; stir until blended. Refrigerate dough 30 minutes. Preheat oven to 325F (165C). Grease 2 large baking sheets. Drop dough by heaping tablespoons 3 inches apart on prepared baking sheets. Bake about 12 minutes for soft cookies and 15 minutes for crisper cookies. Cool completely on racks. If desired, dip cooled cookies halfway into melted chocolate. Place on waxed-paper-lined baking sheets; refrigerate until chocolate sets. Store in an airtight container in a cool place. Makes about 48 cookies.

Peanut-Butter-Kiss Cakes

Tiny peanut-butter-flavored cakes with a chocolate-candy kiss in the middle. Especially for all you peanut-butter and chocolate fans!

1/3 cup chunky peanut butter
1/4 cup butter, softened
1 cup packed brown sugar
2 eggs, room temperature
1 teaspoon vanilla extract
1-1/2 cups all-purpose flour

1-1/2 teaspoons baking powder
1/4 teaspoon salt
1/2 teaspoon ground cinnamon
1/2 cup milk, room temperature
14 milk-chocolate-kiss candies, unwrapped

Generously grease 14 muffin cups or line with paper liners. Preheat oven to 350F (175C). In a large mixer bowl, beat peanut butter, butter and brown sugar until mixture begins to hold together. Add eggs and vanilla; beat until creamy. In a medium bowl, combine flour, baking powder, salt and cinnamon. Add to peanut-butter mixture alternately with milk in 3 additions, beating well after each addition. Spoon into prepared muffin cups until 1/2 to 2/3 full. Bake 10 minutes. Remove from oven. Place a chocolate-kiss candy on center top of each cupcake. Return to oven. Bake 5 to 10 minutes longer or until a wooden pick inserted in center, under candy kiss, comes out clean. If not using paper liners, loosen cupcakes by running a knife around inside edges of muffin cups. Remove cupcakes from pan; cool completely on a rack. Makes 14 cupcakes.

Lemon-Poppy-Seed Cakes

Crisp, poppy-seed-studded cookie cups with a creamy lemon filling—an enticing flavor combination.

Cookie Cups:

1/2 cup butter, softened
1/2 cup powdered sugar
Freshly grated zest from 1 medium lemon
1 egg white
1-1/4 cups all-purpose flour

1/2 teaspoon baking powder
1/4 teaspoon salt
1/4 teaspoon ground ginger
1/4 teaspoon ground cardamom
3 tablespoons poppy seeds

Lemon Filling:

2 eggs
1 egg yolk
1/3 cup sugar
Freshly grated zest from 1/2 medium lemon

1/4 cup lemon juice
1-1/2 tablespoons honey
1/8 teaspoon salt

Cookie Cups:

Grease 12 muffin cups. Do not use paper liners. Preheat oven to 350F (175C). In a small mixer bowl, beat butter, powdered sugar and lemon zest until light and fluffy. Add egg white. Beat until blended; set aside. In a medium bowl, combine flour, baking powder, salt, ginger, cardamom and poppy seeds. Add to butter mixture; stir until mixture holds together. Turn out onto work surface. Form into a log, 12 inches long and 1-1/2 inches in diameter. Cut log into 12 (1-inch) pieces. Place 1 piece of dough in each prepared muffin cup, pressing evenly over bottom and up sides. Bake 12 minutes or until golden. Prepare Lemon Filling while cups are baking.

To complete cakes, fill each hot Cookie Cup with about 1-1/2 tablespoons Lemon Filling. Return to oven; bake 10 to 12 minutes longer or until filling is set. Cool in pan on a rack 3 to 5 minutes. To loosen cakes, run a thin knife around inside edges of muffin cups. Carefully remove cakes; cool on a rack. Serve barely warm or at room temperature. Best served same day as baked. Makes 12 cakes.

Lemon Filling:

In a medium bowl, combine all ingredients; stir until sugar is dissolved.

Confetti Fudgies

This candy-topped cookie brings out the kid in everyone. When I was testing the recipe, my husband's co-workers begged him to bring them more!

1/2 cup butter, melted
1 (8-1/2-oz.) pkg. chocolate-wafer cookies, finely crushed (about 2 cups crumbs)
1-1/2 cups chopped walnuts or pecans

1 cup shredded or flaked coconut
1 (14-oz.) can sweetened condensed milk
1-1/2 cups multi-colored candy-coated chocolate pieces

Preheat oven to 350F (175C). Grease sides only of a 13" x 9" baking pan. Pour in butter. Evenly sprinkle cookie crumbs over butter. Sprinkle nuts over crumbs, then sprinkle coconut over nuts. Drizzle with condensed milk so surface is evenly covered. Sprinkle with candy pieces; press lightly into surface with the back of a fork. Bake 20 to 25 minutes or until golden. Cool on a rack 30 minutes. Using a sharp knife, loosen edges and cut into 32 bars. Cool completely in pan before removing. Store in an airtight container. Makes 32 cookies.

How to Make Chocolate-Cherry Chews

1/Shape dough into 1-1/2-inch balls. Press 1 maraschino cherry deep into center of each ball; close dough over top to seal. Place balls, seam-side down, 2 inches apart on prepared baking sheets.

2/Generously dust cooled cookies with powdered sugar. Place 1 teaspoon chocolate frosting on center-top of cookie, swirling it slightly. Let frosting set before serving.

Chocolate-Cherry Chews   *Photo on page 69.*

Fudgy chocolate-frosted cookies with a cherry surprise—delicious enough for your favorite chocophile!

1 (10-oz.) jar maraschino cherries
1/2 cup butter, softened
1 cup granulated sugar
2 teaspoons vanilla extract
1-1/2 cups all-purpose flour
1/2 cup unsweetened cocoa, sifted

1/2 teaspoon baking soda
1/4 teaspoon salt
1 cup miniature semisweet chocolate pieces
Powdered sugar
3 oz. semisweet chocolate

Drain cherries, reserving juice. Thoroughly blot cherries dry on paper towels; set aside. In a large mixer bowl, beat butter and granulated sugar until light and fluffy. Continue beating, gradually adding 1/4 cup reserved maraschino-cherry juice and vanilla; beat until blended. Mixture will look curdled. Add flour, cocoa, baking soda, salt and chocolate pieces; stir until combined. Cover dough with plastic wrap; refrigerate 1 hour or until firm. Preheat oven to 350F (175C). Grease 2 large baking sheets. Shape dough into about 18 (1-1/2-inch) balls. Press 1 maraschino cherry deep into center of each ball; close dough over top to seal. Place balls, seam-side down, 2 inches apart on prepared baking sheets. Bake 12 to 18 minutes or until cookies flatten slightly and begin to crack on top. Carefully remove from baking sheets; cool completely on racks. Generously dust cooled cookies with powdered sugar. In top of a double boiler, combine 3 ounces chocolate with 2 tablespoons reserved cherry juice. Place double boiler over simmering water. Heat, stirring occasionally, until chocolate melts and mixture is shiny and smooth. Place 1 teaspoon chocolate frosting on center-top of cookie, swirling it slightly. Let frosting set before serving. Store in an airtight container. Makes about 18 cookies.

PUDDINGS, SOUFFLÉS & CUSTARDS

"Life's a pudding full of plums!" These optimistic words were penned by the nineteenth-century poet, William Gilbert. Obviously, Gilbert was paying high tribute to puddings which, since ancient times, have been a British specialty. Indeed, the English are credited with inventing the boiled *"puddynges"* of the fourteenth century.

The word *pudding* is used to describe a plethora of baked, boiled or steamed desserts, usually (but not always) with a soft texture, and served either hot or cold. From this definition, you can see that there's no limit to the variety of puddings one can create. And it's hard to dispute that puddings are one of life's truly "comforting" foods.

Steamed puddings, descendants of the early English boiled puddings, are wonderful, full-flavored creations, perfect for chilly fall and winter evenings. The age-old steaming method creates a moist, firm-textured dessert that smacks of old-fashioned pleasures. Tradition demands steamed puddings be complemented by a sauce and this chapter's Orange-Berry Steamed Pudding follows suit with its Fluffy Hard Sauce or orangey Suzette Sauce.

Baked puddings are usually bolder and heartier than their stirred, stove-top counterparts. Almond-Persimmon and Brandied Bread Puddings, for example, are solid, earthy creations served warm with cream or sauce. By contrast, the creamy Eggnog Chiffon Pudding, cooked briefly on the stove and then chilled, is as light and carefree as an early summer breeze!

Gentleness and care are the watchwords when working with any egg-based mixture. Stirred puddings and custards require a low heat and should be cooked in a heavy saucepan or double boiler. *Constant* stirring is necessary in order for an egg's protein to coagulate evenly. Because egg whites coagulate at a lower temperature than egg yolks, all traces of white must be removed in order to achieve a perfectly smooth pudding or custard. If the recipe calls for whole eggs, straining the mixture through a fine sieve will prevent a lumpy end result.

Custards are generally baked in a water bath, which simply means that the custard containers are halfway immersed in hot water. The water acts as insulation and diffuses the oven heat so the mixture will set without separating. One of my favorite custards is the devilishly good Baked Irish Cream, flavored like the famous imported Irish liqueur. Teetotalers may partake, however, because all the alcohol burns off while the custard bakes!

Whether hot or cold, the airy and flamboyant soufflé is the most ethereal of this dessert genre. Hot soufflés are not as tricky as one might think, and what most cooks don't realize is that their various components can be prepared ahead of time for quick assembly just before baking (see *Hints For Successful Soufflés*, opposite). Something to remember when making soufflés is that one must demonstrate a certain panache. So what if an unexpected catastrophe plunges your cloudlike soufflé into an unattractive puddle? Simply entitle the dessert *English pudding* and serve it with flair!

Soufflés acquire their lightness from stiffly beaten egg whites in which air is entrapped. Oven heat expands the imprisoned air and makes the mixture rise. Too much oven heat and the outside of the soufflé hardens too quickly, preventing it from rising to its maximum. Too little oven heat and the air bubbles collapse from lack of pressure. Our favorite of the hot soufflés is the Aloha Soufflé, created for a luau Ron and I recently hosted. It harmonizes the flavors of banana, coconut and pineapple and is finished with a Hot-Buttered Rum Sauce. A true taste of the islands!

Frozen soufflés are almost as glamorous as hot soufflés and have the advantage of not having to be rushed from oven to table with one's reputation at risk. They're generally made using a soufflé dish with a foil collar which, when removed, gives a high-rising soufflé effect. For show-stopping dessert success, try the Frozen Brandy Alexander Soufflé. Heady with crème de cacao and brandy, this is definitely an "adults only" dessert!

Hints for Successful Soufflés

- A soufflé is comprised of stiffly beaten egg whites which give it the traditional light texture, and a base mixture which provides flavor.
- Recipes calling for more egg whites than egg yolks produce lighter soufflés.
- Position oven rack in center of oven. Preheat oven 15 minutes. Use an oven thermometer for accurate oven temperature.
- A classic soufflé dish is suggested because the straight sides force the expanding soufflé upward.
- Butter a soufflé dish. It is important to use the size dish specified in the recipe.
- To support the side of a soufflé and give it extra height, a collar is added to the soufflé dish. To prepare a collar, cut a piece of foil 2 inches longer than circumference of dish to be used. Fold foil lengthwise in thirds; lightly butter 1 side of foil. Tightly wrap foil, buttered-side in, around outside of soufflé dish. Collar should rise 2 to 3 inches above rim of dish. Securely fasten foil with tape or string. If using string, tie it about 1/2 inch below rim of dish; use a paper clip to secure top edge of foil. Press foil so it conforms to shape of dish.
- Sprinkle dish with about 2 tablespoons sugar, rotating so sugar coats dish and foil collar.
- Egg whites must be beaten so as much air as possible is incorporated. See *Hints for Beating Egg Whites*, page 95.
- Incorporate stiffly beaten egg whites into base mixture immediately after beating. If beaten whites are allowed to stand, they will begin to deflate and your soufflé will not be as light as it should be.
- Stir a small amount of beaten egg whites into soufflé base to lighten mixture and make it easier to fold in remaining egg whites.
- Components of a soufflé may be prepared in advance for easy last-minute assembly. Butter and sugar soufflé dish; set aside unbeaten egg whites in a covered container. Prepare and cover base mixture. If base mixture is refrigerated, allow it to stand at room temperature at least 1 hour before using. Be sure to preheat the oven. At the last minute, simply beat egg whites, fold them into base mixture and bake your soufflé!

Baked Irish Cream

The alcohol burns off while baking, leaving the heady flavor of the famous imported liqueur.

5 eggs
1 (14-oz.) can sweetened condensed milk
3 tablespoons commercial chocolate syrup
1-1/2 tablespoons instant coffee powder or
   granules dissolved in
    1 tablespoon very hot water

1-1/2 cups half and half
3/4 cup Irish whiskey or
   other good-quality whiskey
1-1/2 tablespoons vanilla extract
3/4 cup whipping cream, whipped,
   sweetened to taste

Preheat oven to 300F (150C). Place 8 (6-ounce) custard cups in a large shallow baking pan. In a medium bowl, beat eggs, condensed milk, chocolate syrup and coffee liquid just until blended. Stir in half and half, whiskey and vanilla. Strain through a fine sieve into a pitcher; pour into custard cups. Pour hot water into baking pan to come halfway up sides of custard cups. Cover pan with a large sheet of foil. Bake 45 to 55 minutes or until a knife inserted in center comes out clean. Cool on a rack to room temperature. Cover and refrigerate 3 hours before serving. Place a dollop of sweetened whipped cream on each serving. Makes 8 servings.

Peach Crème Brûlée

Especially created for Sue Bain, this fruited version of the classic "burnt cream" has almonds in the caramelized crust.

1-1/2 cups whipping cream
1-1/2 cups half and half
6 egg yolks
1/3 cup granulated sugar
1/8 teaspoon salt
2 teaspoons vanilla extract
1 cup finely chopped, peeled, ripe peaches
   or unpeeled nectarines (about 2 medium
   peaches or nectarines)

1/8 teaspoon ground nutmeg
2 tablespoons brown sugar
1/3 to 1/2 cup sliced almonds
1/2 to 2/3 cup packed brown sugar

In top of a double boiler, heat cream and half and half over low heat until bubbles appear around edge of pan. While cream heats, in a small mixer bowl, beat egg yolks, granulated sugar and salt until thick and pale. Gradually stir 1 cup hot cream into egg mixture. Stir mixture back into remaining hot cream in pan. Place top of double boiler over simmering water. Cook, stirring constantly, 10 to 15 minutes or until mixture thickly coats the back of a metal spoon. Remove from heat; strain through a fine sieve into a medium bowl. Place bowl in a larger container of iced water. Stir occasionally until custard is room temperature. Stir in vanilla. In a medium bowl, combine peaches or nectarines, nutmeg and 2 tablespoons brown sugar. Divide fruit mixture evenly among 6 (6-ounce) custard cups or sprinkle over bottom of a shallow 1-1/2-quart baking dish. Gently spoon cooled custard over fruit mixture. Cover and refrigerate 8 hours or overnight. Two to 3 hours before serving, preheat broiler. Sprinkle almonds over surface of custard. Using the back of a spoon, press 1/2 to 2/3 cup brown sugar through a sieve over surface of custard. Brown-sugar layer should be even and no thicker than 1/4 inch. Set custard in a large baking pan; surround completely with ice. Place under broiler. Top of custard should be 6 inches from heat. Broil 1 to 2 minutes or until sugar just begins to caramelize and form a hard crust. Watch very carefully and turn custard, if necessary, to prevent sugar from burning. Cool 15 minutes, then refrigerate up to 6 hours before serving. Makes 6 servings.

 To peel peaches: Using a slotted spoon, place 2 to 3 peaches at a time in a pot of boiling water, deep enough to cover them. Let peaches remain in water 20 to 45 seconds; the riper the peach, the less time required. Remove a peach from boiling water with a slotted spoon. Move your thumb firmly across the skin. If it wrinkles, the skin will come off easily. If the skin is resistant, return peach to boiling water for a few seconds. Immediately transfer peaches to a large bowl of iced water. Remove skin with your fingers.

How to Make Peach Crème Brûlée

1/Divide fruit mixture evenly among 6 (6-ounce) custard cups. Gently spoon cooled custard over fruit mixture. Cover and refrigerate 8 hours or overnight.

2/Sprinkle almonds over surface of custard. Using the back of a spoon, press 1/2 to 2/3 cup brown sugar through a sieve over surface of custard. Set custard in a large baking pan; surround completely with ice. Broil 1 to 2 minutes or until sugar just begins to caramelize and form a hard crust.

Eggnog Chiffon Pudding

A heavenly light pudding—drizzle with Praline-Rum Sauce for a sophisticated finale to holiday dining.

1 (1/4-oz.) envelope unflavored gelatin
  (scant 1 tablespoon)
1/3 cup light rum
1-2/3 cups dairy eggnog, not canned
4 eggs, separated, room temperature
1/3 cup sugar
1/4 teaspoon ground nutmeg

1/8 teaspoon salt
1-1/2 teaspoons vanilla extract
1/2 cup whipping cream, whipped
1/4 teaspoon cream of tartar
Praline-Rum Sauce, page 155, or
  Black-Satin Sauce, page 154,
  if desired

In a small bowl, stir gelatin into rum; let stand 5 minutes to soften. In a medium, heavy saucepan, combine eggnog, egg yolks, sugar, nutmeg and salt. Cook over medium-low heat, stirring constantly, until mixture thickly coats the back of a metal spoon. Remove from heat. Add gelatin mixture; stir 1 minute or until dissolved. Strain through a fine sieve into a large bowl; stir in vanilla. Refrigerate, stirring occasionally, until mixture begins to mound when spooned on top of itself. Fold in whipped cream. In a small mixer bowl, beat egg whites and cream of tartar until stiff but not dry. Fold into eggnog mixture. Turn into a 2-quart glass serving bowl or 6 to 8 individual glass dessert dishes. Cover and refrigerate at least 3 hours before serving. Prepare Praline-Rum Sauce or Black-Satin Sauce, if desired. Pass sauce with pudding, if desired. Makes 6 to 8 servings.

Souffléed Rice Pudding

Orange marmalade adds sparkle to this light unbaked version of the old-fashioned favorite.

1 cup golden raisins
1/2 cup orange-flavored liqueur or
   orange juice
1 cup long-grain white rice
3 cups milk
1/4 teaspoon salt
2 (1/4-ounce) envelopes unflavored gelatin
   (about 5 teaspoons)
6 egg yolks
3/4 cup sugar
1/3 cup sweet-orange marmalade
1/2 teaspoon ground cinnamon

1/2 teaspoon ground nutmeg
2 teaspoons vanilla extract
3 egg whites, room temperature
2 tablespoons sugar
1-1/4 cups whipping cream, whipped
1/4 cup sweet-orange marmalade,
   room temperature, mixed with
   1 tablespoon orange-flavored liqueur,
   if desired
Sweetened whipped cream,
   if desired

In a small bowl, combine raisins and orange-flavored liqueur or orange juice. Cover; set aside 3 to 4 hours or overnight to soak. Add rice to 6 cups boiling water in large saucepan; bring to a boil again. Drain; return rice to pan. Add 2 cups milk and salt. Bring to a simmer over medium heat; reduce heat to low. Cover and cook rice 20 to 30 minutes or until tender and milk has been absorbed. Strain raisins, reserving liquid in a small bowl; set raisins aside. Stir gelatin into raisin liquid; let stand 5 minutes to soften. In top of a double boiler, beat egg yolks and sugar until thick and pale. Gradually stir in remaining 1 cup milk. Place top of double boiler over simmering water. Cook egg-yolk mixture, stirring constantly, until mixture coats the back of a metal spoon. Remove from heat. Add gelatin mixture; stir 1 minute or until dissolved. Stir in 1/3 cup marmalade, cinnamon, nutmeg, vanilla and raisins. Stir custard mixture into cooked rice, making sure rice does not clump. Refrigerate, stirring occasionally, until mixture cools and begins to thicken. In a medium bowl, beat egg whites to soft-peak stage. Beating constantly, gradually add 2 tablespoons sugar. Continue beating until whites are glossy and firm. Stir 1/3 of egg-white mixture into rice mixture to lighten it. Fold in remaining egg-white mixture, then whipped cream. Spoon mixture into a 2-1/2- to 3-quart bowl. Stir 1/4 cup orange marmalade until liquid enough to pour. Add 1 tablespoon liqueur, if desired. Spread over top of pudding. Decorate with rosettes of sweetened whipped cream, if desired. Cover and refrigerate at least 3 hours before serving. Makes 10 to 12 servings.

Variation
Holiday Rice Pudding: Substitute 1/2 cup red-maraschino-cherry halves and 1/2 cup green maraschino-cherry halves, thoroughly blotted dry, for 1 cup raisins. Omit orange-marmalade topping and decorate top with additional blotted red- and green-maraschino-cherry halves.

TIP *Use the best ingredients you can afford. Any dish can only be as good as the ingredients that go into it.*

Almond-Persimmon Pudding

Ripe persimmons are very soft. Remove pulp from skin with a spoon before pureeing.

1-1/2 cups very-ripe-persimmon puree
  (4 to 5 persimmons)
3 eggs
1 cup packed brown sugar
1/4 cup butter, melted
1 teaspoon vanilla extract
1 cup all-purpose flour
1/2 cup toasted ground almonds
1 teaspoon baking powder

1/2 teaspoon baking soda
1 teaspoon ground cinnamon
1/2 teaspoon ground nutmeg
1/2 teaspoon salt
1-1/4 cups half and half
3/4 cup raisins, if desired
1/3 cup sliced almonds
Almond Cream, page 152

Grease an 8-inch-square baking pan. Preheat oven to 325F (165C). In a large bowl, combine persimmon puree, eggs, brown sugar, butter and vanilla; set aside. In a medium bowl, combine flour, ground almonds, baking powder, baking soda, cinnamon, nutmeg and salt. Add to persimmon mixture alternately with half and half in 3 additions, stirring well after each addition. Stir in raisins, if desired. Turn into prepared pan. Smooth surface; sprinkle with sliced almonds. Bake 55 to 65 minutes or until set in center and pudding begins to pull away from sides of pan. Prepare Almond Cream; refrigerate. Serve pudding warm or at room temperature with Almond Cream. Refrigerate leftovers. Reheat pudding in top of a covered double boiler over simmering water. Makes 6 to 8 servings.

Variation
Steamed Almond-Persimmon Pudding: Prepare Fluffy Hard Sauce, page 152; refrigerate. Grease a 1-1/2-quart steamed-pudding mold, 2 (1-pound) coffee cans or 4 (1-pound) fruit or vegetable cans. If desired, sprinkle 1 to 2 tablespoons sliced almonds over bottom and sides of container(s). Prepare pudding mixture as directed above. Pour into pudding mold or divide evenly between cans. Secure cover of pudding mold or cover cans tightly with a double layer of regular foil or a single layer of heavy-duty foil. Secure foil with string. Place a rack in a large kettle. Place mold or cans on rack. Add boiling water to come halfway up sides of mold or cans. Cover; bring water to a gentle boil. Steam pudding 2 hours for pudding mold; 1-1/2 hours for coffee cans; or 1 hour for vegetable or fruit cans. Puddings are done when a skewer inserted in center comes out clean. If necessary, add additional boiling water to keep level halfway up sides of mold or cans. Remove mold or cans from water; let stand on a rack 5 minutes. Gently unmold onto a serving plate. Let stand 10 minutes before serving warm with sauce. Reheat leftovers as above. Makes 6 to 8 servings.

 TIP *When you have a pudding which requires lengthy steaming, it is a good idea to put a couple of marbles into the water. You will have a noisy warning when the water level is getting low!*

Orange-Berry Steamed Pudding

Flame this wonderful fall pudding for a stunning and delicious ending to a special meal.

Fluffy Hard Sauce, page 152, or
  Suzette Sauce, page 150
1 cup all-purpose flour
2/3 cup sugar
1-1/2 teaspoons baking soda
1/2 teaspoon salt
1/2 teaspoon ground cinnamon
1/4 teaspoon ground cloves
1/4 teaspoon ground nutmeg
4 cups soft bread crumbs

2 cups cranberries, coarsely chopped
1 cup chopped walnuts
2 eggs
1 cup sweet-orange marmalade
1/2 cup milk
1/2 cup brandy or additional milk
Plain and sugar-dusted cranberries, if desired
Sugar cubes and orange or lemon extract,
  or 1/4 cup brandy, if desired

Prepare sauce of choice; set aside. Generously grease a 7- to 8-cup pudding mold, Bundt pan or other metal mold. In a large bowl, combine flour, sugar, baking soda, salt, cinnamon, cloves, nutmeg, bread crumbs, chopped cranberries and walnuts; set aside. In a medium bowl, combine eggs, orange marmalade, milk and 1/2 cup brandy or additional milk. Add to dry ingredients, stirring until well-blended. Turn into prepared mold. Secure cover of pudding mold or cover tightly with a double layer of regular foil or a single layer of heavy-duty foil. Secure foil with string. Place a rack in a large kettle. Place mold on rack. Add boiling water to come halfway up side of mold. Cover; bring water to a gentle boil. Steam pudding 2-1/2 to 3 hours or until a wooden pick inserted in center comes out clean. If necessary, add more boiling water to keep level halfway up sides of mold. Remove mold from water; let stand on a rack 5 minutes. Gently unmold pudding onto a serving plate. Garnish with plain and sugar-dusted cranberries, if desired. If desired, soak several sugar cubes in orange or lemon extract. Place cubes around top or bottom of pudding; ignite. Or, warm 1/4 cup brandy in a small saucepan just until bubbles appear around edge of pan. Carefully ignite using a long match; pour flaming brandy over pudding. Serve warm with sauce. Makes 10 to 12 servings.

Macadamia Cream Custard

Toasted macadamia nuts add a touch of tropical magic to this easy but incredibly rich custard.

1 cup toasted chopped macadamia nuts
3 cups half and half
4 eggs, room temperature
3 egg yolks, room temperature

2/3 cup packed brown sugar
1-1/2 tablespoons vanilla extract
1/2 recipe Plain Whipped Cream, page 156
About 1/4 cup toasted chopped macadamia nuts

Set aside a 1-1/2- to 2-quart baking dish. Preheat oven to 325F (165C). In a medium saucepan, combine 1 cup macadamia nuts and half and half. Cook over medium heat, stirring frequently, until mixture comes to a boil. Pour into a blender. Begin on lowest speed and gradually increase speed to medium. Process at medium speed 1 minute; set aside. In a large mixer bowl, beat eggs, egg yolks and brown sugar until thick and pale. With mixer running at low speed, gradually add hot nut mixture. Mix only until combined; do not allow mixture to foam. Line a fine sieve with 4 layers of cheesecloth. Strain egg mixture through lined sieve into baking dish. Stir in vanilla. Set dish in a baking pan. Pour hot water into pan to come halfway up side of dish. Bake 35 minutes or until a knife inserted in center of custard comes out clean. Cool completely on a rack; cover and refrigerate at least 4 hours. Prepare Plain Whipped Cream; refrigerate. Before serving, pipe or dollop whipped cream decoratively onto top of custard. Sprinkle with 1/4 cup macadamia nuts. Serve custard chilled. Makes 6 to 8 servings.

Orange-Berry Steamed Pudding, above, with Fluffy Hard Sauce, page 152.

Celestial Cream

Steeping a vanilla bean and fresh orange zest in hot cream gives this dessert a "heavenly" flavor.

1 pint whipping cream (2 cups)
1 cup milk
Freshly grated zest of 1 large orange
2 teaspoons orange-flower water
1 (3-inch) piece vanilla bean,
  cut in 3 pieces
1 (1-inch) piece cinnamon stick
6 egg yolks, room temperature
2/3 cup sugar

1/4 teaspoon salt
1/2 cup all-purpose flour
1 cup orange juice, room temperature
1/2 recipe Spirited Whipped cream, page 156,
  flavored with 1 tablespoon
  orange-flavored liqueur
6 fresh orange slices, membrane removed,
  or Candied Orange Zest, page 143

In top of a double boiler, combine cream, milk, orange zest, orange-flower water, vanilla bean and cinnamon stick. Bring to a simmer over medium heat. Reduce heat to low; cover and simmer 30 minutes. During last 5 minutes of cooking time, combine egg yolks, sugar and salt in a small mixer bowl; beat until thick and pale. Gradually add flour; beat until blended. Beating constantly at low speed, slowly pour 1 cup hot cream mixture into egg mixture. Place top of double boiler over simmering water. Slowly whisk egg mixture back into remaining cream mixture. Stir in orange juice. Cook, stirring constantly, until mixture thickly coats the back of a metal spoon. For a smooth texture, strain mixture through a fine sieve into a medium bowl. Refrigerate, stirring frequently during first hour to release steam and prevent skin from forming. Spoon into 6 stemmed glasses. Cover and refrigerate at least 3 hours. Prepare Spirited Whipped Cream; refrigerate. Before serving, top each portion with whipped cream and an orange slice or Candied Orange Zest. Makes 6 servings.

Zabaglione

Pronounced za-ba-YO-nay, this warm gossamer custard is a true Italian masterpiece!

8 egg yolks, room temperature
1/2 cup sugar
3/4 cup dry Marsala

1 tablespoon finely grated orange or
  lemon zest, if desired

In a large bowl or top of a double boiler, combine egg yolks and sugar. Using a wire whisk or portable mixer, beat until thick and pale. Place bowl or pan over simmering water. Beating constantly, gradually add Marsala. Beat until custard has almost tripled in volume, 10 to 15 minutes. Zabaglione will be very thick, and fluffy enough to form soft peaks. Immediately spoon into 6 to 8 warmed, wide-rimmed, wine glasses, if you have them, or other glass serving dishes. Sprinkle with grated orange or lemon zest, if desired. Serve immediately. Makes 6 to 8 servings.

Variations
Zabaglione Freddo (Cold Zabaglione): Set pan or bowl of tripled Zabaglione in a larger bowl of iced water. Beat constantly 3 to 5 minutes or until mixture is cool. Spoon over fresh fruit or berries.
Amaretto Zabaglione: Substitute amaretto liqueur, Frangelico or other hazelnut-flavored liqueur, or orange-flavored liqueur for Marsala.
To halve the recipe, use 4 egg yolks, 1/4 cup sugar, 6 tablespoons Marsala and 1-1/2 teaspoons grated orange or lemon zest.

Serve hot Zabaglione as a sauce over crumbled angel food or sponge cake.

How to Make Celestial Cream

1/In a double boiler, stir egg mixture until it thickly coats the back of a metal spoon.

2/Spoon chilled mixture into 6 stemmed glasses. Refrigerate at least 3 hours. Before serving, top each portion with whipped cream and Candied Orange Zest, if desired.

Ron's Pots de Crème au Café

My husband taught me to make these rich custards—his favorite—when we were newlyweds.

1-1/2 cups milk
1/2 cup half and half
1 (2-inch) piece vanilla bean,
    split lengthwise
1-1/2 tablespoons instant coffee powder
    or granules

6 egg yolks, room temperature
1/2 cup sugar
2/3 cup whipping cream, whipped with
    1 tablespoon powdered sugar, if desired
6 to 8 coffee-bean candies, if desired

Preheat oven to 275F (135C). In a medium, heavy saucepan, combine milk, half and half, vanilla bean and instant coffee powder or granules. Bring to a boil. Remove from heat. Stir; cover and let stand 10 minutes. Place 8 (3-ounce) pot-de-crème pots or 6 (4-ounce) custard cups in a large baking pan with a cover. If baking pan does not have cover, use a double piece of regular foil or single piece of heavy-duty foil to fit pan. In a large mixer bowl, beat egg yolks with sugar until thick and pale. Stirring constantly, gradually pour hot milk mixture into egg mixture. Do not stir enough to create foam. Strain through a fine sieve into a pitcher. Pour into custard containers. Pour hot water into pan to come halfway up sides of custard containers. If using pot-de-crème pots, cover with lids, if not, place cover on pan or cover securely with foil. Bake 45 to 55 minutes or until a knife inserted in center comes out clean. Remove custards from baking pan. Place on a rack; cool, uncovered, to room temperature. Cover and refrigerate at least 4 hours before serving. Garnish each serving with a rosette of sweetened whipped cream, topped with a coffee-bean candy, if desired. Makes 6 to 8 servings.

Frozen Chocolate-Mint Soufflé

A swirl of creamy chocolate runs through this frosty mint sensation—an elegant variation of after-dinner mints!

6 eggs, separated, barely warm
1 cup sugar
1/8 teaspoon salt
1-3/4 cups whipping cream
1/2 cup green crème de menthe
3 oz. semisweet chocolate, melted

1/2 teaspoon mint extract
1/4 teaspoon cream of tartar
1/2 oz. semisweet chocolate melted with
 1/2 tablespoon butter,
 cooled to barely warm
Black-Satin Sauce, page 154, if desired

Fold a 25-inch length of foil lengthwise in thirds. Lightly oil 1 side of foil. Tightly wrap foil, oiled-side in, around outside of a 1-1/2-quart soufflé dish. Collar should rise 1-1/2 inches above rim of dish. Or, use a 1-quart soufflé dish, making a 3-inch collar. Securely fasten foil with tape or string. If using string, tie about 1/2 inch below rim of dish. Use a paper clip to secure top edge of foil. Press foil so it conforms to shape of dish. In top of a double boiler, whisk egg yolks, 3/4 cup sugar and salt until thick and pale. Gradually stir in 1 cup cream, then crème de menthe. Place top of double boiler over simmering water. Cook, stirring constantly, until mixture is very thick. Turn 3/4 cup custard into a small bowl. Add 3 ounces melted chocolate; stir until thoroughly blended. Set aside to cool at room temperature. Stir mint extract into remaining custard in pan. Refrigerate, stirring frequently, until cold. In a small bowl, beat remaining 3/4 cup cream until stiff. Fold into chilled mint custard; cover and refrigerate. In a large mixer bowl, beat egg whites and cream of tartar to soft-peak stage. Beating constantly, gradually add remaining 1/4 cup sugar, 2 tablespoons at a time. Continue beating until whites are glossy and firm. Fold egg-white mixture into mint mixture, 1/3 at a time. Turn 1/2 of soufflé mixture into prepared dish; smooth surface. Dot with 8 to 9 heaping teaspoons chocolate mixture. Add remaining mint soufflé. Smooth surface; dot with remaining chocolate mixture in 8 or 9 places, randomly spaced. Using the wide side of a dinner knife, cut through mixtures in a wide zigzag pattern to create a marbled effect. Do not marble too much or colors will blend and not contrast. Cover and freeze overnight. Dessert may be tightly covered and frozen up to 1 month. Make a decorator cone out of waxed or parchment paper, page 22; cut an 1/8-inch-wide tip. Fill cone halfway with melted chocolate-butter mixture. Pipe chocolate, following inside of foil collar to create a circular border on surface of soufflé. Drizzle chocolate over center area in a light lacy pattern. Return to freezer until ready to serve. Prepare Black-Satin Sauce, if desired. Before serving, remove foil collar from soufflé. Serve frozen soufflé with sauce, if desired. Makes 8 servings.

Variation

Individual Frozen Chocolate-Mint Soufflés: Following directions above, wrap 15-inch lengths of foil around 6 individual 6-ounce soufflé dishes. Prepare soufflés as above. If desired, do not make chocolate-custard mixture to create marbled effect. Makes 6 servings.

Individual Frozen Chocolate-Mint Soufflés

Bittersweet-Chocolate Soufflé

Most soufflés can be prepared a few hours in advance up to the point of beating and folding in the egg whites.

Tipsy Crème Anglaise, page 149,
  or Black-Satin Sauce, page 154
2 tablespoons granulated sugar
1/3 cup all-purpose flour
1 cup granulated sugar
2/3 cup unsweetened cocoa,
  preferably Dutch process
1/4 teaspoon salt

1-1/4 cups milk
1/4 cup crème de cacao
2 tablespoons butter
7 egg whites, room temperature
5 egg yolks, room temperature
1/4 teaspoon cream of tartar
Powdered sugar

Prepare sauce of choice. Preheat oven to 350F (175C). Butter a 2-quart soufflé dish. Fold a 27-inch length of foil lengthwise in thirds. Lightly butter 1 side of foil. Tightly wrap foil, buttered-side in, around outside of soufflé dish. Collar should rise 2-1/2 to 3 inches above rim of dish. Securely fasten foil with tape or string. If using string, tie about 1/2 inch below rim of dish. Use a paper clip to secure top edge of foil. Press foil so it confirms to shape of dish. Sprinkle dish with about 2 tablespoons sugar, rotating so sugar coats dish and foil collar. In a medium saucepan, whisk together flour, 3/4 cup granulated sugar, cocoa and salt. Gradually add milk and crème de cacao, stirring until smooth. Add butter. Cook over medium-low heat, stirring constantly, until mixture begins to thicken. Remove from heat. Whisk in 1 egg white, then egg yolks, 1 at a time. Let stand 10 minutes, stirring frequently. If preparing in advance, cover and refrigerate up to 8 hours; bring mixture back to room temperature before continuing. In a large mixer bowl, beat remaining 6 egg whites and cream of tartar to soft-peak stage. Beating constantly, gradually add remaining 1/4 cup granulated sugar, 2 tablespoons at a time. Continue beating until whites are glossy and firm. Gently fold cooled chocolate mixture into egg-white mixture, 1/4 at a time. Do not handle any more than necessary. Turn mixture into prepared dish; smooth top. Bake 50 to 60 minutes, depending whether you like the center of your soufflé soft and moist or light and dry. Use a long skewer to test for doneness. Immediately sprinkle baked soufflé with sifted powdered sugar. To prevent soufflé from collapsing too soon, take it to the table with foil collar still attached. Have a plate ready on which to place foil and string or tape. Remove collar to reveal your soufflé in all its glory before it collapses. Serve with sauce. Makes 8 servings.

Variation
Chocolate-Orange Soufflé: Substitute 1/2 cup orange juice for 1/4 cup crème de cacao and 1/4 cup milk. Add freshly grated zest of 1 medium orange before folding in egg whites. Serve with Suzette Sauce, page 150.

TIP *Dutch process cocoa is cocoa in which the acidity has been neutralized by the addition of a small amount of alkali. This method produces a darker, less-bitter cocoa powder.*

How to Make Bittersweet-Chocolate Soufflé

1/Prepare foil collar and attach to dish. Press foil so it conforms to shape of dish.

2/Sprinkle dish with about 2 tablespoons sugar, rotating so sugar coats dish and foil collar.

Almond Curd with Berries

Tossed with fresh berries, this rendition of a Chinese specialty is deliciously refreshing on a hot summer day!

3 (1/4-oz.) envelopes unflavored gelatin (about 2-1/2 tablespoons)
1 cup water
2/3 cup sweetened condensed milk
1-2/3 cups whole milk
1-1/2 teaspoons almond extract

4 cups fresh raspberries, blueberries, chopped strawberries or peaches or a combination of berries and other fruit
1/3 cup kirsch, orange-flavored liqueur or amaretto liqueur

In top of a double boiler, stir gelatin into water; let stand 5 minutes to soften. Place top of double boiler over simmering water. Stir gelatin until dissolved. Remove from heat. Slowly stir in sweetened condensed milk, regular milk and almond extract. Rinse a 9-inch-square baking pan with cold water. Drain, but do not dry. Pour almond mixture into pan. Refrigerate 1 hour or until set. Cut almond curd into 3/4-inch squares. Cover until ready to serve. Thirty minutes before serving, combine fruit and liqueur; refrigerate. Spoon equal amounts of Almond Curd and fruit into each of 8 stemmed glasses. Makes 8 servings.

Brandied Bread Pudding

An age-old favorite dressed up with spirits—unbeatable on a cold winter night!

1 cup packed brown sugar
3/4 teaspoon ground cinnamon
3/4 teaspoon ground nutmeg
1 (1-lb.) loaf 3-day-old bread
5 eggs
3-1/2 cups half and half
1/2 cup brandy, or 1/2 cup orange juice
   and 1 teaspoon imitation brandy extract

1 tablespoon vanilla extract
1 teaspoon freshly grated orange zest
1/2 cup golden raisins
Brandy-Butter Sauce, page 155,
   or whipping cream

Preheat oven to 325F (165C). Lightly butter a 3-quart baking dish. In a small bowl, combine 1/4 cup brown sugar, 1/4 teaspoon cinnamon and 1/4 teaspoon nutmeg for topping; set aside. Cut crusts from bread. Tear or cut bread into 1-inch chunks or cubes. Place in prepared dish; set aside. In a medium bowl, lightly beat eggs. Stir in remaining 3/4 cup brown sugar, 1/2 teaspoon cinnamon, 1/2 teaspoon nutmeg, half and half, brandy, or orange juice and brandy extract, vanilla, orange zest and raisins. Pour over bread chunks, lightly pressing bread into egg mixture. Let stand 10 minutes; stir before baking. If desired, pudding may be covered and refrigerated overnight at this point. Let stand at room temperature 1 hour before baking. To bake, sprinkle spice topping over surface of pudding. Set dish in a shallow baking pan; fill with 1 inch of hot water. Bake 1-1/4 hours or until a knife inserted in center comes out *almost* clean. Preheat broiler. Broil pudding 6 inches from heat 1 to 2 minutes to crisp topping. Cool on a rack 30 minutes. Prepare Brandy-Butter Sauce, if desired. Serve pudding warm with Brandy-Butter Sauce or cream, or both. Makes 8 to 10 servings.

Variations

Orange Bread Pudding: Omit spice topping and broiling. Substitute 1 (11-ounce) can chopped drained mandarin-orange segments for raisins, and 1 cup sweet-orange marmalade for 1/2 cup brandy and 3/4 cup brown sugar. Spread top of baked pudding with additional 1/3 cup sweet-orange marmalade. Serve with Orange Whipped Cream, page 156, if desired.

Tropical Bread Pudding: Omit spice topping. Reduce brown sugar to 1/2 cup. Substitute 1/2 cup rum for brandy. Omit raisins; add 2 small bananas, chopped, and 3/4 cup Toasted Coconut, page 145. Before baking, sprinkle top of pudding with 1/3 cup untoasted shredded coconut. Serve with Tipsy Crème Anglaise, page 149, if desired.

Chocolate Bread Pudding: Omit spice topping. Substitute 1/2 cup commercial chocolate syrup for brandy. Beat eggs with 4 ounces cooled, melted semisweet chocolate before adding remaining ingredients. Omit raisins and orange zest, if desired. Serve with cream.

 TIP *To make lightened whipped cream to serve with desserts, beat 1 egg white until stiff but not dry and fold into 2 cups whipped cream.*

New Orleans Rum Pudding

Created from the memory of a heady concoction Ron and I enjoyed in New Orleans.

1 (1/4-oz.) envelope unflavored gelatin
  (scant 1 tablespoon)
1/3 cup whipping cream
6 eggs, separated, room temperature
3/4 cup packed brown sugar
3/4 cup light rum
1/2 teaspoon ground nutmeg
1/2 cup toasted finely chopped pecans

1/2 cup pecan- or shortbread-cookie crumbs
2 tablespoons brown sugar
1/4 cup granulated sugar
1/2 cup whipping cream
2 tablespoons toasted finely chopped pecans
6 to 8 pecan halves
Plain Whipped cream, page 156, if desired

Set aside a 1-1/2-quart soufflé or casserole dish. A clear glass dish shows off nut-crumb layers better. In top of a double boiler, stir gelatin into 1/3 cup cream; let stand 5 minutes to soften. Add egg yolks and 3/4 cup brown sugar; beat until light. Gradually stir in rum. Place top of double boiler over simmering water. Cook, stirring constantly, over barely simmering water 5 minutes or until gelatin has dissolved and mixture is very thick. Strain through a fine sieve into a large bowl. Stir in nutmeg; cool to room temperature, stirring occasionally. Do not allow mixture to set. In a small bowl, combine 1/2 cup pecans, cookie crumbs and 2 tablespoons brown sugar; set aside. In a large mixer bowl, beat egg whites to soft-peak stage. Beating constantly, gradually add granulated sugar, 2 tablespoons at a time. Continue beating until whites are glossy and firm; set aside. In a small mixer bowl, beat 1/2 cup whipping cream; fold into gelatin mixture. Gently fold in egg-white mixture until thoroughly blended. Spoon 1/3 of pudding into soufflé or casserole dish. Sprinkle 1/2 of nut mixture evenly over top. Repeat layers, ending with pudding. Sprinkle 2 tablespoons chopped pecans in a 1-inch band around outer edge of top. Decorate center with pecan halves. Cover and refrigerate at least 3 hours before serving. Prepare Plain Whipped Cream, if desired; refrigerate. Serve pudding with whipped cream, if desired. Makes 6 to 8 servings.

TIP

If a recipe calls for beating both egg whites and whipping cream, and you only have 1 electric-mixer bowl, try this method. Beat egg whites first. Gently turn out onto a large plate. Use same bowl and beaters to immediately beat whipping cream. Immediately fold whites and whipped cream into base mixture as indicated in recipe.

Frozen Brandy Alexander Soufflé

Softly frozen and delightfully heady, this is definitely a grown-up *dessert!*

1 oz. Grated Chocolate, page 126	2/3 cup crème de cacao
1 (1/4-oz.) envelope unflavored gelatin (scant 1 tablespoon)	1/2 cup brandy
1/2 cup half and half	1/4 teaspoon cream of tartar
5 eggs, separated, room temperature	1-1/3 cups whipping cream, whipped
1/2 cup sugar	Black-Satin Sauce, page 154, if desired

Prepare Grated Chocolate; refrigerate. Fold a 25-inch length of foil lengthwise in thirds. Lightly oil 1 side of foil. Tightly wrap foil, oiled-side in, around outside of a 1-1/2-quart soufflé dish. Collar should rise 2 inches above rim of dish. Securely fasten foil with tape or string. If using string, tie about 1/2 inch below rim of dish. Use a paper clip to secure top edge of foil. Press foil so it conforms to shape of dish. In a small bowl, stir gelatin into half and half; let stand 5 minutes to soften. Place bowl in a pan of very hot water; stir until gelatin dissolves. Cool to room temperature. In a small mixer bowl, beat egg yolks and 1/4 cup sugar 1 minute. Beating constantly, gradually add cooled gelatin mixture, crème de cacao and brandy. Refrigerate, stirring frequently, until mixture begins to mound when spooned on top of itself. In a large mixer bowl, beat egg whites and cream of tartar to soft-peak stage. Beating constantly, gradually add remaining 1/4 cup sugar, 2 tablespoons at a time. Continue beating until whites are glossy and firm; set aside. Fold whipped cream into chilled gelatin mixture. Fold egg-white mixture into cream mixture, 1/3 at a time. Turn into prepared soufflé dish; lightly sprinkle with Grated Chocolate. Cover and freeze overnight. Dessert may be tightly covered and frozen up to 1 month. Prepare Black-Satin Sauce, if desired. Before serving, remove foil collar from soufflé. Serve frozen soufflé with sauce, if desired. Makes 8 servings.

Coconut-Orange Custard

Cream of coconut can be found in the gourmet section of most supermarkets.

1 (8-1/2-oz.) can cream of coconut (about 1 cup)	3 eggs
1 cup sweet-orange marmalade, room temperature	3 egg yolks
	3/4 cup milk
1/4 teaspoon salt	2 tablespoons Toasted Coconut, page 145

Preheat oven to 350F (175C). Lightly grease a 1-1/2-quart baking dish. In a blender, combine cream of coconut, 2/3 cup marmalade and salt; process at medium speed 1 minute. Add eggs, egg yolks and milk. Process only until combined; do not blend until foamy. Turn mixture into prepared dish; place in a large shallow baking pan. Add hot water to come halfway up side of baking dish. Bake 70 minutes or until a knife inserted in center comes out clean. Cool on a rack to room temperature. Place remaining 1/3 cup marmalade in a small bowl. Stir until liquid enough to pour. Spoon marmalade over top of custard; gently spread to cover surface. Sprinkle with Toasted Coconut. Cover and refrigerate at least 3 hours before serving. Makes about 6 servings.

Aloha Soufflé

Bananas, pineapple and coconut harmonize in this airy delight finished with Hot-Buttered-Rum Sauce!

Hot-Buttered-Rum Sauce, page 155
2 tablespoons sugar
2 tablespoons butter
3 tablespoons all-purpose flour
1/4 teaspoon salt
1/2 cup pineapple juice
1/2 cup sugar
6 egg whites, room temperature
5 egg yolks, room temperature
1 cup ripe-banana puree
   (about 2 medium bananas)

1/4 cup light rum, or 1/4 cup milk and
   1/2 teaspoon imitation rum flavoring
1 (8-oz.) can crushed pineapple,
   well-drained
1 cup Toasted Coconut, page 145,
   using shredded coconut
1/4 teaspoon cream of tartar
2 tablespoons untoasted shredded coconut

Prepare Hot-Buttered-Rum Sauce. Preheat oven to 375F (190C). Butter a 1-1/2-quart soufflé dish. Fold a 25-inch length of foil lengthwise in thirds. Lightly butter 1 side of foil. Tightly wrap foil, buttered-side in, around outside of soufflé dish. Collar should rise 2-1/2 inches above rim of dish. Securely fasten foil with tape or string. If using string, tie about 1/2 inch below rim of dish. Use a paper clip to secure top edge of foil. Press foil so it conforms to shape of dish. Sprinkle dish with about 2 tablespoons sugar, rotating so sugar coats dish and foil collar. In a medium saucepan, melt butter over medium heat. Stir in flour and salt; cook 1 minute. Slowly stir in pineapple juice, then 1/4 cup sugar. Cook 1 minute, stirring constantly; remove from heat. Whisk in 1 egg white, then egg yolks, 1 at a time. Mixture should be smooth. Stir in banana puree, rum, or milk and rum flavoring, drained pineapple and Toasted Coconut; set aside. In a large mixer bowl, beat remaining 5 egg whites and cream of tartar to soft-peak stage. Beating constantly, gradually add remaining 1/4 cup sugar, 2 tablespoons at a time. Continue beating until whites are glossy and firm. Gently fold in fruit mixture, 1/3 at a time. Do not handle any more than necessary. Turn into prepared dish; smooth top. Sprinkle with untoasted coconut. Bake 40 to 50 minutes, depending whether you like the center of your soufflé soft and moist or light and dry. Use a long skewer to test for doneness. Reheat Hot-Buttered-Rum Sauce, if necessary. To prevent baked soufflé from collapsing too soon, take it to the table with foil collar still attached. Have a plate ready on which to place foil and string or tape. Remove collar to reveal your soufflé in all its glory before it collapses. Serve with sauce. Makes 6 to 8 servings.

TIP *A gelatin mixture that has set too quickly can be resoftened by placing bowl containing mixture in a larger bowl of warm water and stirring until mixture is desired consistency.*

FRESH-FRUIT DESSERTS

One of my first recollections of fruit comes from the hay-scented loft of our neighbor's barn where my friend Katy and I used to play for hours. I can almost feel the heat of the afternoon sun as it fingered its way into the loft. Dust particles, sparkling like diamond specks, lazily floated all around us. At the back of the barn stood an immense apple tree, its burnished fruit teasing us from the loft's rear door. How much fun it was to reach out, sometimes stretching dangerous lengths, to pluck an apple to share. We pretended the apples were magic and that each bite made us more beautiful!

Though Katy and I didn't know it at the time, apples have long been symbols of beauty, youth and power. In Greek mythology, one of Hercules' labors was to fetch the golden apples from the garden of the Hesperides—beautiful nymphs who guarded the fruit with the aid of a fierce dragon. These precious apples were well-protected because those who possessed them remained forever young and beautiful—in a word, immortal!

You might say that fruit itself is immortal, having been around since the beginning of time. With its great variety and abundance, and easy accessibility, it certainly must be Mother Nature's "convenience food." The most important dictum to remember when working with fresh fruit is that it must be perfectly ripe and blemish free. Plan your fruit desserts according to whatever is in season. Underripe fruit won't deliver the lush flavor you want; bruised or overripe fruit gives an off-taste to your dessert.

One of the easiest ways to prepare a fruit dessert is to begin with fruit puree. *Whips*, the lightest of these desserts, are simple compositions of pureed fruit lightened with stiffly beaten egg whites. The easy and elegant Gingered Pear Whip in Chocolate Cups is a prime example. A delightful English concoction called *a fool* is fruit puree folded into fluffy whipped cream—simplicity at its most delicious! Be "smart" and try Rhu-Berry Fool for a refreshingly tart taste sensation.

Berries, one of nature's sweetest bounties, are all the more special because they're only available fresh during summer. Strawberries—the queen of berries—were once paid great tribute by sixteenth-century author William Butler who wrote: *"Doubtless God could have made a better berry, but doubtless God never did."* Those who agree should be sure and try Spirited Strawberries, featuring large, chocolate-dipped strawberries injected with Grand Marnier!

Raspberries, one of the most delicately flavored of the berry family, may be red, black, purple or yellow in color. Each raspberry is composed of numerous round drupelets—individual parts of a single fruit. Of all the berries, I think raspberries are best adorned with just a kiss of cream. For those who want to gild the lily, try Raspberry-Orange Romanoff. This delightful mélange combines raspberries, oranges, whipped cream and orange sherbet for a refreshingly tangy finish on a warm evening!

A well-chilled bottle of Late Harvest Riesling or French Sauternes is the perfect partner for fruit desserts—whether the elegant Poached Pears enrobed in Crème de Noisette, or a simple fruit and cheese platter. These opulent dessert wines are often referred to as *noble rot* wines because the grapes from which they are made have been attacked by a "desirable" fungus called *botrytis,* which depletes the fruit's moisture and raises its sugar content.

If desserts nostalgic with old-fashioned goodness are your weakness, this chapter's Baked Caramel Apples or Peach-Berry Clafouti are sure to please. Or, if a showstopping sensation is your aim, you can't miss with Cream-Filled Strawberries nestled in Chilled Amaretto Zabaglione. Whatever your pleasure, remember there are hundreds of possibilities when it comes to fresh-fruit desserts.

Hints for Beating Egg Whites

- Bowl and beaters must be spotlessly clean and at room temperature. Even a trace of grease will prevent whites from reaching their full volume.
- Use copper, glass or stainless-steel bowls. Aluminum discolors egg whites and it is difficult to be sure plastic bowls are grease-free.
- Separate eggs while cold. Crack eggs 1 at a time, placing each white in a custard cup before transferring it to a mixing bowl. This prevents accidentally getting any broken yolk into a bowl of whites. A drop of egg yolk, which contains fat, will prevent egg whites from reaching their full volume.
- In order for egg whites to absorb as much air as possible when beaten, they must be at room temperature. To warm cold whites quickly, set bowl of whites in a larger bowl of warm water. Stir occasionally until whites have reached room temperature.
- Use an electric mixer at high speed, or a wire whisk, to beat egg whites to desired stiffness.
- Adding a small amount of acid, such as cream of tartar, lemon juice or vinegar, stabilizes egg whites and allows them to reach their full volume and stiffness. The natural acid on the surface of a copper bowl achieves the same effect.
- It is very important to beat egg whites only until they are stiff, but not dry. Overbeaten egg whites will collapse and begin to reliquefy.
- Egg whites beaten without sugar will not peak as firmly as those beaten with sugar.
- If adding sugar to egg whites to create meringue, first beat whites at high speed until they form soft peaks. Beating constantly, gradually add sugar, 1 to 2 tablespoons at a time. Continue beating until sugar is dissolved and whites are glossy and firm.
- To prevent loss of volume, use egg whites as soon as they are beaten.
- Folding stiffly beaten egg whites into another mixture must be done by hand. Using a large rubber spatula, quickly but gently cut into middle of mixture. Bring bottom of batter up and over remaining mixture. Rotate bowl a quarter turn with each folding motion. Fold gently to retain as much air as possible. Stop folding when no white streaks remain.
- If folding stiffy beaten egg whites into a very thick or heavy mixture, first stir in about a quarter of whites. This will loosen mixture and enable remainder of beaten whites to be folded in with ease.

Mapled Blueberries with Yogurt

The perfect ending for a summer meal—simplicity at its best!

2-1/2 cup fresh blueberries
  (about 1-1/2 pints)
1/4 cup pure maple syrup

2/3 cup vanilla-flavored yogurt
Ground nutmeg

In a medium bowl, toss blueberries with 3 tablespoons maple syrup. Divide evenly between 4 stemmed glasses. Spoon a dollop of yogurt on top of each serving. Drizzle with remaining 1 tablespoon maple syrup; sprinkle lightly with nutmeg. Serve immediately. Makes 4 servings.

Island Baked Alaskas

I created this fruited, slim version of the calorie-laden classic for some friends from Hawaii.

**1-1/2 to 2 cups fresh mixed berries
(blueberries, raspberries, or coarsely
chopped blackberries or strawberries,
about 1 pint)
2 ripe papayas, halved, seeded**

**4 egg whites, room temperature
1/8 teaspoon salt
6 tablespoons sugar
1/2 teaspoon vanilla extract
1/2 cup shredded coconut, if desired**

Position rack in center of oven and preheat to 450F (230C). Select and set aside some attractive berries for garnish. Spoon remaining berries into each papaya half, mounding berries slightly; set aside. In a large mixer bowl, beat egg whites and salt to soft-peak stage. Beating constantly, gradually add sugar, 2 tablespoons at a time. Continue beating until whites are glossy and firm. Beat in vanilla; fold in coconut, if desired. Pipe or spread 1/4 of egg-white mixture over top of each berry-filled papaya, making sure to seal all exposed fruit surfaces. Do not cover base of papaya. Place papayas on a large baking sheet. Bake 3 to 5 minutes or until golden brown. Garnish with reserved berries. Serve immediately. Makes 4 servings.

Ginger-Plum Mousse

Ginger is spicy—chop it finely so your guests won't bite down on a chunk of it.

**1 (1-/4-oz.) envelope unflavored gelatin
(scant 1 tablespoon)
1/4 cup water
1-1/4 cups ripe-purple-plum puree, do not
peel plums (4 to 6 plums)
2 tablespoons lemon juice
1/2 cup sugar
3 tablespoons finely chopped
crystallized ginger**

**1-1/2 cups whipping cream, whipped
1 cup finely chopped purple plums
(2 to 4 plums)
1/2 recipe Plain Whipped Cream,
page 156, if desired
4 to 6 (1/4-inch) plum slices, if desired**

In a small saucepan, stir gelatin into water; let stand 5 minutes to soften. In a medium bowl, combine 1 cup plum puree, lemon juice, sugar and chopped ginger; set aside. Stir gelatin mixture over medium heat just until gelatin dissolves. Stir into plum mixture. Refrigerate, stirring occasionally, until mixture begins to mound when spooned on top of itself. Fold in first amount of whipped cream and chopped plums. Spoon into 4 to 6 stemmed glasses. Refrigerate at least 2 hours. Prepare Plain Whipped Cream, if desired; refrigerate. Immediately before serving, drizzle each portion with some of remaining 1/4 cup plum puree. Garnish with dollops of Plain Whipped Cream and plum slices, if desired. Makes 4 to 6 servings.

Variation
Ginger-Persimmon Mousse: Substitute 1-1/4 cups persimmon puree for plum puree, 1 cup finely chopped persimmon for chopped plums. Garnish with persimmon slices.

How to Make Island Baked Alaskas

1/Pipe or spread 1/4 of egg-white mixture over top of each berry-filled papaya, making sure to seal all exposed fruit surfaces.

2/Place papayas on a large baking sheet. Bake 3 to 5 minutes or until golden brown. Garnish with reserved berries.

Gingered Pear Whip in Chocolate Cups

Ripe pears give the fullest flavor—the amount of sugar needed depends on the natural sweetness of the fruit.

10 Chocolate Cups, page 130
1 (1/4-oz.) envelope unflavored gelatin
  (scant 1 tablespoon)
1/4 cup pear nectar or water
1 lb. ripe pears (2 to 3 medium pears)
  peeled, cored, cut in chunks
1/2 tablespoon lemon juice

1 to 2 tablespoons brown sugar
2 teaspoons finely chopped
  crystallized ginger
Salt
3 egg whites, room temperature
10 candied violets, if desired

Prepare Chocolate Cups; set aside. Chocolate Cups may be prepared several days in advance and refrigerated. In a small saucepan, stir gelatin into pear nectar or water; let stand 5 minutes to soften. Stir over medium heat just until gelatin dissolves; set aside. In a blender, combine pears, lemon juice, brown sugar, ginger and a pinch of salt. Process until pureed, stopping and scraping down sides as necessary. With blender running at low speed, slowly add hot gelatin mixture. Increase speed to high; process 30 seconds. Turn into a medium bowl. Refrigerate, stirring occasionally, until mixture begins to mound when spooned on top of itself. In a small mixer bowl, beat egg whites and a pinch of salt until stiff but not dry. Gently fold, 1/3 at a time, into pear mixture. Spoon into Chocolate Cups, mounding high in center; refrigerate. Immediately before serving, top each cup with a candied violet, if desired. Makes 6 servings.

Chocolate-Dipped Fruits & Nuts

Surprise your friends with these beautiful and delicious temptations—easier to make than they look!

6 to 8 oz. semisweet, milk or
white chocolate, coarsely chopped
1 tablespoon vegetable oil

About 1 lb. fruits or nuts of your choice,
prepared as suggested below

Combine chocolate and oil in top of a double boiler over simmering water. When chocolate is partially melted, remove from heat; stir until smooth. Or, place chocolate, without oil, in a medium glass bowl; microwave at 50% power 3 to 5 minutes. Remove from microwave oven; stir until completely melted. Pour chocolate into a small bowl, deep enough for dipping. Cool to room temperature. Line a large baking sheet with waxed paper. Fruit to be dipped must be *absolutely dry.* Using a wooden pick to spear fruit or 2 forks to cradle nuts, dip into chocolate. Drain excess chocolate on rim of bowl. Place on prepared baking sheet. Refrigerate until firm. If chocolate begins to harden before you have finished dipping, gently reheat using 1 of the melting methods given above. Any leftover melted chocolate may be poured onto a piece of waxed paper and refrigerated until set. Store at room temperature; melt and reuse at a later date. Makes 4 to 6 servings.

Chocolated-Dipped Whole Strawberries: Photo on page 129.
Brush berries with a pastry brush to remove soil; do not wash. Holding strawberries by stems, dip into chocolate, covering 2/3 of each berry. If a strawberry has no stem, hold by leaves or spear through center top with a wooden pick.

Chocolate-Dipped Halved Strawberries: Cut strawberries in 1/2 vertically, cutting through leaves. Lay strawberries, cut-side down, on 2 layers of paper towels; let stand 5 minutes. Dip into chocolate to coat cut side completely; only coat 1/2 of outside of strawberry.

Chocolate-Dipped Cherries: In a medium bowl, combine 24 stemmed maraschino cherries with 1/4 cup kirsch. Freeze 1 hour, stirring occasionally. Working with 6 cherries at a time, thoroughly blot cherries dry on paper towels. Holding cherries by stems, dip into chocolate to coat completely.

Chocolate-Dipped Banana Slices: Cut peeled bananas into 1/2-inch slices immediately before dipping. Spear with a wooden pick; dip into chocolate to coat completely.

Chocolate-Dipped Seedless Grapes: Divide grapes into clusters of 3, stems attached. Holding by stems, dip into chocolate, covering 1/2 of each grape.

Chocolate-Dipped Fresh Coconut: Cut coconut into 1-inch chunks. Dip partially or completely into chocolate.

Chocolate-Dipped Lemon or Orange Slices: Using a citrus stripper, score fruit lengthwise at 1/2-inch intervals. Cut off and discard ends. Cut fruit into 1/8-inch-thick slices; cut each slice in 1/2. Place slices on 2 layers of paper towels; blotting surface with more paper towels. Reblot with new towels, if necessary, to remove as much moisture as possible. Using the back of a teaspoon, spread melted chocolate over 1 side of fruit, leaving peel exposed. Do not allow any moisture from fruit to get into bowl of chocolate. Refrigerate until set. Turn slices over; remove any seeds. Spread second side with chocolate; place on waxed paper.

Chocolate-Dipped Dried Fruits: Dip fruit halfway into melted chocolate, then into finely chopped nuts, if desired.

Chocolate-Dipped Apples: Core unpeeled apple; cut into eighths immediately before dipping. Spear slices with a wooden pick; dip exposed fruit into chocolate, leaving most of skin uncoated.

Chocolate-Covered Raspberries & Blueberries: Thickly spread about 1 teaspoon melted chocolate over bottom and up sides of miniature paper or foil bon bon cups. Refrigerate until set. Place 1 or 2 berries in center of each chocolate-coated cup. Spoon melted chocolate over fruit to cover completely; refrigerate until set. Gently peel off paper cup before serving.

Chocolate-Dipped Nuts: Use perfect walnut or pecan halves or whole almonds, macadamias or cashews. Dip into chocolate, covering 1/2 of each nut.

Cream-Filled Strawberries with Chilled Amaretto Zabaglione, page 100.

Cream-Filled Strawberries with Chilled Amaretto Zabaglione

Photo on page 99.

Understated elegance is the keynote of these luxurious cream-filled berries nestled in a pool of liqueur-scented sauce.

18 extra-large strawberries
1 (8-oz.) pkg. cream cheese, softened
1/4 cup amaretto liqueur
1/3 cup powdered sugar
1 pint whipping cream (2 cups), whipped
Amaretto Zabaglione, page 84

1/3 cup amaretti crumbs or other crisp almond-macaroon-cookie crumbs, if desired
1/2 cup Raspberry Jewel Sauce, page 150, if desired

Rinse strawberries; thoroughly blot dry with paper towels. Hull berries, being careful not to cut too deeply into fruit. From the pointed end, split each berry into quarters or sixths to within 1/4 inch of base. Place on a waxed-paper-lined baking sheet; refrigerate. In a large mixer bowl, beat cream cheese until perfectly smooth. Gradually add amaretto liqueur and powdered sugar; beat until smooth and creamy. Fold in whipped cream. Place in a pastry bag fitted with a large (1/2-inch) star tip. Generously pipe cream-cheese mixture into each strawberry; berries will open like flowers as mixture is piped into them. Refrigerate. No more than 3 to 4 hours before serving, prepare Amaretto Zabaglione. Place pan or bowl of hot zabaglione in a larger bowl of iced water. Beat 3 to 5 minutes or until mixture is cool; refrigerate. Stir before serving to incorporate any separation. To serve, ladle even amounts of zabaglione onto 6 dessert plates. Arrange 3 cream-filled strawberries in sauce on each plate. If desired, sprinkle tops of berries with cookie crumbs and add some Raspberry Jewel Sauce to decorate zabaglione. Makes 6 servings.

Spirited Strawberries

Every bite of these liqueur-infused, chococolate-covered berries is bursting with irresistible flavor!

15 to 20 large strawberries with stems
6 to 8 oz. semisweet or white chocolate, melted, cooled
1/4 to 1/3 cup Grand Marnier or other orange-flavored liqueur

Coventry Cream, page 148;
Tipsy Crème Anglaise, page 149, flavored with Grand Marnier; or Spirited Whipped Cream, page 156, flavored with Grand Marnier

Line a baking sheet with waxed paper. Dip strawberries in melted chocolate as directed on page 98, covering entire berry up to leaves with chocolate. Place berries on lined baking sheet; refrigerate until chocolate is set. Check bottom of each dipped berry; if there is a thin place or hole in chocolate, patch it with melted chocolate using a teaspoon. Weak spots in chocolate shell will allow liqueur to leak through. Refrigerate again until set. Fill a small basting needle with liqueur; slowly inject liqueur through top of leaves into berry. Be careful not to force too much liqueur into fruit or berry will expand causing chocolate shell to crack; watch for liqueur overflowing at the stem end. Refrigerate until ready to serve, preferably no more than 6 hours. Prepare Coventry Cream, Tipsy Crème Anglaise or softly whipped Spirited Whipped Cream. Place in a bowl in center of a large serving plate for dipping. Surround with chocolate-covered berries. Makes about 6 servings.

How to Make Cream-Filled Strawberries with Chilled Amaretto Zabaglione

1/From the pointed end, split each strawberry into quarters or sixths to within 1/4 inch of base.

2/Generously pipe cream-cheese mixture into each strawberry; berries will open like flowers as mixture is piped into them.

Rhu-Berry Fool

Fools are deliciously "smart" compositions of pureed fresh fruit and fluffy whipped cream—M-m-m-m!

1-1/2 lbs. rhubarb, cut in 1-inch pieces	1 teaspoon vanilla extract
3/4 cup granulated sugar	1/4 cup powdered sugar
1/4 cup water	2 to 3 tablespoons orange-flavored liqueur,
1 pint strawberries, hulled	if desired
1-1/4 cups whipping cream	6 to 8 whole medium strawberries

In a medium saucepan, combine rhubarb, granulated sugar and water. Cover and cook over medium heat until tender, 15 to 20 minutes. Cool to room temperature. Drain off excess liquid. Turn rhubarb into a blender; process until smooth. Add 1 pint strawberries; process until smooth. Strain fruit through a sieve into a medium bowl. Refrigerate 2 to 3 hours or until very cold. In a large bowl, beat cream and vanilla to soft-peak stage. Add powdered sugar; beat until stiff. If desired, gradually add liqueur, beating constantly so cream mixture remains stiff. Fold fruit puree, 1/3 at a time, into cream mixture. Spoon into 6 to 8 stemmed glasses. Top each serving with a whole strawberry. Refrigerate until ready to serve. Makes 6 to 8 servings.

Poached Pears with Crème de Noisette

Noisette *is French for hazelnut. This elegant warm dessert can be made ahead and assembled quickly just before serving.*

4 cups dry vermouth
1 large cinnamon stick, broken lengthwise then crosswise in 4 pieces

Crème de Noisette:
6 eggs, beaten
1/2 cup sugar
1/4 teaspoon salt
1 cup milk

Strips of zest from 1 medium lemon
1 cup sugar
6 firm ripe pears

1/2 cup reserved vermouth poaching syrup
3/4 cup toasted finely ground hazelnuts
2 to 3 tablespoons toasted chopped hazelnuts

In a medium saucepan, combine vermouth, cinnamon, lemon zest and sugar. Bring to a boil, stirring to dissolve sugar. Working with 3 pears at a time, core pears from the top, cutting to within 1/2 inch of bottom. Some seeds will remain in base of pear. If necessary, cut off a thin slice from bottom of pears with a knife so they will sit upright for serving. Peel pears just before poaching. Reduce heat so liquid is simmering. Place 3 peeled and cored pears on their sides in poaching liquid; cover. Simmer, turning pears halfway through cooking time, only until pears are tender when pierced with a fork, about 10 minutes. Remove cooked pears from liquid. Stand upright in a large deep casserole with a cover. Repeat poaching with remaining 3 pears. Reserve poaching liquid. Pears may be covered and left at room temperature up to 6 hours. Or, refrigerate pears; let stand at room temperature 1 hour before serving. Bring reserved poaching mixture to a boil. Cook over high heat until thick, syrupy and reduced to 1/2 cup. Strain through a fine sieve; use to prepare Crème de Noisette.
To complete dessert, spoon 2 to 3 tablespoons warm Crème de Noisette onto each of 6 dessert plates. Set a room-temperature pear upright in center of sauce. Fill pear cavities with more sauce, allowing a little to drizzle down sides. Sprinkle each pear with about 1 teaspoon chopped hazelnuts. Pour any additional Crème de Noisette into a small pitcher to pass with dessert. Makes 6 servings.
Crème de Noisette:
In top of a double boiler, combine eggs, sugar, salt, milk and 1/2 cup reduced poaching liquid. Cook over simmering water, stirring constantly, until very thick. Strain into a bowl; stir in ground hazelnuts.

Fruit-Cream Chemise   *Photo on page 151.*

A rich fruity topping for cobblers, cakes, cold soufflés or fresh fruit!

1 egg yolk
2 tablespoons powdered sugar
1/2 cup pureed fresh or thawed, frozen, loosepack fruit, strained, if desired

1 tablespoon liqueur of choice, if desired
1/2 cup whipping cream

In a medium bowl, beat egg yolk and powdered sugar until light and creamy. Stir in fruit puree and liqueur, if desired; set aside. In a small mixer bowl, beat cream until soft peaks form. Fold into fruit mixture. Cover and refrigerate up to 1 week. Let stand at room temperature 15 minutes and stir before serving. Makes about 2 cups.

Note: If using peaches or nectarines for fruit, add 2 teaspoons lemon juice to puree.

Pineapple with Avocado Cream

This beautiful pale-green dessert is a refreshing ending for any spicy meal.

1 medium, ripe avocado, peeled,
  pitted, quartered
1 tablespoon lemon juice
1/4 cup dairy sour cream
2 teaspoons finely chopped
  crystallized ginger
1/2 teaspoon ground ginger

1/3 cup sugar
1/8 teaspoon salt
1-1/2 cups whipping cream, whipped
3 cups diced fresh pineapple, thoroughly
  drained (1 medium pineapple)
Freshly grated or ground nutmeg

In a blender or food processor fitted with a metal blade, combine avocado, lemon juice, sour cream, crystallized ginger, ground ginger, sugar and salt. Process until smooth; pour into a medium bowl. Fold in whipped cream; cover and refrigerate up to 8 hours. Immediately before serving, fold in pineapple. Spoon into 6 stemmed glasses or dessert dishes. Sprinkle lightly with nutmeg. Makes 6 servings.

Blueberry-Mango Crisp

Use only firm ripe mangos to lend a touch of tropical magic to this old-fashioned favorite.

1 cup all-purpose flour
1 cup rolled oats, regular or quick-cooking
1/2 cup packed brown sugar
1/2 cup granulated sugar
1 teaspoon baking powder
1/2 teaspoon ground cinnamon
1/2 teaspoon ground nutmeg
1/8 teaspoon salt
1/2 cup butter, melted

2 cups chopped peeled mangos
  (about 2 medium mangos)
2 cups fresh or drained, thawed,
  frozen blueberries (about 1 pint)
Freshly grated zest from 1/2 medium lemon
1/3 cup chopped almonds
Fruit-Cream Chemise, opposite,
  using mango puree, or Plain
  Whipped Cream, page 156, if desired

Preheat oven to 350F (175C). Grease an 8-inch-square baking dish. In a medium bowl, combine flour, oats, sugars, baking powder, cinnamon, nutmeg and salt. Add butter; stir with a fork until mixture is crumbly. To make crust, firmly press 1/2 of mixture over bottom of prepared baking dish. Layer mangos evenly over crust; dot with blueberries and lemon zest. Stir almonds into remaining flour mixture. Sprinkle evenly over fruit. Bake 55 to 65 minutes or until deep golden brown. Prepare Fruit-Cream Chemise or Plain Whipped Cream, if desired. Serve dessert warm with Fruit-Cream Chemise or whipped cream, if desired. Makes 6 servings.

Tropical-Fruit Strudelettes

Individual strudels that don't require a fork—perfect for picnics or buffets!

2 cups finely chopped ripe papaya or
  mango (about 2 medium papaya or mangos)
1/4 cup sugar
1/2 cup shredded or flaked coconut
1 tablespoon minced crystallized ginger
1/4 teaspoon ground nutmeg

1/2 cup toasted ground macadamia nuts or
  almonds
1 tablespoon all-purpose flour
About 12 sheets filo dough
About 3/4 cup butter, melted

Preheat oven to 375F (190C). In a medium bowl, combine papaya or mango, sugar, coconut, ginger, nutmeg, nuts and flour; set aside. Cover filo sheets with plastic wrap and a slightly damp towel. On a large work surface, stack 2 filo sheets; generously brush with melted butter. Using a sharp knife, cut lengthwise into 4 (3-inch-wide) strips. Place a heaping teaspoon of fruit mixture in corner of each strip. Fold corner over filling, making a triangle. Continue folding strip as in a flag fold, maintaining triangle shape. Place, seam-side down and 1 inch apart, on an ungreased baking sheet; brush top with some of the melted butter. Repeat with remaining filo sheets and filling. May be covered and refrigerated at this point, if desired. Bake 20 to 25 minutes or until golden brown. Serve warm or at room temperature. Makes about 24 strudelettes.

Baked Caramel Apples

A rich caramel sauce bakes on the inside and glazes the outside of these delicious treats.

Hot Caramel Sauce, page 155
6 large, firm, tart apples, cored
About 3/4 cup apple juice or apple cider

Almond Cream, page 152, or
  Plain Whipped Cream, page 156

Prepare Hot Caramel Sauce; set aside. Preheat oven to 350F (175C). Grease a shallow baking pan large enough for apples. Core apples from the top, cutting to within 1/2 inch of bottom. Using a vegetable peeler or paring knife, remove a 1/2-inch strip of peel around top of each apple. Arrange apples upright in prepared pan. Add just enough apple juice or cider to cover bottom of pan. Using about 1 cup caramel sauce, fill cavity of each apple with sauce. Spread some around peeled rim to prevent discoloration. Bake, uncovered, 30 to 40 minutes or until apples are tender when pierced with a fork. Prepare Almond Cream or Plain Whipped Cream, refrigerate. Place apples on a serving platter or individual dessert plates. Spoon additional caramel sauce into center and over top of each apple, allowing excess to drizzle down sides. Serve with Almond Cream or Plain Whipped Cream. Makes 6 servings.

How to Make Tropical-Fruit Strudelettes

1/Place a heaping teaspoon of fruit mixture in corner of each filo strip. Fold corner over filling, making a triangle.

2/Continue folding filo strip as in a flag fold, maintaining triangle shape. Place, seam-side down, on an ungreased baking sheet; brush top with melted butter.

Raspberry-Orange Romanoff

Fresh raspberries and oranges caressed in a mélange of orange sherbet and whipped cream!

1/2 pint whipping cream (1 cup)
4 large oranges, halved crosswise
2 cups fresh raspberries (1 pint)
1/4 cup raspberry-flavored liqueur

2 pints orange sherbet, slightly softened
Biscotti or Mama's Sugar Snaps,
** page 64**

Up to 6 hours before serving, beat cream until stiff. Cover and refrigerate. Using a grapefruit spoon or knife, remove orange segments, making sure no pith is attached. Coarsely chop orange segments. Set aside 8 attractive raspberries for garnish. In a medium bowl, combine oranges and any juice, remaining raspberries and liqueur. Cover and refrigerate up to 6 hours. When ready to serve, strain liqueur from fruit. Gradually whisk or beat liqueur into whipped cream so cream remains stiff; set aside. Turn sherbet into a large bowl. Add fruit; stir until mixture is combined. Sherbet mixture should be soft but still hold its shape. Fold in whipped-cream mixture. Immediately spoon into 8 stemmed glasses; top each serving with a whole raspberry. Serve with Biscotti or Mama's Sugar Snaps, if desired. Makes 8 servings.

Honeyed Rainbow Fruit

Honey and lime juice combine in a simple yet elegant glaze for this multi-colored fruit dessert.

1/3 cup lime juice
1/2 cup honey
3/4 teaspoon vanilla extract
1-1/2 cups chopped, seeded, peeled mango or papaya (about 2 small mangos or papaya)
1-1/2 cups peeled orange segments, membrane removed (about 2 medium oranges)

1-1/2 cups sliced, peeled kiwifruit (about 4 kiwifruit)
6 star fruit, if desired
1-1/2 cups fresh raspberries (3/4 pint)
6 mint sprigs, if desired
About 1-1/2 cups extra-dry champagne, if desired

In a small bowl, stir together lime juice, honey and vanilla until blended; set aside. In a large bowl, combine fruit and berries. Pour honey-lime glaze over fruit; toss lightly to coat fruit. Cover and refrigerate up to 4 hours before serving. Spoon into 6 stemmed goblets or small glass dessert bowls. Garnish each serving with a mint sprig, if desired. If desired, pour about 1/4 cup champagne over each portion immediately before serving. Makes 6 servings.

Peach-Berry Clafouti

A simple country dessert that originated in France—traditionally made only with dark sweet cherries. Fresh is best but drained, thawed, loosepack fruit may also be used with delicious results.

2 cups chopped peeled peaches (about 4 medium peaches)
2 cups blueberries or raspberries or 1 cup each (1 pint)
1 cup sliced almonds
3/4 cup all-purpose flour
2/3 cup sugar
1/2 teaspoon baking powder

1/2 teaspoon ground cinnamon
1/8 teaspoon salt
3 eggs, lightly beaten
3/4 cup milk
2 tablespoons melted butter
2 teaspoons vanilla extract
1 tablespoon sugar
Coventry Cream, page 148

Preheat oven to 350F (175C). Butter a 2-quart oval au gratin dish or other shallow baking dish. Evenly distribute fruit over bottom of dish; set aside. Coarsely grind 1/2 cup almonds. In a medium bowl, combine ground almonds, flour, 2/3 cup sugar, baking powder, cinnamon and salt. Add eggs, milk, butter and vanilla; stir until blended. Pour batter over fruit in dish; make sure all fruit is covered with batter. Sprinkle with remaining 1/2 cup almonds, then 1 tablespoon sugar. Bake 50 minutes to 1 hour or until top is browned and puffy. Prepare Coventry Cream. Serve pudding warm with Coventry Cream. Makes 6 to 8 servings.

Variations
Streusel-Topped Clafouti: In a small bowl, combine 1/2 cup sugar, 1/3 cup all-purpose flour and 1/2 teaspoon ground cinnamon. Using a pastry blender or 2 knives, cut in 1/4 cup firm cold butter until mixture resembles coarse crumbs. Sprinkle over top of clafouti batter before baking.
Cherry-Peach Clafouti: Substitute 2 cups pitted, dark, sweet cherries for berries; add 1/4 teaspoon almond extract to batter.
Peach-Plum Clafouti: Substitute 2 cups chopped unpeeled plums for berries. Substitute 3/4 cup peach nectar for milk, if desired.

FROZEN & REFRIGERATED DESSERTS

It's logical to assume that ice cream and other frozen desserts weren't created until the advent of mechanical refrigeration. Not true! Like so many other culinary delights, the Chinese are credited with formulating the first iced sweets. But it wasn't until 1295, when Marco Polo returned from China with a sherbet recipe, that frozen milk- and cream-based desserts were introduced to Europe.

For centuries, because they were so expensive to store, iced desserts were the privilege of the affluent and the influential. But by the early 1800s ice creams and sherbets were available to everyone—from kings and presidents to factory workers. Americans have loved ice cream from the start. George Washington was rumored to have spent $200 on it during a single summer. And Thomas Jefferson is credited with introducing America to "French-style" ice cream, made with egg custard.

Homemade ice cream is fun to make and delicious. Making your own eliminates the problems of objectionable stabilizers and emulsifiers often found in commercial products. The number of homemade ice-cream flavors is unlimited! I've created nine variations for the creamy-rich Royal Vanilla Ice Cream. It's impossible to choose a favorite, but I love the Vanilla-Swiss Almond, featuring chunks of chocolate-covered almonds. My husband Ron favors the dark magic of the kirsch-scented, cherry-studded Black Forest, a variation of Rich Fudge Ice Cream.

Remember that coldness mutes taste, so ice-cream mixtures should be more strongly flavored than other desserts. Chilling the mixture in the canister for several hours will speed processing. Ice cream, sherbet and sorbet must be continually stirred during the freezing process. This aerates the mixture, prevents the formation of large ice crystals and creates a silky-smooth texture. Homemade ice cream is often consumed immediately after it's frozen, when very soft. Or, you may prefer to "ripen" it for two to three hours in the freezer, allowing the texture to firm and the flavors to blend.

Frozen desserts aren't strictly limited to ice cream. Consider the superb Frozen Praline Mousse—a praline-crowned dessert spectacular, drizzled with Hot Caramel Sauce. Or, the rum-laced Macaroon Madness, a frozen temptation with only five main ingredients! And, for those who enjoy fruitful finales, there's Instant Berry Sorbet, prepared in a blender, and tangy Raspberry-Yogurt Freeze, which has no added sugar.

The delightful mousse, made fluffy by the addition of stiffly beaten egg whites or whipped cream, also plays an important role in this chapter. Literally translated, the French word *mousse* means *froth*. A mousse is sometimes fortified with the aid of unflavored gelatin which, unless properly used, can produce disastrous results. Too much, and the dessert will be rubbery and tough; too little and it won't hold its shape. Generally, one envelope of unflavored gelatin will gel two cups of liquid. A mandatory step is always to soak gelatin in cold water, or other liquid, three to five minutes *before* stirring in a hot liquid. This method softens and swells the gelatin granules so they will readily dissolve when heated. Combining a hot liquid with dry gelatin causes it to form lumps and prevents it from dissolving properly. This reduces gelatin's thickening capacity and produces a grainy dessert.

Mousse can be served in individual goblets or a large dessert dish. The beauty of its fluffy texture is best displayed in clear or cut-glass containers. White-Chocolate Mousse, for example, is layered with sparkling ribbons of Raspberry Jewel Sauce. The dramatic layering would, of course, lose its effect in a plain ceramic bowl.

One of the attractions of serving chilled desserts is that their very nature demands advance preparation, leaving the host or hostess plenty of time for last-minute details. So, when it comes to keeping your "cool" in the kitchen, think of serving easy, delicious, make-ahead frozen and refrigerated desserts. You're bound to get a warm response for your efforts!

Instant Berry Sorbet

Frozen summer berries create a refreshingly delicious sorbet in less than five minutes!

**3-1/2 cups fresh strawberries,
    blueberries, blackberries or
    pitted cherries (about 1-3/4 pints)**
**1 cup fruit juice or fruit nectar,
    same flavor as fruit used, chilled**

1/4 to 1/3 cup sugar
1/2 teaspoon vanilla extract
**Additional 1/2 to 3/4 cup fresh berries
    or cherries, if desired**

Line a large baking sheet with waxed paper. Spread 3-1/2 cups fruit in an even layer on waxed paper. Freeze 1 hour or until frozen solid. A few minutes before serving, remove frozen fruit from freezer. Place fruit juice or fruit nectar, sugar and vanilla in a blender. Process 5 seconds. With speed set on high, drop frozen fruit, a few pieces at a time, through hole in top of blender lid. Stop motor and scrape down sides of blender jar as necessary. Continue until all fruit has been added and sorbet is smooth. A food processor may also be used and gives a softer sorbet. Spoon into 4 to 6 stemmed glasses. Top with additional fresh fruit, if desired. Serve immediately. Makes 4 to 6 servings.

Variations
Instant Berry Ice Cream: Substitute 1 cup whipping cream for 1 cup fruit juice. For **Enriched Instant Berry Ice Cream,** increase berries to 4 cups; add 2 egg yolks to cream mixture. For **Spirited Instant Berry Ice Cream,** substitute 1/4 cup kirsch, orange liqueur or amaretto liqueur for 1/4 cup of cream.
Frozen Berry Yogurt: Substitute 8 ounces (1 cup) plain yogurt for 1 cup fruit juice or nectar. Less fruit may be needed depending on thickness of yogurt.

Note: Amount of sugar added depends on the natural sweetness of the fruit you use. Raspberries are not suggested for this recipe because their large seeds create an unpleasant texture.

Making Ice Cream in the Freezer

If you do not have an ice-cream maker, ice cream and sherbet can be frozen successfully in metal pans in the freezer. Set the freezer setting to the lowest temperature. Freeze prepared mixture until slushy. Scrape it away from the sides of the pan. Stir well to break up ice crystals. Freeze again until firm. Turn into a large bowl. Beat with an electric mixer 1 minute to incorporate air to lighten the mixture. Or, beat in a food processor fitted with a metal blade. Refreeze until firm. Serve as soon as possible. Ice crystals continue to form quickly, causing the texture of the frozen dessert to deteriorate.

Royal Vanilla Ice Cream

Use the finest pure vanilla extract you can buy for this ultra-rich queen of frozen desserts!

1 pint half and half (2 cups)	**1/4 teaspoon salt**
6 egg yolks, room temperature	**1 pint whipping cream (2 cups), chilled**
3/4 cup sugar	**1 tablespoon vanilla extract**

In a small saucepan, scald half and half by heating over medium heat until bubbles form around edge of pan. In a large mixer bowl, beat egg yolks, sugar and salt until thick and pale. Beating constantly, gradually add hot half and half; beat 1 minute. Stir in whipping cream and vanilla. Freeze in an ice-cream maker according to manufacturer's directions or follow freezer directions, page 109. Remove dasher and serve ice cream soft. Or, remove dasher and replace lid. Cover lid with foil. Place ice cream in freezer to ripen 2 to 4 hours or until firm. Makes about 2 quarts.

Variations

Vanilla-Swiss-Almond Ice Cream: Melt 2 ounces semisweet chocolate with 2 tablespoons butter. Add 1 cup coarsely chopped almonds; stir to coat almonds completely with chocolate. Turn out onto a waxed-paper-lined baking sheet. Using 2 forks, separate almonds into single pieces. Refrigerate or freeze until chocolate is set. Break up chocolate-covered almonds. Stir into ice cream after freezing but before ripening.

Cappuccino Ice Cream: Add 1/4 cup instant coffee powder or granules, 1 tablespoon unsweetened cocoa and 1/4 teaspoon ground cinnamon to half and half. Stir until smooth before scalding. Increase sugar to 1 cup; reduce vanilla to 1 teaspoon.

Cookies'n Ice Cream: Stir 3 cups coarsely crushed cream-filled chocolate cookies into ice cream after freezing but before ripening.

Orange-Dream Ice Cream: Add finely grated zest of 2 medium oranges to half and half before scalding. Omit vanilla; add 2-1/2 tablespoons orange-flower water and 1/3 cup thawed frozen orange-juice concentrate.

Peppermint-Candy Ice Cream: Add 3/4 cup crushed peppermint-stick candy to half and half before scalding. Reduce sugar to 1/3 cup; omit vanilla. Stir 1/2 cup crushed peppermint-stick candy into ice cream after freezing but before ripening.

Cinnamon Ice Cream: Add 1 (1-ounce) can cinnamon sticks, broken in small pieces, to half and half; simmer 10 minutes. Strain through a fine sieve before adding to egg yolks. Reduce vanilla to 1 teaspoon.

Fresh-Fruit Ice Cream: Twenty-four hours before making ice cream, combine 2 cups chopped fresh fruit with 1/2 cup of sugar in recipe. If using peaches, apricots or bananas, add 1 tablespoon lemon juice to prevent discoloration. Cover and refrigerate. Puree 1/2 of fruit with all of the juice; add with whipping cream. Reduce vanilla to 1 teaspoon. Stir remaining fruit into ice cream after freezing but before ripening.

Hazelnut Ice Cream: Stir 3/4 cup toasted ground hazelnuts into half and half; simmer 10 minutes. Strain through a fine sieve. Substitute 3/4 cup packed brown sugar for granulated sugar; reduce vanilla to 1 teaspoon. Stir additional 1 cup toasted chopped hazelnuts into ice cream after freezing but before ripening.

Fudge-Ripple Ice Cream: Prepare Fudge Velvet Sauce, page 150, or use commercial fudge sauce. You will need 1/2 cup sauce; serve remaining sauce with ice cream. After freezing ice cream, remove dasher. Insert a long bread knife randomly in ice cream. Pull knife to side to create a hole; pour 1/3 of fudge sauce into hole. Repeat with 2 more holes and remaining fudge sauce. Using the broad edge of knife, cut through ice cream in a wide zigzag pattern to create a marbled effect. Do not marble too much or colors will blend and not contrast. Cover canister and place in freezer to ripen.

Rich Fudge Ice Cream

For a super ice-cream experience, try the Fudge-Chocolate-Chunk or Black Forest variations!

3-1/2 cups whipping cream
8 oz. semisweet chocolate, coarsely chopped
2 eggs, room temperature
4 egg yolks, room temperature

1/2 cup sugar
1/4 teaspoon salt
2 teaspoons vanilla extract

In a small saucepan, scald 1-1/2 cups cream by heating over medium heat until bubbles form around edge of pan. Remove from heat; add chocolate. Stir or whisk until chocolate is melted and mixture is smooth; set aside. In a large mixer bowl, beat eggs, egg yolks, sugar and salt until thick and pale. With mixer running at low speed, slowly add hot chocolate mixture. Beat until blended. Stir in vanilla and remaining 2 cups cream. Freeze in an ice-cream maker according to manufacturer's directions or follow freezer directions, page 109. Remove dasher and serve ice cream soft. Or, remove dasher and replace lid. Cover lid with foil. Place ice cream in freezer to ripen 2 to 4 hours or until firm. Makes about 2 quarts.

Variations

Fudge-Chocolate-Chunk Ice Cream: Chop 3 ounces semisweet or white chocolate, or 1-1/2 ounces of each, into 3/8-inch chunks. Stir into ice cream after freezing but before ripening.

Mocha-Chocolate-Chunk Ice Cream: Add 1/4 cup instant coffee powder or granules to cream before scalding. Reduce chocolate to 6 ounces. Chop another 3 ounces semisweet chocolate in 3/8-inch chunks. Stir into ice cream after freezing but before ripening.

Black Forest Ice Cream: Add only 6 ounces semisweet chocolate to scalded cream. Add 1/4 cup kirsch or brandy with second addition of cream. Melt remaining 2 ounces chocolate with 1 tablespoon butter. Drip hot chocolate mixture into ice-cream mixture. Let stand 1 minute; stir. Freeze as directed above. Stir 1 (16-ounce) can pitted, dark, sweet cherries, well-drained and coarsely chopped, into ice cream before ripening.

White-Chocolate-Fudge-Flake Ice Cream: Substitute 8 ounces white chocolate for 8 ounces semisweet chocolate, and 1/2 cup white crème de cocoa for 1/2 cup sugar. Melt 2 ounces semisweet chocolate with 1 tablespoon butter. Drip hot chocolate mixture into ice-cream mixture. Let stand 1 minute; stir. Freeze as directed above.

Rocky-Road Ice Cream: Add 1 cup miniature marshmallows with second addition of cream. After freezing, but before ripening, stir in additional 2 ounces finely chopped semisweet chocolate and 3/4 cup toasted chopped almonds.

Chocolate-Marmalade Ice Cream: Add 1 cup sweet-orange marmalade to cream before scalding. Reduce chocolate to 6 ounces; omit sugar. Add 1/3 cup orange-flavored liqueur with second addition of cream.

Peanut-Butter-Fudge Ice Cream: Add 2/3 cup chunky peanut butter to hot chocolate mixture. Stir until combined before adding to egg mixture.

 TIP *Calorie-counters may wish to substitute equal amounts of whole milk for half and half, or half and half for cream.*

Peach-Melba Bavarian

Have the fruit purees and whipped cream ready in the refrigerator before starting this recipe.

1 (1/4-oz.) envelope plus 1 teaspooon
   unflavored gelatin
   (about 3-1/2 teaspoons)
1/4 cup water
5 egg yolks
1 cup half and half
3/4 cup sugar
1-1/2 cups whipping cream, whipped

1/2 cup strained raspberry puree
   (about 1/2 pint fresh raspberries)
1-1/4 cups peach puree
   (2 to 3 medium peaches)
1/2 recipe Plain Whipped Cream, page 156,
   if desired
Whole raspberries and peach slices,
   if desired

In a small bowl, stir gelatin into water; let stand 5 minutes to soften. In a medium saucepan, whisk egg yolks and half and half together; stir in sugar. Cook over medium-low heat, stirring constantly, until mixture thickly coats the back of a metal spoon. Remove from heat. Add gelatin mixture; stir 1 minute or until dissolved. Strain through a fine sieve into a large bowl. Set in another large bowl filled with iced water. Stir constantly with a rubber spatula just until mixture is cool. Do not allow mixture to become so cold that it sets. Immediately remove from iced water. Working quickly, gently fold in first amount of whipped cream, 1/3 at a time. Remove 1-1/2 cups mixture to a medium bowl. Fold in raspberry puree; set aside. Fold peach puree into remaining cream mixture; set aside. Rinse a 6-cup decorative mold with cold water. Drain thoroughly, but do not dry. Turn peach mixture into dampened mold. Spoon raspberry mixture into center of peach mixture to within 1-1/2 to 2 inches of edge. Using the back of a spoon, lightly press raspberry mixture down into peach mixture so surface is level. Refrigerate 3 to 4 hours or until set. Prepare Plain Whipped Cream, if desired; refrigerate. Dip mold into hot water 5 to 10 seconds. Invert and unmold onto a serving plate. If bavarian will not release from mold, insert a thin knife between mold and bavarian mixture to break the suction. Redip in hot water a few seconds, if necessary. Garnish with rosettes of Plain Whipped Cream, raspberries and peach slices, if desired. Serve immediately or refrigerate until serving time. Makes 8 to 10 servings.

Razz-Ma-Jazz

Raspberry-flavored liqueur adds a provocative touch to rich vanilla ice cream in this sparkling dessert!

1 qt. Royal Vanilla Ice Cream, page 110,
   softened, or 1 pint each commercial
   vanilla ice cream and raspberry sherbet,
   softened, mixed together
1/2 cup Chambord or other
   raspberry-flavored liqueur,
   (do not use raspberry-flavored brandy)

3 cups fresh raspberries (about 1-1/2 pints)
   or thawed, frozen, loosepack raspberries
2 tablespoons sugar
1/2 cup crisp almond-macaroon-cookie crumbs

In a large bowl, combine ice cream or ice-cream-sherbet combination and 5 tablespoons liqueur. Cover and refreeze ice cream 6 hours. In a medium bowl, combine raspberries, sugar and remaining 3 tablespoons liqueur. Cover and refrigerate 4 to 6 hours, stirring occasionally. At serving time, place 1 scoop ice cream in each of 6 stemmed goblets. Using 1/2 of raspberries and their juice, distribute evenly over ice cream; sprinkle with 1/2 of cookie crumbs. Top with another scoop of ice cream. Repeat with remaining raspberries and cookie crumbs. Serve immediately. Makes 6 servings.

How to Make Peach-Melba Bavarian

1/Spoon raspberry mixture into center of peach mixture to within 1-1/2 to 2 inches of edge. Using the back of a spoon, lightly press raspberry mixture down into peach mixture so surface is level.

2/Unmold bavarian and garnish as desired.

Macaroon Madness

Your guests will drive you "crazy" asking for more of this frozen rum-laced delight!

4 eggs, separated, room temperature
1 cup sugar
3/4 cup light rum
4-1/4 cups crisp coconut- or
  almond-macaroon-cookie crumbs

1/4 teaspoon salt
1-1/2 cups whipping cream, whipped

Fold a 25-inch length of foil lengthwise in thirds. Lightly oil 1 side of foil. Tightly wrap foil, oiled-side in, around outside of a 1- or 1-1/2-quart soufflé dish. Collar should rise 2 inches above rim of dish. Securely fasten foil with tape or string. If using string, tie about 1/2 inch below rim of dish. Use a paper clip to secure top edge of foil. Press foil so it conforms to shape of dish. In a large mixer bowl, beat egg yolks and sugar until thick and pale. Gradually stir in rum, then 4 cups macaroon crumbs. Beat 1 minute at medium-high speed or until well-combined; set aside. In a small mixer bowl, beat egg whites and salt until stiff but not dry. Gently fold whites, then whipped cream into macaroon mixture. Turn into prepared dish; smooth top. Sprinkle remaining 1/4 cup macaroon crumbs in a 1-1/2-inch band around outer edge of top. Gently press into surface with the back of a spoon. Cover and freeze 6 hours. May be tightly covered and frozen up to 1 month. Remove foil collar; let dessert stand at room temperature 20 to 30 minutes before serving. Makes 6 to 8 servings.

Chocolate-Tortoni Torte

Amaretto and chocolate rendezvous in this spectacular make-ahead dessert, crowned with chocolate leaves!

3 eggs, separated, room temperature
3/4 cup sugar
1/8 teaspoon salt
1 cup half and half
4 oz. semisweet chocolate, finely chopped
1/2 cup amaretto liqueur
1/8 teaspoon cream of tartar

1 pint whipping cream (2 cups), whipped
1 cup amaretti or other crisp
    almond-macaroon-cookie crumbs
1/2 recipe Chocolate Whipped Cream, page 156
Chocolate Leaves, page 126
Coffee-bean candies

In top of a double boiler, combine egg yolks, 1/2 cup sugar and salt. Gradually stir in half and half. Place top of double boiler over simmering water. Cook, stirring constantly, until mixture thickly coats the back of a metal spoon. Remove top of double boiler from bottom pan; place on a towel-lined work surface. Add chocolate to egg-yolk mixture; stir until melted. Stir in liqueur; turn into a large bowl. Cool to room temperature or refrigerate, stirring frequently, until cool. Lightly oil a 9-inch springform pan. In a small mixer bowl, beat egg whites and cream of tartar to soft-peak stage. Beating constantly, gradually add remaining 1/4 cup sugar, 2 tablespoons at a time. Continue beating until whites are glossy and firm. Fold egg-white mixture, whipped cream and cookie crumbs into cooled chocolate mixture. Turn into prepared pan; smooth top. Cover with foil; freeze 4 to 5 hours or overnight. Prepare Chocolate Whipped Cream and Chocolate Leaves; refrigerate. To loosen torte, run a thin knife around inside edge of pan; remove side of pan. Using 2 large metal spatulas, carefully slide torte off pan bottom onto a serving plate. Decorate with Chocolate Whipped Cream and coffee-bean candies. Place Chocolate Leaves, pinwheel-fashion, fanning out from center of torte. Makes 12 servings.

Chocolate-Raspberry Mousse

Serve this beguiling mousse in Lacy Chocolate Cups and you'll get rave reviews!

3 cups fresh raspberries
    (about 1-1/2 pints) or 2 (10-oz.) pkgs.
    thawed frozen raspberries in syrup,
    well-drained
1 (8-oz.) pkg. cream cheese, softened
6 oz. semisweet chocolate, melted, cooled
4 eggs, separated, room temperature

1 teaspoon vanilla extract
1 tablespoon Chambord or other
    raspberry-flavored liqueur, if desired
1/4 teaspoon cream of tartar
1/3 cup sugar
6 Lacy Chocolate Cups, page 131
1/2 recipe Plain Whipped Cream, page 156

Set aside 6 attractive raspberries for garnish. If using frozen berries, spread them out on a double layer of paper towel. Top with another layer of paper towel. Blot berries thoroughly; set aside. In a small bowl, beat cream cheese until perfectly smooth. Gradually add chocolate; beat until blended. Beat in egg yolks, vanilla and liqueur, if desired; set aside. In a large mixer bowl, beat egg whites and cream of tartar to soft-peak stage. Beating constantly, gradually add sugar, 2 tablespoons at a time. Continue beating until whites are glossy and firm. Stir 1/4 of egg-white mixture into chocolate mixture to lighten it. Gently fold in remaining egg-white mixture and raspberries. Cover and refrigerate 2 hours or until very thick. Prepare Lacy Chocolate Cups and Plain Whipped Cream. Spoon mousse into chocolate cups. Garnish with a rosette or dollop of whipped cream, topped with a raspberry. Refrigerate until ready to serve. Makes 6 servings.

Mocha-Macadamia Ice-Cream Torte

Cracker crumbs are used to extend expensive macadamia nuts in this sensational make-ahead dessert.

1-1/4 cups sugar
2 teaspoons instant coffee powder rather than granules, if possible
1-1/2 tablespoons unsweetened cocoa
5 egg whites, room temperature
1/2 teaspoon cream of tartar
1 (5-oz.) can macadamia nuts, ground, toasted (about 1-1/4 cups)

2/3 cup Ritz-cracker crumbs (about 16 crackers)
1 qt. slightly softened mocha ice cream or 1 pint each slightly softened coffee and chocolate ice cream, combined
1/2 recipe Sugar-Nut Crumble, page 146, using macadamia nuts

Preheat oven to 300F (150C). Grease and flour a 9-inch springform pan. In a small bowl, combine sugar, coffee powder and cocoa; set aside. If using instant coffee granules, crush to a powder before using. In a large mixer bowl, beat egg whites and cream of tartar to soft-peak stage. Beating constantly, gradually add sugar mixture, 2 tablespoons at a time. Continue beating until whites are glossy and firm. Fold in nuts and cracker crumbs. Turn into prepared pan; smooth top. Bake 30 to 40 minutes or until a wooden pick inserted in center comes out clean. To loosen torte, gently run a thin knife around inside edge of pan. Let cool in pan on a rack 10 minutes. Gently press down outside edge of torte slightly with your fingertips. Top should be almost level. Cool on rack to room temperature. Spread ice cream over surface; smooth top. Cover and freeze 3 hours or until ice cream is firm. Torte may be tightly covered and frozen up to 1 month. Prepare Sugar-Nut Crumble; set aside. Remove torte from freezer 15 to 20 minutes before serving. Run knife between torte and edge of pan; remove side of pan. Using 2 large metal spatulas, carefully slide torte off pan bottom onto a serving plate. Sprinkle with Sugar-Nut Crumble; lightly press into surface of torte with the back of a spoon. Makes 10 to 12 servings.

Frozen Zabaglione Mousse

Zabaglione's intense sweetness is tempered by the addition of egg whites and whipped cream.

1/2 recipe Zabaglione Freddo, page 84
1/2 cup whipping cream, whipped
2 egg whites, room temperature

1/8 teaspoon cream of tartar
8 to 12 tablespoons crisp almond-macaroon-cookie crumbs

Prepare Zabaglione Freddo. Fold in whipped cream; set aside. In a small bowl, beat egg whites with cream of tartar until stiff but not dry. Fold into zabaglione. Spoon 1/2 of mixture into 4 to 6 stemmed glasses. Sprinkle each serving with 1 tablespoon cookie crumbs. Top with remaining zabaglione mixture; sprinkle with remaining cookie crumbs. Freeze 3 hours before serving. If mousse is frozen more than 3 hours, remove from freezer and let stand at room temperature 10 to 15 minutes before serving. Makes 4 to 6 servings.

Variation
Frozen Chocolate-Zabaglione Mousse: Place 1 tablespoon unsweetened cocoa in a small bowl. Gradually add whipping cream, stirring constantly until mixture is smooth. Refrigerate 30 minutes before beating. Substitute chocolate-wafer-cookie crumbs for almond-macaroon-cookie crumbs.

How to Make Toffee-Butter Torte

1/Sprinkle 1/3 cup candy mixture over bottom and halfway up sides of prepared pan.

2/Sprinkle remaining 2/3 cup candy mixture over final layer of egg mixture.

Toffee-Butter Torte

A ribbon of chocolate runs through the middle of this frozen fantasy—ideal for elegant entertaining!

2 oz. semisweet chocolate, coarsely chopped
2 tablespoons butter
1/3 cup whipping cream
3 oz. Grated Chocolate, page 126
1/2 cup finely and 1 cup coarsely crushed chocolate-covered toffee or almond-roca candy

1-1/2 cups butter, softened
1 cup packed brown sugar
1 tablespoon vanilla extract
3 eggs, room temperature
2/3 cup whipping cream, whipped

In a small saucepan, warm chopped chocolate, 2 tablespoons butter and 1/3 cup whipping cream over low heat. Stir occasionally until chocolate melts and mixture is smooth. Cool to room temperature. Prepare Grated Chocolate. Generously grease a 9-inch springform pan. In a medium bowl, combine Grated Chocolate and 1/2 cup finely crushed candy. Sprinkle 1/3 cup over bottom and halfway up sides of prepared pan; set aside. In a large mixer bowl, beat 1-1/2 cups butter, brown sugar and vanilla until light and fluffy. Add eggs, 1 at a time, beating with an electric mixer a full 3 minutes after each addition. *Lengthy beating is important and necessary to incorporate eggs into butter mixture.* Fold in whipped cream and 1 cup coarsely crushed candy. Turn 1/2 of cream mixture into pan. Drizzle melted and cooled chocolate mixture over surface to within 1/2 inch of outside edge. Smooth chocolate layer. Gently spoon remaining cream mixture over chocolate; smooth top. Sprinkle with remaining 2/3 cup chocolate-candy mixture. Using the back of a spoon, lightly press into surface of torte. Cover and freeze at least 4 hours. Torte may be tightly covered and frozen up to 1 month. To loosen torte, run a thin knife around inside edge of pan; remove side of pan. Using 2 large metal spatulas, carefully slide torte off pan bottom onto a serving plate. Serve immediately. Makes 8 to 10 servings.

Lemon-Berry Mousse

Brilliant swirls of raspberry puree create an exciting contrast in this zesty lemon mousse.

1 (1/4-oz.) envelope unflavored gelatin
  (scant 1 tablespoon)
3/4 cup lemon juice
6 eggs, separated, room temperature
1 cup sugar
3 tablespoons butter
1 (10-oz.) pkg. thawed frozen raspberries
  in syrup

1/4 teaspoon salt
3/4 cup whipping cream, whipped
1-1/2 cups fresh raspberries (about 3/4 pint)
  mixed with 2 tablespoons sugar, or
  Raspberry Jewel Sauce, page 150,
  if desired

In a small bowl, stir gelatin into 1/4 cup lemon juice; let stand 5 minutes to soften. In a medium saucepan, combine remaining 1/2 cup lemon juice, egg yolks, 3/4 cup sugar and butter. Cook, stirring constantly, over medium-low heat until mixture coats the back of a metal spoon. Remove from heat. Add gelatin mixture; stir 1 minute or until dissolved. Turn into a large bowl. Refrigerate, stirring frequently, until mixture begins to mound when spooned on top of itself. While lemon mixture is cooling, drain syrup from raspberries. Discard or reserve for another use. Press berries through a fine sieve into a small bowl. You should have about 1/3 cup puree; set aside. In a large mixer bowl, beat egg whites and salt to soft-peak stage. Beating constantly, gradually add remaining 1/4 cup sugar, 2 tablespoons at a time. Continue beating until whites are glossy and firm. Stir 1/3 of egg-white mixture into lemon mixture to lighten. Gently fold in remaining egg-white mixture, then whipped cream. Spoon 1/2 of mousse into a 1-1/2-quart clear glass soufflé dish or serving bowl. Using about 1/2 of raspberry puree, drop teaspoonfuls randomly in 6 or 7 places in lemon mousse. Using the flat edge of a dinner knife, cut through mixture to create a marbled effect. Do not marble too much or colors will blend and not contrast. Spoon remaining mousse on top. Dot with remaining raspberry puree; repeat marbling action. Cover and refrigerate 2 hours or until set. Prepare Raspberry Jewel Sauce, if desired. Serve mousse with fresh sugared raspberries or Raspberry Jewel Sauce on the side, if desired. Makes 6 servings.

Raspberry-Yogurt Freeze

No added sugar in this frozen finale—top with Sweetened Crème Fraîche for extra pizzazz!

Sweetened Crème Fraîche, page 156,
  or Raspberry Jewel Sauce,
  page 150, if desired
1 (10-oz.) pkg. thawed frozen raspberries
  in syrup

16 oz. raspberry-flavored yogurt (2 cups)
3 egg whites, room temperature
1/4 teaspoon cream of tartar

Prepare Sweetened Crème Fraîche or Raspberry Jewel Sauce, if desired; refrigerate. Pour raspberries and their juice into a blender; process until smooth. Strain through a fine sieve into a small mixer bowl. Add yogurt; whisk until smooth. Set aside. In a small mixer bowl, beat egg whites and cream of tartar until stiff but not dry. Fold into raspberry mixture. Spoon into 4 to 6 stemmed glasses. Cover with foil; freeze overnight. Remove dessert from freezer immediately before serving. Dollop dessert with crème fraîche or drizzle with sauce, if desired. Makes 4 to 6 servings.

How to Make Lemon-Berry Mousse

1/Using about 1/2 of raspberry puree, drop teaspoonfuls randomly in 6 or 7 places in lemon mousse.

2/Using the flat edge of a dinner knife, cut through mixture in a wide zigzag pattern to create a marbled effect.

Black-Magic Mousse

Photo on page 153.

The most chocolatey mousse imaginable—created for my chocolate-crazy friend, Donna. Brandied orange sauce adds a stylish finish.

**12 oz. semisweet chocolate,
  coarsely chopped
2 tablespoons instant coffee powder or
  granules dissolved in
  1 tablespoon very hot water
3 tablespoons Kahlúa or other
  coffee-flavored liqueur**

**5 eggs, separated, room temperature
1/4 teaspoon cream of tartar
1/4 cup sugar
1 pint whipping cream (2 cups), whipped
Suzette Sauce, page 150, if desired**

In top of a double boiler, combine chocolate, dissolved instant coffee and liqueur. Place top of double boiler over simmering water. Stir until chocolate is halfway melted. Remove top of double boiler from bottom; place on a towel-lined work surface. Stir until chocolate is completely melted. Whisk in egg yolks, 1 at a time. Turn mixture into a large bowl. Cool to room temperature, stirring occasionally. Do not allow mixture to set. In a large mixer bowl, beat egg whites and cream of tartar to soft-peak stage. Beating constantly, gradually add sugar, 2 tablespoons at a time. Continue beating until whites are glossy and firm; set aside. Stir 1/3 of whipped cream into chocolate mixture to lighten. Gently fold in remaining whipped cream, then egg-white mixture. Spoon into a 2-quart glass bowl or 8 to 10 stemmed glasses. Cover and refrigerate at least 2 hours. Prepare Suzette Sauce, if desired. Serve mousse with sauce, if desired. Makes 8 to 10 servings.

White-Chocolate Mousse with Raspberry Jewel Sauce

Photo on page 153.

A sparkling red-raspberry sauce creates an enticingly tart finish for this ultra-rich and creamy mousse.

1 (1/4-oz.) envelope unflavored gelatin
  (scant 1 tablespoon)
1/2 cup white crème de cacao
4 eggs, separated, room temperature
2 whole eggs, room temperature
1/2 cup sugar
1-1/4 cups milk

1/2 cup butter
8 oz. white chocolate, coarsely chopped
Raspberry Jewel Sauce, page 150
1/4 teaspoon salt
1-1/2 cups whipping cream, whipped
6 to 8 fresh raspberries, if desired

In a small bowl, stir gelatin into crème de cacao; let stand 5 minutes to soften. In a medium saucepan, combine 4 egg yolks, 2 whole eggs, sugar, milk and butter. Cook over medium heat, stirring constantly, until mixture coats the back of a metal spoon. Remove from heat. Add gelatin mixture; stir 1 minute or until dissolved. Strain through a fine sieve into a large bowl. Add chocolate pieces; let stand 5 minutes. Stir until chocolate is melted and mixture is smooth. Refrigerate, stirring occasionally, until mixture begins to mound when spooned on top of itself. Prepare Raspberry Jewel Sauce; set aside. In a small mixer bowl, beat 4 egg whites and salt until stiff but not dry. Stir 1/3 of whites into chocolate mixture to lighten. Fold in remaining egg whites, then whipped cream. Spoon 1/2 of mousse into 6 to 8 stemmed wine or sherbet glasses. Leave top uneven, so sauce can form a decorative design. Drizzle each serving with about 2 tablespoons Raspberry Jewel Sauce. Spoon remaining mousse into glasses; drizzle with more sauce or serve with mousse. Garnish each serving with a fresh raspberry, if desired. Cover and refrigerate 4 hours or until set. Makes 6 to 8 servings.

Ice-Cream 'n Cookie Sandwiches

Use your favorite ice cream and cookies to create this homemade treat. Dip in chocolate to double your fun!

1 gallon ice cream of your choice,
  slightly softened
About 24 (3- to 3-1/2-inch) Spicy Oat
  Cookies, page 66, or other cookies

About 2/3 cup jam or peanut butter,
  if desired
8 oz. semisweet chocolate, melted, cooled
  to room temperature, if desired

Line 2 (13" x 9") baking pans with plastic wrap using 2 (18-inch) lengths placed crosswise in each pan; let ends hang over edges of pans. Spoon 1/2 gallon softened ice cream into each lined pan. Smooth and level surface of ice cream with a rubber spatula. Freeze until very firm. Measure diameter of cookies. Set aside a round cookie cutter or a drinking glass with a rim equal to diameter of cookies. Spread bottoms of cookies with a thin layer of your favorite jam or peanut butter, if desired. Working with 1 pan of ice cream at a time, use edges of plastic wrap to lift solid ice cream out of pan and onto work surface. Use cookie cutter or rim of glass to cut ice cream into 6 rounds. Sandwich each round between 2 cookies. Place on a baking sheet; freeze until firm. Repeat with remaining ice cream and cookies. If desired, after ice-cream sandwiches have been frozen 2 hours, dip 1/2 of each sandwich into melted chocolate. Place on a waxed-paper-lined baking sheet; freeze until chocolate sets. Wrap each sandwich individually in plastic wrap, or place individually in small plastic bags and seal. Store in freezer up to 1 month. Makes 12 ice-cream sandwiches.

Strawberry-Champagne Silk

Photo on pages 4 and 5.

Straining the strawberry puree gives this elegant dessert a silky-smooth texture.

1 (1/4-oz.) envelope unflavored gelatin
  (scant 1 tablespoon)
3/4 cup whipping cream
1/3 cup sugar
1/4 teaspoon salt
1-1/4 cups dry champagne

About 2 cups strawberry puree (about 2 pints)
1 pint strawberry ice cream,
  slightly softened
6 to 8 whole strawberries with leaves,
  if desired

In a small saucepan, stir gelatin into cream; let stand 5 minutes to soften. Stir over low heat just until gelatin dissolves. Turn into a large bowl. Stir in sugar, salt and champagne. Refrigerate 30 to 45 minutes or until mixture begins to mound when spooned on top of itself. Press strawberry puree through a fine sieve to yield 1-1/2 cups strained puree. Add to champagne mixture; beat until smooth. Beat in softened ice cream. Spoon mixture into 6 to 8 champagne or sherbet glasses. Cover and refrigerate 3 to 4 hours. Immediately before serving, top each portion with a whole strawberry, if desired. Makes 6 to 8 servings.

Variation
Frozen Strawberry-Champagne Cups: Line 10 muffin cups with foil liners. Divide mixture evenly between cups. Cover and freeze 4 hours. May be tightly covered and frozen up to 1 month. Gently peel off foil cup. Let stand at room temperature 5 to 10 minutes before serving. If desired, garnish with rosettes of whipped cream and tiny whole strawberries.

Frozen Praline Mousse with Hot Caramel Sauce

The contrast of hot and cold adds drama to this meltingly delicious dessert.

Praline Crunch, page 145
1/2 cup half and half
1/2 cup packed brown sugar
3 eggs, separated, room temperature
3 tablespoons butter, softened

2 tablespoons praline-flavored liqueur,
  if desired
1/4 teaspoon cream of tartar
1-1/2 cups whipping cream, whipped
Hot Caramel Sauce, page 155

Prepare Praline Crunch; set aside. Butter a 9-inch springform pan. In top of a double boiler, combine half and half, brown sugar and egg yolks. Place top of double boiler over simmering water. Cook, stirring constantly, until smooth and slightly thickened, about 5 minutes. Turn into a large mixer bowl. Beat until cool, 3 to 5 minutes. Add butter and liqueur, if desired; beat until blended. In a small mixer bowl, beat egg whites and cream of tartar until stiff but not dry. Fold whites, whipped cream and all but 1/2 cup Praline Crunch into egg-yolk mixture. Spoon into prepared pan; smooth surface. Sprinkle reserved Praline Crunch over top. Cover with foil; freeze overnight. To loosen mousse, run a thin knife around inside edge of pan; remove side of pan. Using 2 large spatulas, carefully slide mousse off pan bottom onto a serving plate. Return mousse to freezer until ready to serve. Hot Caramel Sauce may be prepared the night before and refrigerated. Reheat sauce before serving. Pour into a glass pitcher or bowl and pass with mousse. Makes 8 to 10 servings.

Giant Black Forest Cream-Puff Sundae

Cream puffs filled with black-cherry ice cream and drizzled with fudge sauce—perfect for parties!

Cream-Puff Pastries, page 139
Fudge Velvet Sauce, page 150
About 1/2 gallon black-cherry ice cream,
  slightly softened

1/2 cup finely chopped almonds, if desired

Prepare Cream-Puff Pastries; cool. Prepare Fudge Velvet Sauce; cool. Lightly grease a 10-inch springform pan. Line with 3 (20-inch) lengths of plastic wrap, allowing ends to drape over edge of pan. Cut top 1/3 off pastries. Remove any soft dough from centers. Spoon slightly softened ice cream into top and bottom of each pastry. Overfill slightly so ice cream oozes out when top is replaced on bottom of puff. Place a ring of ice-cream-filled cream puffs around inside edge of prepared pan. Fill center with second ring of cream puffs. Entire space should be filled. Generously drizzle cream puffs with fudge sauce. When frozen, excess ice cream and fudge sauce act as cement to hold giant sundae together. Sprinkle with nuts, if desired. Freeze, uncovered, 4 hours. When sundae is frozen, it may be tightly covered and stored in freezer up to 2 months. Release side of springform pan. Working quickly, gently remove plastic wrap. Place giant sundae on a serving plate. Return to freezer until 10 minutes before serving time. To serve, pull puffs apart with 2 forks. Makes about 10 servings.

Low-Calorie Choco-Berry Mousse

Guaranteed to satisfy the most ardent chocoholic, this tofu-enriched dessert only has 210 calories per serving!

1 (1/4-oz.) envelope unflavored gelatin
  (scant 1 tablespoon)
2/3 cup diet chocolate-, raspberry- or
  strawberry-flavored soda
8 oz. part skim milk ricotta cheese (1 cup),
  drained, if necessary
1/4 cup sugar
8 oz. soft tofu, rinsed, blotted dry,
  cut in 8 pieces

5 oz. semisweet chocolate, melted, cooled
2 cups fresh raspberries or chopped fresh
  strawberries (about 1 pint)
4 egg whites, room temperature
1/4 teaspoon cream of tartar
8 Chocolate Leaves with Berries, page 126

In a small saucepan, stir gelatin into soda; let stand 5 minutes to soften. Stir over medium heat just until gelatin dissolves; set aside. In a blender, combine ricotta cheese and sugar. Process, scraping sides of container as necessary, until mixture is perfectly smooth. Add tofu; process until smooth. With blender at low speed, slowly add warm gelatin mixture, then melted chocolate. Increase speed to high; blend until creamy and smooth, scraping sides of blender as necessary. Turn into a large bowl. Refrigerate, stirring frequently, until mixture mounds thickly when spooned on top of itself. Fold in 2 cups berries; set aside. In a large mixer bowl, beat egg whites and cream of tartar until stiff but not dry. Fold egg whites, 1/3 at a time, into chocolate mixture. Spoon into 8 stemmed glasses or small dessert bowls, mounding high in center. Refrigerate at least 3 hours before serving. Prepare Chocolate Leaves with Berries. Use to garnish each serving. Makes 8 servings.

How to Make a Giant Black Forest Cream-Puff Sundae

1/Place a ring of ice-cream-filled cream puffs around inside edge of prepared pan. Fill center with second ring of cream puffs. Entire space should be filled.

2/Generously drizzle cream puffs with Fudge Velvet Sauce.

Frosty Peach Cream

Sour cream gives this quick peach ice cream a tart refreshing tang! Fresh peaches give the fullest flavor but frozen loosepack peaches may be used when fresh are unavailable.

2 lbs. ripe peaches, peeled,
  pitted, sliced
3 tablespoons lemon juice
1 pint dairy sour cream or
  vanilla-flavored yogurt (2 cups)

3/4 cup sugar
1/2 teaspoon ground ginger
1/4 teaspoon ground cinnamon
Additional peach slices, if desired
Mint sprigs, if desired

Line 1 or 2 large baking sheets with plastic wrap. In a large bowl, toss peaches with lemon juice. Spread peaches in a single layer on lined baking sheets. Freeze 1-1/2 hours or until solid. Immediately before serving, place frozen peaches in a large food processor fitted with a metal blade. If using a small food processor, make ice cream in 2 batches use 1/2 of ingredients at a time. Process peaches until finely chopped, scraping down sides of bowl as necessary. Add sour cream or yogurt, sugar, ginger and cinnamon. Process until mixture is smooth. Spoon into stemmed glasses. Top each serving with a single peach slice and mint sprig, if desired. Serve immediately. Makes about 1-1/2 quarts.

POTPOURRI

This chapter's title says it all. In it you'll find a tempting array of miscellaneous sweets and dessert accompaniments. Some recipes are old, passed down to me as part of my culinary heritage. Others were scribbled hastily on a sheet of note paper as the idea came to me, then tested until true. There are indulgent confections, beautiful and easy-to-make chocolate decorations, stunning chocolate baskets and cups, and caramel-glazed nuts—just to name a few. In short, a wonderful assortment of delicious odds and ends!

Caramel Crowns, for example, are lacy caps of sparkling, hardened caramel that can turn the most ordinary dessert into an instant sensation. Small caramel crowns may be set on top of individual servings of mousse, fruit compote or chocolate cups filled with ice cream. Large crowns might adorn a special cake, torte or cheesecake. The trick to working with caramel in this case is to have it at the right temperature. It must be thick enough to form long threads when drizzled over the mold. Once the caramel has hardened, the "crown" is removed from its mold. It should either be used the same day or stored in an *airtight* container to be used within two days. Humidity is the enemy of these filigreed decorations. Caramel is made of sugar, and sugar melts when confronted with moisture!

Chocolate Cups are beautiful, edible containers for all kinds of delightful fillings. They're a cinch to make! Melted chocolate—dark or white—is simply spread over the inside of paper cupcake liners. The chocolate-coated paper liners are then placed in muffin tins so they hold their shape until the chocolate sets. That's as hard as it gets! My favorite way to serve these wonderful confections is to make Harlequin Cups (half white and half dark chocolate), filling the white-chocolate half with Black-Magic Mousse, and the dark chocolate half with White-Chocolate Mousse. The raves one gets for this simple creation are embarrassing—but nice!

In many circles it's becoming popular to serve just a bite of sweetness after the cheese course. I like to pass a pretty cut-glass plate with a choice of three or four homemade candies. Guests love picking and choosing and, more often than not, end up trying them all. Chocolate fans will love the divinely decadent Chocolate Truffles, with flavor variations ranging from Espresso to Grand Marnier. And then there are Chocolate-Covered Potato Chips. Don't laugh—they really *are* delicious. The crispness of the low-salt chips makes a perfect foil for the creamy-smooth chocolate coating.

For a true touch of elegance, serve the diminutive Mocha Creams. Tiny, one-inch chocolate cups are filled with Mocha Buttercream, then decorated with coffee-bean candies. Apricot-Amaretto Confections are dried-apricot "sandwiches" filled with almond cream, then dipped in chocolate. You can use the same filling to stuff dates, dipping them in white chocolate to create Saturday-Night Dates!

Nothing I've ever served has elicited such raves as the Woven Chocolate Basket, filled to the brim with chocolate-dipped fruits, nuts and cookies. This beautiful chocolate creation is about eight inches in diameter and 12 inches tall including the handle. I present it on a footed glass cake plate garnished with fresh flowers. You can imagine what an impressive sight it is! Creating the basket takes a little time, but the technique isn't at all difficult. The fabulous bonus with this beautiful basket is that it can be used over and over again! After the basket is emptied, simply use a paper towel to remove any moisture left by the fruit. Place the basket in a large bowl for protection, cover it securely with plastic wrap and refrigerate. I've kept a chocolate basket in the refrigerator for several months, refilling it with chocolate-dipped goodies whenever we entertained. Each group of guests thought it was made especially for them—and I didn't tell them any differently!

Chocolate Truffles

Photos on pages 5 and 135.

Work quickly when making truffles or they'll melt in your hands— instead of your mouth!

1/2 cup whipping cream
1/2 cup butter
8 oz. semisweet chocolate, coarsely chopped
3 tablespoons rum or other liqueur

2-1/2 tablespoons unsweetened cocoa mixed
with 2 tablespoons sugar, or toasted
finely chopped nuts, or Chocolate Coating,
see below

Chocolate Coating:
12 oz. semisweet or white chocolate

1 tablespoon vegetable oil

Line an 8-inch-square baking pan with plastic wrap, allowing excess to hang over edges; lightly oil plastic wrap. In a medium saucepan, combine cream and butter over medium heat. Heat, stirring occasionally, until butter melts. Add chocolate, stirring constantly, until chocolate is melted and mixture is smooth. Remove from heat; cool on a rack 5 minutes. Stir in rum or liqueur. Pour into prepared pan, spreading mixture evenly into corners. Refrigerate 1 to 2 hours or until very firm. Place cocoa and sugar or chopped nuts in a small bowl; set aside. Line a large baking sheet with waxed paper. Grasping edges of plastic wrap in baking pan, lift truffle mixture out of pan; place on work surface. Cut mixture into 36 squares. Return 18 squares to refrigerator. Dust your palms with powdered sugar occasionally to prevent mixture from sticking to your hands. Working quickly, shape each square of mixture into a rough ball using your fingers or roll pieces between your palms. Roll in cocoa mixture or chopped nuts or leave plain if using Chocolate Coating. If mixture becomes too soft to handle, place in freezer 15 minutes before continuing. Place coated truffles on lined baking sheet. Refrigerate or freeze cocoa- or nut-covered truffles. Repeat with remaining 18 chilled squares truffle mixture. If dipping truffles in Chocolate Coating, place uncoated truffles on lined baking sheet. Freeze at least 1 hour before dipping. To coat truffles, prepare Chocolate Coating. Place in a small bowl. Remove 6 truffles at a time from freezer. Using 2 forks to cradle each truffle, dip into chocolate mixture. Allow excess chocolate to drain before placing truffles on another waxed-paper-lined baking sheet. Repeat with remaining truffles. Refrigerate to set coating. If truffle mixture shows through Chocolate Coating, use a wooden pick to dab some melted chocolate over hole; refrigerate to set. If desired, use a fork to drizzle melted chocolate of the opposite color (white on dark, dark on white) lightly over chocolate-coated truffles. Store in an airtight container in refrigerator up to 2 weeks or freeze up to 2 months. Let refrigerated truffles stand at room temperature 15 minutes before serving; let frozen truffles stand 30 minutes. Makes 36 truffles.

Chocolate Coating:
Melt chocolate in top of a double boiler over simmering water, stirring until smooth. Add oil; stir until blended. Cool to room temperature before dipping truffles.

Variations
White-Chocolate Truffles: Reduce cream to 1/4 cup. Substitute white chocolate for dark chocolate.
Espresso Truffles: Add 1 tablespoon instant espresso coffee powder or other instant coffee powder or granules to cream before heating. Substitute coffee-flavored liqueur for rum. Roll truffles in a mixture of 2 tablespoons cocoa, 1 tablespoon instant coffee powder and 2 tablespoons sugar.
Grand Marnier Truffles: Add 2 teaspoons freshly grated orange zest to cream before heating. White chocolate may be substituted for dark chocolate, if desired. Substitute Grand Marnier or other orange-flavored liqueur for rum. Dip in melted white or dark chocolate.
Praline Truffles: Prepare White-Chocolate Truffles, adding 1/3 cup packed brown sugar to cream before heating. Cook until sugar is dissolved before stirring in white chocolate. Use praline-flavored liqueur, if desired. Add 1/2 cup toasted finely chopped pecans. Roll in toasted chopped pecans.

Chocolate Decorations

Use dark or white chocolate to create these beautiful garnishes for cakes, pies, mousses—whatever!

Grated Chocolate: Use semisweet or bittersweet chocolate in a large chunk for ease in handling. Place grater over a piece of waxed paper. Hold 1 end of chocolate in a piece of paper towel to prevent the heat of your hands from melting chocolate. Firmly rub chocolate over coarse side of grater. Or, use a Mouli rotary grater for fast and easy results. Let curls drop onto waxed paper. Refrigerate in an airtight container until ready to use.

Chocolate Curls: Use a large long chocolate bar. If chocolate is too cold, shavings will be brittle and break. Hold chocolate firmly to warm slightly or place in warm location (90F) about 15 minutes. Place a piece of waxed paper on work surface. Holding chocolate in 1 hand and using a swivel-blade vegetable peeler in the other, firmly draw blade toward you along edge of bar. Pressure you apply will determine thickness of curl. Let curls drop onto waxed paper. Refrigerate in an airtight container until ready to use.

Chocolate Cigarettes: Line a large baking sheet with waxed paper. Melt 6 ounces chocolate. Pour onto a smooth work surface such as marble, formica or back of a baking sheet. Using a narrow, metal, spreading spatula, spread chocolate about 1/8 inch thick over work surface. Let cool until firm but not hard. Starting at 1 end of chocolate and at side closest to you and using a flexible pastry scraper or wide metal spatula tilted at a 45-degree angle, slowly and firmly move spatula forward. Spatula's edge will lift chocolate and cause it to roll around itself. Use spatula to transfer cigarettes gently to lined baking sheet; refrigerate until firm. Refrigerate in an airtight container until ready to use.

Chocolate Leaves: Line a large baking sheet with waxed paper. Choose 6 to 8 *firm* non-poisonous leaves, such as camellia, orange or lemon, with stems attached. Wash and *thoroughly* dry leaves. Melt 2 ounces chocolate. Using a small metal spatula or the back of a kitchen teaspoon, thickly spread melted chocolate over undersides of leaves. Be careful not to let chocolate run over edges of leaves. Use your fingertip to remove any excess chocolate from edges. Place leaves, chocolate-side up, on prepared baking sheet; refrigerate until chocolate is set. Patch any bare spots with additional chocolate; refrigerate until set. Remove leaf from chocolate by grasping stem and pulling leaf gently away from chocolate. Refrigerate in an airtight container until ready to use.

Chocolate Leaves with Berries: Attach a fresh raspberry or small strawberry to center of a Chocolate Leaf using a tiny blob of melted chocolate as "glue." Refrigerate in an airtight container up to 8 hours.

Chocolate Triangles: Line a large baking sheet with waxed paper. Draw an 8- or 9-inch circle on waxed paper. Spread 3 ounces melted chocolate evenly within circle. Refrigerate until almost set. Using a large sharp knife, cut chocolate circle into 10 to 12 pie-shaped pieces. Refrigerate until completely set. Gently break triangles apart; peel away waxed paper, handling chocolate as little as possible. Refrigerate in an airtight container until ready to use.

Chocolate Cutouts: Line a large baking sheet with waxed paper. Spread 2 ounces melted chocolate 1/16 to 1/8 inch thick on lined baking sheet. Refrigerate until almost set. Using canapé cutters, small cookie cutters or a pointed knife, cut out desired shapes in chocolate. Refrigerate until completely set. Gently break shapes apart; peel away waxed paper, handling chocolate as little as possible. Refrigerate in an airtight container until ready to use.

Chocolate Doilies: Doilies may be made any shape and size—large for cakes and tortes; small for individual servings of mousse, ice cream, etc. Draw design of choice or large or small circles on white paper; place under waxed paper on a baking sheet. Melt 2 ounces chocolate; cool to room temperature. Spoon chocolate into a decorator cone made out of waxed or parchment paper, page 22; cut a 1/16- to 1/8-inch-wide tip. To make a regular doily, pipe chocolate around circumference of circle showing through waxed paper. Continue to pipe chocolate inside circle in a lacy design, making sure all lines connect. Do not make design too open or doily will be fragile. Or, pipe melted chocolate onto waxed paper tracing alternative design. Refrigerate until chocolate is set. Gently peel away waxed paper, handling chocolate as little as possible. Refrigerate in an airtight container until ready to use.

How to Make Chocolate Cutouts & Doilies

Using canapé cutters, small cookie cutters or a pointed knife, cut out desired shapes in chocolate. Refrigerate until completely set. Gently break shapes apart; peel away waxed paper.

Draw design of choice on white paper; place under waxed paper on baking sheet. Pipe melted chocolate onto waxed paper, tracing design.

Chocolate-Covered Potato Chips

Low-salt potato chips transform into crisp and delicious treats when thinly coated with chocolate.

12 oz. semisweet, sweet or white chocolate, melted

3 oz. low-salt rippled potato chips (about 4 cups)

Line 2 large baking sheets with waxed paper. Place chocolate in a medium, shallow bowl. Lay 1 potato chip at a time in chocolate. Using a small rubber spatula or the back of a spoon, thoroughly coat top of chip. Using your index finger and thumb, pick up chip with ripples vertical to bowl. Shake chip up and down to remove all excess chocolate. Lay chip, curved-side up, on lined baking sheet. If necessary, use a spoon to dab some melted chocolate where your fingers left an imprint in chocolate. Repeat with remaining chips. If chocolate begins to thicken, warm slightly to thin. Place chocolate-dipped potato chips in refrigerator to set chocolate. Remove from refrigerator immediately before serving. Makes about 1 pound chocolate-covered potato chips.

Variation
Chocolate-Covered Pretzels: Substitute 5 to 6 ounces thin low-salt pretzels for potato chips. White chocolate is especially good with pretzels.

Woven Chocolate Basket

A gorgeous creation that's time-consuming but not difficult—and you can use it over and over again!

16 to 20 oz. semisweet chocolate, melted,
  cooled to room temperature
Candied violets or rosebuds

Candied mint leaves or tinted
  White-Chocolate Leaves, page 126

To make mold, invert a 1-1/2-quart soufflé dish or other flat-bottomed bowl on a work surface. *Firmly press a large sheet of heavy-duty foil over top and down sides of soufflé dish or bowl, leaving a 1- to 2-inch "collar" around base. Heavy-duty foil must be used for this project.* Use scissors to cut away excess foil. Surface of foil should be as smooth as possible and form a sharp crease at base of bowl where collar begins. Mold will be shaped like a man's hat. Making sure foil is pressed as tightly as possible against bowl will insure a strong mold. Gently lift foil mold off bowl. Place mold, open-end down, on a small cutting board or baking sheet that will fit into your refrigerator.

To make basket, make a decorator cone out of waxed or parchment paper, page 22, or use a pastry bag. Fit decorator cone or pastry bag with a #5 writing tip. Fill cone or pastry bag halfway with melted chocolate. Chocolate must be fairly cool so it will hold its shape without running. Refill cone or bag with melted chocolate as necessary. Starting at the mold's center top, which will become the bottom of your basket, pipe chocolate in straight lines, radiating like the spokes of a wheel. Lines should be about 1/2 inch apart at top edge of mold and continue down sides of mold. Refrigerate 10 minutes or until chocolate is firm. For second weave of chocolate basket, pipe melted chocolate in a close pinwheel design on top of mold. Pipe horizontal lines, about 1/2 inch apart, down sides of mold and going all the way around it. It is helpful to place mold on a lazy Susan when piping around mold. Refrigerate until chocolate is firm. Final basket weave of chocolate will be lines piped directly over first rows of chocolate. Refrigerate 30 minutes. Using a sharp pointed knife, cut away any excess chocolate that has run down onto collar of mold. Turn chocolate basket and mold right-side-up; place on a cutting board or baking sheet. *Carefully* peel foil away from inside of chocolate basket. Do not touch basket any more than necessary or the heat of your hands will cause it to melt. Using a #18 star tip, pipe chocolate rosettes around top rough edge of basket. Chocolate must be fairly cool in order for star pattern to show. Refrigerate until rosettes are firm.

To make basket handle, line a large baking sheet that will fit into your refrigerator with waxed paper. Measure the diameter of your chocolate basket. Using a pencil, draw a line equal to basket's diameter along 1 long side of waxed paper, 1-1/2 inches from edge of baking sheet. Draw an arc in the shape of a handle, connecting the 2 ends of the line. Using a #18 or #20 star tip, pipe an open zigzag, following the handle pattern. Pipe a second zigzag over the first, going in the opposite direction to form a woven-look handle. Chocolate must be fairly cool for star pattern to show in chocolate. Refrigerate 15 minutes or until firm. Gently peel waxed paper from back of chocolate handle. Return handle, flat-side up, to lined baking sheet. Pipe chocolate in a double zigzag pattern as for first side. Refrigerate until chocolate is firm.

To complete basket, remove handle from waxed paper. Attach to basket using 2 ample blobs of melted chocolate as "glue." Lightly balance handle in place with the palm of your hand a few seconds until chocolate sets and handle stands by itself. If desired, reinforce handle by dabbing additional melted chocolate around handle base. Attach candied violets or roses, and mint leaves or tinted White-Chocolate Leaves at the side of handle with chocolate "glue." Refrigerate until ready to use. Fill with Chocolate-Dipped Fruits, Nuts or cookies, page 98. Pass Spirited Whipped Cream, page 156, Tipsy Crème Anglaise flavored with orange-flavored liqueur, page 149, or Coventry Cream, page 148, into which the fruit can be dipped. To reuse chocolate basket, remove contents; dry any moist places left by the fruit with paper towel. Place basket in a large bowl to protect sides; cover with plastic wrap. This basket will keep several months in your refrigerator. Makes 1 large chocolate basket.

How to Make a Woven Chocolate Basket

1/Starting at the mold's center top, pipe chocolate in straight lines, radiating like the spokes of a wheel. Lines should be about 1/2 inch apart at top edge of mold and continue down sides of mold.

2/For second weave of chocolate basket, pipe chocolate in a pinwheel design on top of mold. Pipe horizontal lines, about 1/2 inch apart, down sides of mold and going all the way around it.

3/Pipe an open zigzag, following the handle pattern. Pipe a second zigzag over the first, going in the opposite direction to form a woven-look handle.

4/Attach garnishes of choice to handle of chocolate basket. Refrigerate until ready to use. Fill basket with Chocolate-Dipped Fruits.

Chocolate Cups

Photo on pages 4 and 5.

These incredibly easy creations are all the more appealing because they're made in advance. Harlequin Cups filled with white- and dark-chocolate mousse are stunning!

8 to 10 oz. semisweet, sweet or white chocolate

16 to 24 (2-1/2-inch) fluted foil or paper baking cups

Melt chocolate in top of a double boiler over simmering water. Remove from heat when chocolate is halfway melted. Stir until completely melted and smooth; cool to room temperature. Place 1 baking cup inside another, forming a double thickness. Using the back of a regular teaspoon, spread melted chocolate over bottom and up sides of paper cups. Push chocolate into ridges; make surface of inside as smooth as possible. Chocolate should be about 1/8 inch thick. As each baking cup is coated, place in a muffin cup to support sides. Refrigerate 15 minutes or until chocolate is firmly set. Check cups to be sure there are no thin spots. If so, dab additional melted chocolate on those places in need of repair. Refrigerate again until set. Gently peel off paper or foil. Be careful not to handle chocolate too much because the heat of your hands will cause it to melt. Return chocolate cups to refrigerator until ready to fill. Cups can be made a month in advance, covered and refrigerated. Makes 8 to 12 cups.

Variations
Harlequin Cups: Use 1/2 white chocolate and 1/2 dark chocolate. Spread melted white chocolate over 1/2 of bottom and side of each paper cup. Refrigerate until set. Spread remaining 1/2 with melted dark chocolate; refrigerate until set.
Chocolate-Mint Cups: Add 1 teaspoon mint extract to chocolate before melting.
Miniature Chocolate Cups: Use 60 (1-1/2-inch) miniature paper cups. Place 1 cup inside another, forming 30 cups with a double thickness. Proceed as for large cups. The tiny size of these cups makes them particularly vulnerable to the heat of your hands. Remove only 4 to 5 cups from refrigerator at a time; carefully peel off paper. Return to refrigerator while working on remaining cups.

Summer-Fruit Fudge

White chocolate makes magic in this no-cook confection dotted with fresh blueberries and toasted almonds.

1 (8-oz.) pkg. cream cheese, softened
1/2 teaspoon ground cinnamon
1/4 teaspoon ground nutmeg
1/4 teaspoon salt
12 oz. white chocolate, melted, cooled

3 cups sifted powdered sugar
1-1/4 cups toasted, finely chopped, blanched almonds
1 cup fresh blueberries (do not use frozen)

Line an 8-inch-square baking pan with a 15-inch length of foil. Tightly press foil into corners and against sides to make a smooth lining. In a large mixer bowl, beat cream cheese, cinnamon, nutmeg and salt until perfectly smooth. Beat in white chocolate. Beating at medium-low speed, add powdered sugar, 1 cup at a time. Increase speed to high; beat fudge 2 minutes. Fold in 1 cup nuts, then blueberries. Turn fudge into prepared pan; smooth top. Sprinkle with remaining 1/4 cup nuts; lightly press into surface. Cover and refrigerate 8 hours or overnight. Turn out fudge onto work surface; carefully peel off foil. Turn fudge right-side up; cut into squares. Store in refrigerator. Serve cold. Makes about 2-1/2 pounds candy.

Lacy Chocolate Cups

Fill these delicious edible cups with your favorite mousse, ice cream or chocolate-dipped fruit for a show-stopping finale!

**12 to 14 oz. semisweet chocolate, melted, cooled
  to room temperature**

To make mold, invert a 4-ounce custard cup on a work surface. *Firmly* press foil over top and down sides of cup, leaving a 1-inch "collar" around base. Use scissors to cut away excess foil. Surface of foil should be as smooth as possible and form a sharp crease at base of cup where collar begins. Mold will be shaped like a man's hat. Making sure foil is pressed as tightly as possible against cup will insure a strong mold. Gently lift foil mold off custard cup. Repeat 5 more times to make 6 foil molds. Place molds, open-end down, on a baking sheet that will fit into your refrigerator.

To make cups, make a decorator cone out of waxed or parchment paper, page 22, or use a pastry bag. Fit decorator cone or pastry bag with a #3 or #4 writing tip. Fill cone or pastry bag halfway with melted chocolate. Chocolate should be fairly cool in order to hold its shape when piped. Pipe a circle of chocolate around bottom edge of mold, being careful not to get any chocolate on foil collar. Continue piping chocolate in a continuous drizzle over bottom and sides of each mold in a open lacy design. Refrigerate 10 minutes or until chocolate is set. Refill cone or pastry bag with melted chocolate as necessary. Repeat with a second layer of chocolate drizzle, this time making sure bottoms of cups are almost solid chocolate so any soft filling will not seep through. Sides of chocolate cups should be in a tight lacy pattern. Refrigerate 30 minutes. Using a sharp pointed knife, cut away any excess chocolate that may have run down onto collar of molds.

To complete cups, place right-side-up on a baking sheet. Remove foil by slowly and *carefully* pulling it away from sides, then bottom of chocolate cups. Do not handle chocolate any more than necessary or the heat of your hands will cause it to melt. Using a #14 or #16 star tip, pipe chocolate rosettes around top edge of cups. Chocolate must be fairly cool in order for star pattern to show. Refrigerate until rosettes are firm. Fill cups with your favorite mousse, ice cream or Chocolate-Dipped Fruits & Nuts, page 98. Mousse must be quite thick in order not to seep through sides of cups. Return filled cups to refrigerator, or freezer for ice-cream filling, until ready to serve. Unfilled cups may be covered with plastic wrap and stored several weeks in your refrigerator. Makes 6 cups.

Delicious Fillings for Chocolate Cups

Spoon your favorite filling into white- or dark-chocolate cups to create an exciting dessert!
Zabaglione Freddo, page 84, flavored with orange-flavored liqueur
Macaroon Madness, page 113
Strawberry-Soirée filling, page 16
Strawberry-Champagne Silk, page 121
Black-Magic Mousse, page 119
Celestial Cream, page 84
Gingered Pear Whip, page 97
White-Chocolate Mousse, page 120
Your favorite ice cream.

Chocolate Clay

For years, pastry chefs have used this pliable chocolate to create beautiful and easy decorations. It looks spectacular and tastes delicious. Go ahead and have some fun with it!

8 oz. semisweet chocolate, coarsely chopped	**1/3 cup light corn syrup**
	Powdered sugar

To make Chocolate-Clay sheets, line a small baking sheet with plastic wrap. Place chocolate in top of a double boiler over simmering water until almost melted. Remove top of double boiler from heat; stir chocolate until completely melted. Add corn syrup; stir until mixture is smooth, Turn out onto lined baking sheet; spread to a 1/4-inch thickness. Cover with another layer of plastic wrap. Set aside in a cool place 4 to 6 hours or until mixture becomes firm enough to knead. Or, refrigerate 30 to 45 minutes. Knead 1 to 2 minutes or until pliable.

To roll out Chocolate-Clay sheets by hand, lightly sprinkle a smooth work surface with powdered sugar. Work with 1/2 of clay at a time; cover remaining clay. Using a rolling pin dusted with powdered sugar, roll mixture into 1/16- to 1/8-inch-thick sheets. Brush excess powdered sugar off clay using a pastry brush.

To roll out Chocolate-Clay sheets with a pasta machine, set machine to widest setting. Divide chocolate into about 6 pieces. Cover pieces you are not working on. Run each piece through pasta machine at widest setting. Adjust machine to next thinner setting; run chocolate pieces through machine. Repeat with thinner settings until chocolate sheets are about 1/16 to 1/8 inch thick. If chocolate sticks to machine, let sheets stand, uncovered, 10 minutes to dry.

Cut rolled-out clay into designs or shape as directed below. Unused chocolate clay may be wrapped and refrigerated several months.

To resoften, place plastic-wrapped clay in a microwave oven set at 50% power 10 to 20 seconds. Or, place wrapped mixture in a 200F (95C) oven 2 to 5 minutes. Knead until mixture is pliable.

Variations

White-Chocolate Clay: Substitute white chocolate for semisweet chocolate. If desired, immediately after stirring in corn syrup, use paste food coloring to tint chocolate.

Chocolate-Clay Strips: Use to wrap around cakes, cheesecakes, tortes and other desserts. Measure the circumference and height of the dessert you are banding with clay. Add 1/4 inch to circumference measurement to allow for an overlap. Cut a chocolate strip to equal those measurements. If your chocolate sheets are not long enough to cut the length of strip you need, cut 2 strips, each 1/2 of length of the dessert's circumference (adding a 1/4 inch to both strips for overlap). Wrap chocolate strips around sides of dessert, overlapping and pressing the ends together. Lightly press chocolate-clay strips into sides of dessert. Refrigerate until ready to serve.

Chocolate Nests: Pastel-colored white-chocolate clay makes beautiful nests for Easter eggs. Line a large baking sheet with waxed paper. Run chocolate sheets through fettuccine attachment of pasta machine to create chocolate strands. To clean machine, run a folded piece of paper towel through attachment. Chocolate sheets can also be cut into strands about 1/4 inch wide using a sharp knife. On prepared baking sheet, place mounds of strands the size you wish the finished nest(s) to be. Using your hands, lightly toss each mound until strands randomly intertwine. Press down in center of nest to form a flat bottom; pull up side strands to form nest's raised rim. Cover and refrigerate until firm. Use a large metal spatula to transfer nest(s) to a serving plate. Fill with Marzipan Easter Eggs, page 136, Chocolate-Dipped Fruit or Nuts, page 98, or other candies or candy-coated nuts in this chapter.

Chocolate-Clay Fettuccine: Use to decorate tops of cakes, cheesecakes, pies and other desserts. Prepare chocolate strands as for Chocolate Nests, above. Strands should be no longer than 8 inches. Toss strands to entwine.

How to Make Chocolate Clay

1/Run Chocolate Clay through pasta machine, adjusting settings until sheets are about 1/16 to 1/8 inch thick. Cut rolled-out clay into designs or shape as desired.

2/To make Chocolate-Clay Nests or Fettuccine, run clay through fettuccine attachment of pasta machine to create chocolate strands. Shape as desired.

Chocolate-Clay Scrolls: Stand scrolls vertically to decorate sides of cakes, tortes or other desserts. Or, arrange them horizontally on a loaf-shaped dessert, or in a pinwheel fashion on a round dessert. Cut chocolate-clay sheets into 2-inch-wide strips. Measure width or height of dessert you wish to garnish; cut strips to conform to your measurements. Use your hands to roll each strip into a tight scroll shape, overlapping edge 1/4 to 1/8 inch. Refrigerate until firm. Garnish dessert with scrolls, seam-side down.
Harlequin Chocolate-Clay Scrolls: Use half white-chocolate clay and half dark-chocolate clay to create scrolls.

Note: To give chocolate-clay creations an added sheen, spray lightly with vegetable cooking spray.

TIP

Before melting chocolate, lightly butter inside of pan. When chocolate melts, it won't stick to the pan.

Cappuccino-Fudge Roll

An easy Kahlúa-laced fudge, scented with cinnamon and rolled in toasted nuts.

1 (8-oz.) pkg. cream cheese, softened
3/8 teaspoon ground cinnamon
1/8 teaspoon salt
1/4 cup Kahlúa, other coffee-flavored
    liqueur or whipping cream
1 tablespoon instant coffee powder or
    granules dissolved in
    2 teaspoons very hot water

6 oz. unsweetened chocolate, melted, cooled
About 5 cups sifted powdered sugar
2 to 2-1/2 cups toasted finely chopped
    almonds, walnuts or pecans

In a large mixer bowl, beat cream cheese, cinnamon and salt until perfectly smooth. Gradually beat in liqueur or cream, and coffee liquid. Add melted chocolate; beat until blended. Add powdered sugar, 1 cup at a time, beating well after each addition. Stir in 1 cup nuts. Cover and refrigerate 1 hour or until firm enough to shape. Place remaining 1 to 1-1/2 cups nuts on a baking sheet or large plate. Divide fudge into 4 equal portions. Working with 1 portion of fudge at a time, place fudge in center of a 12-inch length of plastic wrap. Fold long sides of plastic wrap over fudge. With your palms, roll wrapped fudge into a log, 1-1/2 inches in diameter. Carefully remove plastic wrap and roll log in chopped nuts. Wrap in plastic wrap; twist ends to seal. Repeat with remaining 3 portions of fudge and nuts. Refrigerate overnight. Cut into 1/2-inch slices. Let stand at room temperature 20 minutes before serving. Fudge can be refrigerated up to 1 month. Makes about 2-1/4 pounds candy.

Mocha Creams

Photos opposite and on page 5.

Tiny chocolate cups filled with luscious mocha cream—wonderful with after-dinner coffee.

Miniature Chocolate Cups, page 130
1/2 cup butter, softened
4 oz. cream cheese, softened
1/3 cup powdered sugar
2 egg yolks

8 oz. semisweet chocolate, melted, cooled
1 tablespoon instant espresso coffee powder
    dissolved in 1 tablespoon very hot water
30 coffee-bean candies

Prepare Miniature Chocolate Cups; refrigerate. In a small mixer bowl, beat butter, cream cheese and powdered sugar until light and fluffy. Add egg yolks, 1 at a time, beating well after each addition. Add chocolate and coffee liquid; beat until smooth. If mixture is very soft, refrigerate 30 minutes until firm enough to pipe. Using a pastry bag fitted with a 1/2-inch plain round tip or a large star tip, pipe cream-cheese mixture into chocolate cups. Place a coffee-bean candy on top of each confection, pressing down slightly to anchor. Cover and refrigerate until ready to serve. May be tightly covered and frozen up to 2 months. Makes 30 confections.

Chocolate Truffles, page 125; Coffee-Glazed Macadamia Nuts, page 143; and Mocha Creams, above.

Marzipan Easter Eggs in Baskets

These tiny temptations are so much fun to make that kids of all ages will be begging to help!

1/4 cup margarine, softened
1/2 cup almond paste, softened
1 (7-oz.) jar marshmallow creme
1/8 teaspoon salt
1 teaspoon vanilla extract
4 to 5 cups powdered sugar
Paste food coloring

Jelly beans and toasted, whole,
    blanched almonds, if desired
6 to 8 oz. semisweet or milk chocolate,
    if desired, melted, cooled
Miniature White-Chocolate Easter Baskets,
    page 138

Line 1 or 2 large baking sheets with waxed paper. In a small mixer bowl, beat margarine and almond paste until smooth. Add marshmallow creme, salt and vanilla; beat until blended. Stir in 4 cups powdered sugar, 1 cup at a time, blending well after each addition. Turn out mixture onto a work surface dusted with powdered sugar. Knead in enough additional sugar until mixture is firm, smooth and has the consistency of putty. Divide marzipan into as many portions as you wish different Easter-egg colors. Flatten each section into a 3-inch circle; dot in 3 to 4 places with food coloring. Be careful, a little coloring goes a long way, and light pastel shades are traditional for Easter. Fold marzipan over color dots and gently knead dough until coloring has evenly tinted entire piece. For marbled eggs, stop kneading while color is still in streaks. Work with 1 section of marzipan at a time, covering remaining sections with plastic wrap.

To form eggs, pinch off a piece of marzipan about the size of a small prune. Roll it between your palms to form a ball; gently taper ends to form egg shape. For two-tone eggs, pinch off 2 pieces of marzipan, each the size of 1/2 a small prune. Roll each piece between your palms to form 2 (3-inch) ropes. Twist ropes together, then form eggs as directed above. If desired, place a jelly bean or whole almond inside marzipan before forming egg. Marzipan eggs may be decorated by dipping a wooden pick or fine-tipped brush into food color then drawing designs on egg. Place finished eggs on lined baking sheets. Let stand uncovered overnight or until surface is dry to the touch and eggs are firm. If desired, spear dried eggs with a wooden pick and dip into melted chocolate. Place chocolate-dipped eggs on a waxed-paper-lined baking sheets; refrigerate until chocolate is set. Store undipped eggs in an airtight container at room temperature. Store chocolate-dipped eggs, covered, in refrigerator. Eggs can be kept up to 3 months. If refrigerated, let eggs stand at room temperature 30 minutes before serving. Arrange eggs in Miniature White-Chocolate Easter Baskets. Makes about 40 (1-1/2-inch) Easter eggs.

 TIP *Leftover almond paste can be wrapped airtight and frozen. Defrost at room temperature before using.*

How to Make Marzipan Easter Eggs in Baskets

1/For two-tone eggs, pinch off 2 pieces of marzipan, each the size of 1/2 a small prune. Roll each piece between your palms to form 2 (3-inch) ropes. Twist ropes together, then roll between your palms to form an egg.

2/Fill Miniature White-Chocolate Easter Baskets with flowers, if desired, and Marzipan Easter Eggs.

Apricot-Amaretto Confections

Apricots stuffed with amaretto cream and jacketed in chocolate, deliver a delightful sweet-tart taste!

1/4 cup packed almond paste, softened
1 tablespoon butter, softened
1-1/2 tablespoons amaretto liqueur
Dash of salt

64 moist-pack dried-apricot halves
6 oz. semisweet chocolate, melted, cooled
About 1 cup toasted finely chopped almonds,
   if desired

Line a large baking sheet with waxed paper. In a small bowl, beat almond paste, butter, liqueur and salt until creamy. Place a scant 1/2 teaspoon almond mixture in center of 32 apricot halves. Top with remaining apricot halves, matching sizes as closely as possible. Lightly press halves together to spread filling evenly. Place melted chocolate in a small deep bowl. Dip apricot "sandwiches" halfway into chocolate; drain excess chocolate on rim of bowl. Dip chocolate portion into almonds, if desired. Place on prepared baking sheet; refrigerate until set. Let stand at room temperature 10 minutes before serving. If desired, place each confection in a paper candy cup; arrange on pretty serving plate. Makes 32 confections.

Variation
Saturday-Night Dates: Substitute 32 pitted dates for apricot halves. Cut dates in half lengthwise; fill and press halves together as directed above. Dip into 6 ounces melted white chocolate instead of semisweet chocolate.

Miniature White-Chocolate Easter Baskets

Photo on page 137.

Fill these beautiful baskets with Marzipan Easter Eggs for an Easter brunch surprise.

16 oz. white chocolate, melted, cooled
Paste food coloring, if desired
6 candied violets, if desired
12 candied mint leaves, if desired

Fresh flowers, if desired
Easter grass, if desired
Marzipan Easter Eggs, page 136, if desired

For pastel Easter baskets, tint melted white chocolate with paste food coloring. Using a wooden pick, add tiny amounts of paste food coloring and blend until chocolate reaches desired color. Make chocolate baskets following directions for Lacy Chocolate Cups, page 131. Handles are optional for these Easter baskets.

To make handles, use a large baking sheet that will fit into your refrigerator; line with waxed paper. Measure diameter of a chocolate basket. Using a pencil, draw 6 well-spaced lines equal to the basket's diameter on the waxed paper. Draw an arc in the shape of a handle, connecting the 2 ends of each line. Using a #14 or #15 star tip, pipe chocolate in an open zigzag following the handle pattern. Pipe a second zigzag over the first, going in the opposite direction to form a woven-look handle. Chocolate must be fairly cool for star pattern to show in chocolate. Refrigerate 15 minutes or until firm. Gently peel waxed paper from back of chocolate handles. Return handles, flat side up, to waxed paper-lined baking sheet. Pipe chocolate in a double zigzag pattern as for first side. Refrigerate until chocolate is firm.

To complete baskets, remove handles from waxed paper. Attach to baskets using 2 ample blobs of melted chocolate as "glue." Lightly balance handle in place with the palm of your hand a few seconds until chocolate sets and handle stands by itself. If desired, reinforce handles by dabbing additional melted chocolate around handle bases. If desired, attach a candied violet and 2 mint leaves at the center top of each handle with chocolate "glue." Refrigerate until ready to use. Fill with fresh flowers, Easter grass and Marzipan Easter Eggs, if desired. These baskets may be made well in advance. Cover well with plastic wrap; refrigerate until ready to use. Cover and store handles separately and attach before filling. Makes 6 miniature chocolate baskets.

TIP

Paste food coloring is a highly concentrated coloring sold in cake-decorating-supply shops and the gourmet section of some supermarkets. It must be used when tinting white chocolate because liquid coloring would cause the chocolate to harden and clump. Paste food coloring is also wonderful for buttercream frostings because it does not dilute the mixture. Dip a wooden pick into the paste color, then into the mixture you are coloring. Blend in a little at a time until desired tint is reached.

Cream-Puff Pastries

Years ago, Maida Heatter gave me the inspiration for the delicious chocolate version of this classic.

1 cup water	1 cup all-purpose flour
1/2 cup butter, cut in 6 pieces	4 eggs
1/8 teaspoon salt	1 teaspoon vanilla extract
1 tablespoon sugar	

If you do not have double ovens, it is best to make these pastries in 2 batches, rather than crowding them in 1 oven. Position rack in center of oven and preheat to 400F (205C). Lightly grease 2 large baking sheets. Place each greased baking sheet on another ungreased baking sheet. Double sheets will prevent bottoms of pastries from becoming too brown. In a medium saucepan, combine water, butter, salt and sugar. Cook over medium heat until butter melts and water comes to a boil. Remove from heat; reduce heat to low. Add flour all at once; stir rapidly with a wooden spoon until mixture leaves sides of pan. Return pan to low heat. Stirring occasionally, cook 2 to 3 minutes to dry flour mixture. This drying procedure creates a mixture called a *panade*. Transfer panade to a small mixer bowl. Beat at medium speed 1 minute to reduce temperature of mixture to 145F (65C). A higher temperature will coagulate the eggs and prevent the paste from rising to its maximum in the oven. With mixer set at medium-low speed, add eggs, 1 at a time, beating until mixture is smooth after each addition. Beat in vanilla. Or, use a wooden spoon and beat by hand. Batter will separate into clumps after the addition of each egg, but will become smooth with beating. Drop by heaping tablespoons 2 to 3 inches apart on prepared baking sheets. Mounds should be high and rounded. Or, spoon batter into a pastry bag fitted with a large, round, 5/8-inch tip. Pipe into mounds about 2 inches wide and 1-1/2 inches high. Wet your fingertip and smooth any sharp peaks. Bake 25 to 30 minutes or until crisp and golden brown. Don't open oven during first 15 minutes baking time. Remove pastries from oven; turn off oven. Stick the point of a small knife in 2 or 3 places in sides of each pastry. Return pastries to oven 1 hour to continue drying with oven door propped open 1 to 3 inches. Remove pastries from baking sheets; cool completely on racks. To fill, cut top 1/3 off each pastry. Remove any soft dough from center. Fill with Black-Magic Mousse, page 119, Lemon-Berry Mousse, page 118, or Strawberry-Champagne Silk, page 121. Or, use for Raspberry Cream Puffs, page 141, Giant Black Forest Cream-Puff Sundae, page 122, or Paris-Brest with Praline Cream, page 140. Unfilled pastries may be prepared a day in advance and wrapped airtight until ready to use. They may also be sealed in a plastic bag and frozen up to 3 months. Recrisp by baking frozen pastries 5 to 10 minutes at 325F (165C). Makes about 12 to 14 pastries.

Variation

Chocolate Cream-Puff Pastries: Increase sugar to 2 tablespoons; reduce flour to 3/4 cup. Stir 2 tablespoons unsweetened cocoa into flour before adding to hot liquid. Bake puffs an additional 5 minutes.

Amaretto Cream-Puff Pastries: Omit sugar. Substitute 1/2 cup amaretto liqueur for 1/2 cup water. Substitute 3/4 teaspoon almond extract for 1 teaspoon vanilla extract.

Spiced Cream-Puff Pastries: Add 1/2 teaspoon ground cinnamon and 1/2 teaspoon ground nutmeg to water before bringing to a boil.

Paris-Brest with Praline Cream *Photo on page 5.*

A large cream-puff-pastry ring filled with praline cream—très élégante!

Cream-Puff paste (dough), page 139
1 egg mixed with 1 tablespoon cream
  for glaze

1/3 cup sliced almonds
Praline Cream, see below
Powdered sugar

Praline Cream:
1-1/2 cups sugar
1 tablespoon lemon juice
2 cups toasted finely chopped almonds

2-1/2 cups whipping cream
1/3 cup amaretto liqueur, if desired

Preheat oven to 425F (220C). Lightly grease and flour a large baking sheet; set on another ungreased baking sheet. Invert a 9-inch bowl or pan on center of prepared baking sheet. Twist slightly then remove to mark a circle in flour. Prepare Cream-Puff paste. Spoon into a large pastry bag fitted with a 1/2-inch plain tip. Pipe paste in 3 thick rings; the first following the outline in the flour; the second just inside the first; and the third on top, centered on the first 2 rings. Smooth section where ends of rings meet with your wet fingertip. Brush rings with egg glaze; sprinkle with sliced almonds. Bake 10 minutes. Reduce oven temperature to 375F (190C); bake 25 minutes longer. Remove ring from oven. Stick the point of a small knife into lower edge of pastry every 2 inches to allow steam to escape. Return to oven; bake 10 minutes longer or until crisp and golden brown. Turn off oven. Let pastry ring cool in oven 1 hour with oven door propped open 1 to 3 inches. Using a metal spatula, gently loosen ring from baking sheet; transfer to a rack to cool completely. Prepare Praline Cream. Using a long-bladed serrated knife, split ring in half. Remove any soft dough from center. Place bottom 1/2 of ring on a serving plate. Pipe or spoon Praline Cream into ring. Lightly dust top of ring with powdered sugar; place over filling. Refrigerate up to 6 hours. Makes 10 to 12 servings.

Praline Cream:

Generously grease a 15" x 10" jelly-roll pan. In a large heavy skillet, combine sugar and lemon juice. Cook over low heat without stirring until sugar begins to melt. Continue cooking, stirring constantly, until mixture turns a rich caramel color. Remove from heat; stir in 1-1/4 cup almonds, coating nuts thoroughly. Immediately pour nut mixture into prepared pan; spread in pan. Cool until hardened. Break into 1-inch pieces; place in a blender or food processor fitted with a metal blade. Process to a coarse powder; set aside. If using a blender, it will be necessary to grind praline pieces in 2 or 3 batches. In a large mixer bowl, beat cream to soft-peak stage. Beating constantly, gradually drizzle in liqueur, if desired. Beat until cream is stiff. Gently fold in praline powder and remaining 3/4 cup almonds.

TIP *Remove lumps from powdered sugar by processing 30 seconds in a food processor.*

Raspberry Cream Puffs

An easy dessert to assemble if you prepare puffs, filling and sauce ahead of time.

Raspberry Filling, see below
Cream-Puff Pastries, page 139

Fudge Velvet Sauce, page 150
Chocolate Curls, page 126

Raspberry Filling:
**2 (10-oz.) pkgs. thawed frozen
  raspberries in syrup**
1 (3-oz.) pkg. raspberry-flavored gelatin

1-1/3 cups whipping cream, firmly whipped
Fresh raspberries, if desired
Mint leaves, if desired

Place thawed raspberries in a colander set in a medium bowl. Cover and refrigerate overnight to drain thoroughly; reserve juice. Prepare Cream-Puff Pastries. Using a serrated knife, split 8 pastry puffs horizontally in half; keep tops and bottoms together. Remove and discard any soft dough from center. Set halved puffs aside. Wrap and freeze remaining pastries for another use. Prepare Fudge Velvet Sauce; set aside at room temperature. Complete preparation of Raspberry Filling; refrigerate. Prepare Chocolate Curls; refrigerate.

To complete cream puffs, using a pastry bag with a large star tip, decoratively pipe raspberry mixture into bottom half of each pastry puff. Place on individual dessert plates. Place top half of each puff over raspberry-cream mixture; drizzle each filled puff with Fudge Velvet Sauce. Garnish each serving with Chocolate Curls, fresh raspberries and mint leaves, if desired. Pass additional sauce with dessert. Makes 8 servings.

Raspberry Filling:
Sprinkle gelatin over bottom of a small bowl or 2-cup glass measuring cup; set aside. Pour 1 cup reserved raspberry juice into a small saucepan; bring to a boil. Pour hot juice over gelatin in bowl; stir to dissolve. Pour hot mixture into a blender; add drained raspberries. Process until pureed. Using a rubber spatula, work raspberry mixture through a fine sieve into a large bowl. Refrigerate, stirring occasionally, until mixture begins to mound when spooned on top of itself. Gently fold in whipped cream, 1/3 at a time. Continue folding until no streaks remain. Refrigerate 30 minutes or until mixture is consistency of very firm whipped cream.

Note: If Fudge Velvet Sauce becomes too thick, place it in a container and set in a large bowl of hot water. Stir until desired consistency.

TIP

If you accidentally overbeat whipping cream so that it begins to turn buttery, gradually whisk in additional cream, 1 tablespoon at a time. Do not beat any more than necessary.

Turinois Terrine

Layers of white chocolate, chestnut puree and Candied Orange Zest ribbon this spectacular dessert terrine.

Candied Orange Zest, opposite
1 (3-oz.) pkg. cream cheese, softened
3 oz. white chocolate, melted,
  cooled until slightly warm
2 egg yolks
1/2 teaspoon vanilla extract
1 (15- to 16-oz.) can unsweetened
  chestnut puree

1/3 cup butter, softened
1/2 cup powdered sugar
8 oz. semisweet chocolate, melted, cooled
1/4 cup Strega liqueur, orange-flavored
  liqueur or whipping cream
Tipsy Crème Anglaise, page 149, if desired,
  flavored with orange-flavored liqueur
Bittersweet-Chocolate Glaze, page 147

Prepare Candied Orange Zest; set aside.

To prepare mold, tear off a 16″ x 12″ piece of foil. Cut lengthwise into 2 strips; 1 measuring 16″ x 3-1/2″, and the other measuring 16″ x 8-1/2″. Fit 8-1/2-inch-wide piece of foil crosswise in an 8″ x 4″ loaf pan. Firmly press foil against sides of pan, allowing excess to hang over edges of pan. Foil should be as smooth as possible so surface of terrine is smooth when unmolded. Repeat with 3-1/2-inch-wide strip of foil, placing it lengthwise in pan. Upper corners of pan will not be completely covered with foil. Lightly oil foil and exposed pan corners.

To make terrine, beat cream cheese, white chocolate, 1 egg yolk and vanilla until smooth in a small mixer bowl. Fold in 2/3 cup Candied Orange Zest; set aside. In a large mixer bowl, beat chestnut puree, butter, powdered sugar and remaining egg yolk until smooth. Gradually beat in semisweet chocolate, then liqueur. Spoon 1/2 of chestnut mixture, about 1-3/4 cups, into prepared pan. Press down firmly with the back of a spoon, making sure surface is level. Cover with white-chocolate mixture; smooth and level surface. Top with remaining chestnut mixture. Smooth surface, spreading mixture into corners of pan. Fold excess foil over terrine so it touches and completely seals surface. Refrigerate overnight. Prepare Tipsy Crème Anglaise, if desired; refrigerate at least 4 hours before serving. Prepare Bittersweet-Chocolate Glaze; cool to room temperature. Line a small baking sheet with waxed paper.

To loosen terrine, run a thin knife around inside edges of pan, between pan and foil. Gently remove terrine from pan by lifting with flaps of foil used to cover terrine. Invert foil-covered terrine onto prepared baking sheet; gently remove foil. Dampen a metal spoon with water. Use back of spoon to smooth any indentations in terrine.

To complete terrine, pour 1/3 of Bittersweet Chocolate Glaze over surface of terrine. Using a narrow, metal, spreading spatula, smooth glaze evenly over top and down sides of terrine. Refrigerate 5 minutes to set glaze. Repeat glazing and refrigerating process with 1/2 of remaining glaze. Spread on remaining glaze. Immediately after last layer of glaze has been smoothed over terrine, sprinkle top with remaining 1/3 cup Candied Orange Zest. Lightly press into surface. Refrigerate until ready to serve. Immediately before serving, use a knife to trace around base of terrine on waxed paper. This will separate any chocolate glaze that has drizzled down onto waxed paper. Using 2 large metal spatulas, carefully slide terrine off waxed paper onto a serving plate. Use a thin sharp knife to cut terrine into thin slices. If necessary, wipe blade of knife with a paper towel between slices. If desired, ladle about 1/4 cup Tipsy Crème Anglaise onto each serving plate; place a slice of Turinois Terrine in center of sauce. Makes 10 to 12 servings.

Candied Orange Zest
Photo on page 151.

Use any citrus zest to form these delicate shimmering strands—instant elegance for any dessert!

2 medium oranges
1 cup sugar

1/2 cup water

Using a citrus zester, remove outer zest of oranges in long thin strands. Or, using a sharp paring knife, remove colored part of peel from orange; julienne finely. In a small saucepan, combine 3/4 cup sugar, water and orange zest over high heat. Bring to a full rolling boil; reduce heat to simmer. Cover and cook without stirring 15 minutes. Strain off syrup; reserve for pancakes or waffles, if desired. Place orange zest on a large lightly greased plate. Using 2 forks, separate zest into individual strands. Cool 10 minutes. Sprinkle cooled zest with remaining 1/4 cup sugar. Using your fingers or 2 forks, toss zest with sugar as you would pasta. Peel must be thoroughly coated with sugar. Transfer zest and sugar to a sheet of waxed paper, making sure strands are separate. Let dry overnight in sugar. Remove zest from sugar. Store in an airtight container at room temperature up to 2 weeks. May be refrigerated up to 3 months. Makes about 1 cup.

Coffee-Glazed Macadamia Nuts
Photo on page 135.

Let the sweet coffee-flavored glaze melt in your mouth before biting into the delectable macadamias.

2/3 cup water
2 cups sugar
1/3 cup instant coffee powder or
** granules dissolved in 3 tablespoons**
** very hot water**

4 cups toasted macadamia nuts or
** toasted whole blanched almonds**

Grease 2 large baking sheets. In a medium, heavy saucepan, combine water and sugar. Cook over medium heat without stirring until a medium caramel color. Remove from heat. Slowly and carefully add coffee liquid, using a long-handled wooden spoon to stir. Be careful because mixture will bubble and steam. Add nuts, stirring rapidly to coat evenly with glaze. Immediately turn out onto prepared baking sheets. Using 2 forks, quickly pull nuts apart as much as possible. Set on racks on sheets until completely cool. Break nuts apart, if desired. Store in an airtight container up to 3 weeks. Makes about 6 cups.

 TIP

A good-quality citrus zester is necessary to obtain long thin strands of citrus zest. Press firmly as you draw the zester down along the skin of a citrus fruit.

CROWNING TOUCHES

Some desserts simply demand a crowning touch—either by tradition, like steamed puddings with their sauces—or by necessity, as with the frosting on most cakes. Ice cream doesn't really need a topping, but somehow becomes more festive when drizzled with a gooey-good sauce or sprinkled with crunchy praline. Fruit pies certainly don't require adornment, but become doubly delicious with just a dollop of Plain Whipped Cream or one of the many variations suggested in the recipe. And, though strawberries are perfectly wonderful on their own, they are eminently more elegant when lightly dipped into Grand Marnier-scented Tipsy Crème Anglaise. The simple truth is that sauces, frostings and other toppings often add the perfect finishing touch to an otherwise rather everyday dessert.

A dessert sauce should complement or reflect the flavor of the dish it adorns. But it should also be delicious on its own! Sauces may be hot or cold; cooked or uncooked. Many uncooked sauces acquire their flavor and body from fruit puree, and can easily be tailored to a particular dessert by changing the fruit.

Other sauces are sugar-based and thickened by cooking. A candy thermometer aids in testing these mixtures. The thermometer bulb should be completely immersed in the liquid being cooked, but must not touch the bottom of the pan. If not handled correctly, a cooked sugar sauce can turn from a smooth, homogeneous mixture into a gritty, o-paque mass—all within the blink of an eye! This calamity is referred to as *sugaring* or *crystallization*. It's usually caused by stirring the sugar crystals clinging to the sides of a pan back down into the bubbling sugar mixture, which has a completely different crystal structure. This problem is why some recipes instruct that the sauce *not* be stirred. One easy way to dissolve unwanted sugar crystals is to cover the pan for two or three minutes. This creates steam, which melts the clinging crystals and washes them down into the liquid below.

Many sauce recipes reduce the crystallization problem by adding corn syrup, which won't crystallize, or butter, which lubricates the mixture and prevents crystals from forming. Hot Caramel Sauce has a high ratio of de-crystallization aids in the form of corn syrup, butter and cream. It can therefore be stirred without risk of sugaring. Corn syrup is used in many cooked frostings for the same reason.

Whether you call it *frosting* or *icing* depends on what part of the country you're from. But we all know both words refer to a delicious, sugary coating for everything from cakes to cookies. *"It's the frosting on the cake!"* is a phrase sometimes used to describe a wonderful occurrence. And, for many people, it's the frosting that makes the cake worth eating. Before frosting a cake, use a pastry brush to whisk any crumbs from its surface. If a cake is extremely soft, a *crumb coating* will prevent excess crumbs from being pulled into the frosting, marring its finish. Simply spread a *very* thin coating of frosting on the cake to seal the surface, set the crumbs and fill in any imperfections. Allow this coating to dry before applying the remaining frosting. Whether working with a thick, fluffy frosting like Chocolate-Ganache Soufflé, or a thin, liquid mixture like Bittersweet-Chocolate Glaze, a flexible, metal, spreading spatula greatly aids spreading.

Toppings add eye appeal and flavor excitement to almost any dessert. They can range from billowy, cloudlike frostings to silky smooth sauces to butter-crunchy crumbles. They can be simple, exotic or just plain fun! Dry toppings, such as Praline Crunch, Toasted Coconut and Sugar-Nut Crumble can be made well in advance, stored in airtight containers, and used at a moments notice. Remember, any dessert can be turned into an "event" with the simple addition of a delicious "crowning touch!"

144

Toasted Coconut

Photo on page 151.

Wonderful as a garnish for pies, cake and puddings—great sprinkled over your favorite ice cream!

1 cup shredded or flaked coconut

Preheat oven to 350F (175C). Spread coconut in a single layer over bottom of an ungreased jelly-roll pan. Stirring frequently, toast in oven 5 to 8 minutes or until crisp and golden brown. Store in an airtight container at room temperature several months. Makes about 1 cup.

Praline Crunch

Photo on page 151.

This beautiful shiny candy will add a sparkling finish to any dessert.

3 tablespoons water   **1 cup toasted chopped pecans**
2/3 cup sugar

Grease a medium jelly-roll pan. In a small heavy saucepan, stir together water and sugar. Cook over medium heat, without stirring, until a medium caramel color. Add nuts; stir to coat evenly with caramel. Pour praline into prepared pan, spreading evenly. Cool until hardened. Coarsely crush praline into 1/4-inch pieces by sealing in a plastic bag and using a rolling pin. Store praline in an airtight container at room temperature up to 1 month. Makes about 1-1/2 cups.

Mocha Candy Topping

A quick candy topping that's great sprinkled over chocolate- and coffee-flavored desserts.

1/2 cup sugar   **1 teaspoon unsweetened cocoa**
2 tablespoons water   **1/8 teaspoon ground cinnamon**
1/2 teaspoon instant coffee powder
  or granules

Grease a small baking sheet. In a small saucepan, combine sugar and water. Cook over high heat, without stirring, until mixture turns a light caramel color; remove from heat. Add remaining ingredients; stir just until blended. Pour onto prepared baking sheet. Cool on a rack until hard. Break into pieces; crush to desired texture by sealing in a plastic bag and using a rolling pin. Store in an airtight container at room temperature up to 3 months. Makes 1/2 cup.

TIP *For a change of pace, try the unsweetened flaked or chipped coconut found in health-food stores. Toasted, it's a delightfully crunchy, sugar-free snack, or topping for fresh fruit.*

Sugar-Nut Crumble

Photo on page 151.

Sprinkle this crunchy topping over ice cream, fresh fruit, puddings or mousses.

1 cup chopped nuts	**1 tablespoon cornstarch**
1/2 cup packed brown sugar	**3 tablespoons butter, melted**

Preheat oven to 325F (165C). In a medium bowl, stir together nuts, brown sugar and cornstarch. Add butter; stir until combined. Pat mixture over bottom of an ungreased 13″ x 9″ baking pan. Bake about 15 minutes or until lightly browned. Cool in pan on a rack. Crumble finely or coarsely, as desired. Store in an airtight container in refrigerator up to 1 month or freeze up to 3 months. Makes about 2 cups.

Fluffy Frosting

Use one of the many variations of this easy frosting as a delicious finish for your favorite cake.

1-1/4 cups sugar	**3 egg whites, room temperature**
1/3 cup water	**2 tablespoons sugar**
1 tablespoon light corn syrup	**1 teaspoon vanilla extract**
1/8 teaspoon salt	

In a medium saucepan, stir together 1-1/4 cups sugar, water, corn syrup and salt. Cook over medium heat, without stirring, until mixture comes to a full rolling boil and sugar has dissolved. Remove from heat. While sugar mixture is heating, beat egg whites to soft-peak stage in a large mixer bowl. Beating constantly, gradually add 2 tablespoons sugar. Continue beating until mixture is stiff but not dry. With mixer running at high speed, *slowly* drizzle hot sugar syrup into egg whites. Add vanilla; beat until frosting is fluffy and stands in stiff peaks. Fills and frosts 1 (2- or 3-layer) 8- to 10-inch cake. Makes about 6 cups.

Variations
Lane-Cake Frosting: Substitute 3 tablespoons dark corn syrup for 1 tablespoon light corn syrup.
Fluffy Praline Frosting: Substitute packed dark brown sugar for granulated sugar, and dark corn syrup for light corn syrup. Fold 1 cup toasted finely chopped pecans into finished frosting.
Fluffy Orange Frosting: Substitute thawed frozen orange-juice concentrate for water. Omit vanilla. Fold freshly grated zest from 1 medium orange into finished frosting.
Maple-Fluff Frosting: Substitute 1/2 cup plus 2 tablespoons sugar for 1-1/4 cups sugar, and 2/3 cup pure maple syrup for 1/3 cup water and 1 tablespoon corn syrup.
Fluffy Chocolate Frosting: Fold 3 ounces cooled, melted unsweetened chocolate into finished frosting.
Rocky-Road Frosting: Fold 3/4 cup *each* miniature marshmallows and chopped walnuts, and 2 ounces cooled, melted unsweetened chocolate into finished frosting.
Jelly-Fluff Frosting: Substitute 1/2 cup fruit-flavored jelly for 1/3 cup water.
Fluffy Mocha Frosting: Add 1 tablespoon instant coffee powder or granules to sugar-syrup mixture before boiling. Fold 2 ounces cooled, melted unsweetened chocolate into finished frosting.
Cherry-Fluff Frosting: Substitute maraschino-cherry juice for water. Fold 1/2 cup finely chopped maraschino cherries, thoroughly blotted dry, into finished frosting.

Chocolate-Ganache Soufflé
Photo on page 4.

Jacques Pépin taught me this classic frosting. The additional step of beating the ganache creates a lighter frosting that is referred to as a ganache soufflé.

1 pint whipping cream (2 cups)
1 tablespoon instant coffee powder or
   granules

1 lb. semisweet chocolate, coarsely chopped
1 tablespoon rum or brandy

In a medium, heavy saucepan, combine cream, instant coffee powder or granules, and chocolate. Cook over medium-low heat, stirring constantly, until chocolate has melted and mixture comes to a boil. Turn into a large mixer bowl. Let stand, stirring occasionally, until cool and very thick. Mixture may be refrigerated to speed cooling but watch carefully so it does not set. Add rum or brandy; beat at high speed until frosting is thick and fluffy. Be careful not to overbeat or frosting will become too stiff to spread easily. Fills and frosts 1 (2- or 3-layer) 8- to 10-inch cake. Makes about 5 cups.

Bittersweet-Chocolate Glaze
Photo on page 49.

Dress up cakes, tortes—even cookies—with this delicious glossy glaze made in minutes!

6 oz. bittersweet or semisweet chocolate,
   coarsely chopped
1/3 cup rum, brandy, your favorite liqueur,
   or whipping cream

3 tablespoons butter

In a small heavy saucepan, or in top of a double boiler over simmering water, combine chocolate, rum, liqueur or cream, and butter. Cook over low heat, stirring frequently, until chocolate is partially melted. Remove from heat, stir until chocolate is completely melted and glaze is satiny and smooth. Cool to room temperature; stir well before using. To speed cooling, place pan in a bowl of iced water. Stir constantly until room temperature. Makes about 1-1/3 cups.

Chocolate-Buttercream Frosting

A quick creamy-rich frosting with a delicate chocolate flavor.

3-1/3 cups powdered sugar
1/3 cup unsweetened cocoa
2/3 cup butter, softened

3 tablespoons light corn syrup
1-1/2 teaspoons vanilla extract
3 to 5 tablespoons whipping cream

In a small mixer bowl, stir together powdered sugar and cocoa. Add butter, corn syrup, vanilla and 3 tablespoons cream. Beat 1 minute at medium speed. Add 1 to 2 more tablespoons cream, beating until frosting is thick and creamy. Fills and frosts 1 (2-layer) 8- to 10-inch cake. Makes about 3 cups.

Caramel Crowns

Photo on pages 4 and 5.

Top individual desserts with these sparkling caramel creations for a crowning finish to a special meal.

1-1/3 cups sugar
1/8 teaspoon cream of tartar

1/3 cup water

Cover a cutting board with a piece of waxed paper. Generously oil exterior of 8 custard cups, 6 (4-inch) round-bottom bowls, a Bundt pan or a large (1-1/2- to 2-quart) round-bottom bowl; set aside, inverted, on covered cutting board. Size of mold chosen depends on whether you want Caramel Crown to sit on top of your dessert or completely enclose it. In a medium, heavy saucepan, combine sugar and cream of tartar. Add water; stir to combine. Cook over medium-low heat, without stirring, until mixture comes to a boil. Cover and continue boiling 3 minutes. Remove cover; continue boiling until a candy thermometer registers 310F (155C), hard-crack stage, or until mixture separates into brittle threads. Do not stir. Remove from heat. Set pan in a large bowl filled with iced water to stop cooking process. Stir caramel occasionally. Remove from iced water when caramel is thick enough to form long threads. Hold bowl(s) or pan on cutting board close to saucepan. Dip a small spoon or fork into caramel. Drizzle threads of caramel back and forth over surface of bowl(s) or pan to form a lacy pattern. Threads must be long in order for crown to be sturdy enough not to break when removed from mold. Continue draping threads of caramel over bowl(s) or pan until crown has an attractive lacy pattern. Rewarm caramel if it becomes too thick to drizzle. Set caramel-covered molds aside until caramel hardens. Line a large baking sheet with waxed paper. Gently push on bottom edge of caramel until it loosens from mold. Remove and set on lined baking sheet. Store in a cool dry place up to 6 hours before serving. Or, prepare a day ahead and store in an airtight container. Immediately before serving, place crowns on top of or over your favorite fruit compote, mousse, pudding or Chocolate Cups, page 130, filled with ice cream. Large Caramel Crowns may also top cakes and cheesecakes. Makes about 8 small or 1 large Caramel Crown.

Variation
Caramel Doily: Draw a circular pattern on a waxed-paper-lined baking sheet that matches the size of your dessert. For example, a 9-inch circle for a 9-inch cake or cheesecake; 3- or 4-inch circles for individual desserts. Lightly oil waxed paper. Drizzle caramel in a circle, following pattern outline. Fill in center of circle with drizzled caramel in a lacy design. Set aside until hardened. Immediately before serving, peel Caramel Doily off waxed paper; place on dessert.

Coventry Cream

Dip Chocolate-Dipped Fruits, page 98, into this delicious, enriched cream for a delectable treat!

2 egg yolks, room temperature
1/3 cup powdered sugar

1/2 teaspoon vanilla extract
1 cup whipping cream, whipped

In a small mixer bowl, beat egg yolks, powdered sugar and vanilla until light and creamy. Fold in whipped cream. Makes about 2-1/3 cups.

How to Make a Caramel Crown

1/Drizzle threads of caramel back and forth over surface of oiled Bundt pan to form a lacy pattern.

2/Large Caramel Crowns can be used to top cheesecakes and cakes.

Tipsy Crème Anglaise

Classic English custard cream *emboldened with spirits—cook custards over low heat to prevent curdling.*

1-3/4 cup milk
6 egg yolks, room temperature
3/4 cup sugar
1/8 teaspoon salt

1/3 cup light rum, amaretto liqueur,
    Frangelico or other hazelnut-flavored
    liqueur or orange-flavored liqueur
1 teaspoon vanilla extract

In a medium saucepan, scald milk by heating until bubbles form around edge of pan; remove from heat. While milk is heating, in a large mixer bowl, combine egg yolks, sugar and salt. Beat at high speed 3 to 4 minutes or until mixture is thick and pale. Gradually whisk into hot milk. Return pan to low heat. Cook, stirring constantly, until mixture thickly coats the back of a metal spoon. Remove from heat; whisk in rum or liqueur. Strain custard through a fine sieve into a medium bowl. Cool at room temperature, stirring occasionally. Stir in vanilla. Place a piece of waxed paper directly on surface of custard. Refrigerate at least 4 hours before serving. May be refrigerated up to 5 days. Makes about 2-3/4 cups.

Suzette Sauce

Buy the best marmalade you can afford for this luscious sauce named after the famous crepe dessert.

2 cups sweet-orange marmalade
1/4 cup orange-flavored liqueur

1/3 cup brandy
1/4 cup firm cold butter, cut in 6 pieces

In a small saucepan, combine marmalade, liqueur and brandy. Cook over medium heat, stirring occasionally, until marmalade melts and mixture is blended. Remove from heat. Add butter; stir quickly until butter melts. Serve barely warm or at room temperature. Makes about 2-2/3 cups.

Raspberry Jewel Sauce

Drizzle this brilliant sauce over lemon sherbet for a visually stunning and delicious finale!

2 (10-oz.) pkgs. thawed frozen raspberries
in syrup
1 tablespoon cornstarch
1/8 teaspoon salt

1 tablespoon lemon juice
2 tablespoons Chambord liqueur, Framboise
or kirsch, if desired

Strain syrup from 1 package of raspberries into a blender. Place berries in a small bowl; cover and refrigerate. Add second package of raspberries with their syrup to blender; process until smooth. Strain through a fine sieve into a small bowl. In a small saucepan, combine cornstarch and salt. Slowly add 1/4 cup raspberry puree; stir until perfectly smooth. Stir in remaining puree and lemon juice. Bring mixture to a boil over medium heat, stirring occasionally. Cook, stirring frequently, 3 minutes or until thickened and clear. Remove from heat. Stir in liqueur, if desired. Cool at room temperature, stirring occasionally. Cover and refrigerate up to 1 week. Before serving, stir in reserved raspberries. Makes about 1-1/2 cups.

Fudge Velvet Sauce

Sinfully thick, this seductive sauce is delectable over orange or cherry ice cream!

1/2 cup unsweetened cocoa,
preferably Dutch process
1 cup sugar

1/8 teaspoon salt
3/4 cup whipping cream
2 tablespoons butter

In a medium, heavy saucepan, combine cocoa, sugar and salt; stir until cocoa is no longer lumpy. Gradually stir in cream. Bring mixture to a boil over medium heat, stirring constantly. Reduce heat to low. Cook 2 minutes, stirring frequently. Remove from heat. Add butter; whisk until melted. Serve warm or at room temperature. Sauce will thicken as it cools. Cover and refrigerate up to 1 month. To reheat after refrigeration, warm in top of a double boiler over simmering water. Makes about 1-1/3 cups.

Shown clockwise starting at top right: Sugar-Nut Crumble, page 146; Fruit-Cream Chemise, page 102; Toasted Coconut, page 145; Suzette Sauce, above; Praline Crunch, page 145; Raspberry Jewel Sauce, above; and Candied Orange Zest, page 143.

Almond Cream

Especially good with warm fruit desserts and baked puddings!

1/2 pint whipping cream (1 cup)	**2 tablespoons powdered sugar**
2 drops almond extract	**1 tablespoon amaretto liqueur**
1/4 teaspoon freshly grated lemon zest	**1/4 cup toasted ground almonds**

In a small mixer bowl, beat cream, almond extract and lemon zest until soft peaks form. Add powdered sugar and liqueur; beat until stiff. Gently fold in almonds. Spoon or pipe into a pretty glass serving bowl. Refrigerate. Makes about 2-1/2 cups.

Fluffy Hard Sauce   *Photo on page 83.*

This delicious paradox is lightened with the addition of beaten egg whites.

1-1/2 cups powdered sugar	**1 teaspoon vanilla extract**
1/3 cup butter, softened	**2 to 3 tablespoons brandy**
1/8 teaspoon salt	**2 egg whites, room temperature**
1 egg yolk	**1/4 teaspoon cream of tartar**

Set aside 2 tablespoons powdered sugar. In a small mixer bowl, beat remaining powdered sugar, butter and salt until light and fluffy. Add egg yolk and vanilla; beat 1 minute. Add brandy, 1 tablespoon at a time, beating 1 minute after each addition. Mixture will separate unless beaten thoroughly after each addition of liquid. Set sugar mixture aside. In a small mixer bowl, beat egg whites and cream of tartar to soft-peak stage. Beating constantly, gradually add reserved 2 table-spoons powdered sugar. Continue beating until whites are glossy and firm. Fold egg-white mixture, 1/3 at a time, into butter mixture. Spoon into a glass compote or sauce boat. Cover and refrigerate at least 3 hours. May be refrigerated up to 3 days. Makes about 2 cups.

Variation
Traditional Hard Sauce: Beat all of powdered sugar with butter and salt. Omit egg whites and cream of tartar. Spoon into a decorative 1-1/2-cup mold. Refrigerate 4 hours or until firm. When ready to serve, dip mold into very hot water for 15 seconds; unmold onto a serving plate.

Chocolate-Sour-Cream Topping

Wonderful on chocolate cheesecakes, pies or cakes—makes a great dip for strawberries!

1/2 pint dairy sour cream (1 cup)	**2 teaspoons cocoa, preferably Dutch process**
3 tablespoons powdered sugar	**1 teaspoon vanilla extract**

In a medium bowl, combine all ingredients; stir until smooth. Makes 1 cup.

White-Chocolate Mousse with Raspberry Jewel Sauce, page 120, and Black-Magic Mousse, page 119.

Black-Satin Sauce

This luxurious sauce epitomizes what many people strive to be—thin and rich!

1/2 cup light corn syrup
1 cup sugar
1/8 teaspoon salt
1/4 cup brandy, Kahlúa or other coffee-
  or orange-flavored liqueur or water

5 oz. unsweetened chocolate,
  coarsely chopped
3/4 cup whipping cream
1 teaspoon vanilla extract

In a medium saucepan, combine corn syrup, sugar, salt and brandy, liqueur or water. Bring to a boil over medium heat. Remove from heat. Add chocolate; stir until melted. Gradually stir in cream. Return to medium-low heat. Cook 4 minutes, stirring constantly; do not let boil. Remove from heat. Cool to room temperature; stir in vanilla. Serve slightly warm or at room temperature. Refrigerate leftover sauce up to 2 weeks. To reheat, stir over low heat until desired thickness. Makes about 2-1/2 cups.

Variations
Chocolate-Orange Sauce: Add finely grated zest of 1 medium orange to corn-syrup mixture before bringing to a boil. Substitute 1/4 cup thawed frozen orange-juice concentrate for 1/4 cup of the cream.
Chocolate-Mint Sauce: Add 1 teaspoon mint extract to finished sauce.
Chocolate-Raspberry Sauce: Reduce sugar to 2/3 cup. Substitute 1 (10-ounce) package thawed frozen raspberries and their syrup for cream.
Mocha Sauce: Add 3 tablespoons instant coffee powder or granules to 1/4 cup *hot* water before adding to corn-syrup mixture.

Sweet-Cherry Sauce

Spoon over ice cream, then top with whipped cream and grated chocolate for a delicious cherry sundae.

1 (15-1/2-oz.) can pitted, dark,
  sweet cherries in heavy syrup
Water
1-1/2 tablespoons cornstarch

1/4 cup sugar
2 teaspoons lemon juice
1/4 teaspoon almond extract
1/4 cup kirsch or additional water

Drain cherries, reserving syrup; set aside cherries. Add enough water to syrup to equal 1-1/3 cups liquid; set aside. In a medium saucepan, combine cornstarch and sugar; stir until lumps have disappeared. Gradually stir in 2 tablespoons cherry liquid; stir until blended. Slowly stir in remaining cherry liquid and lemon juice. Cook over medium heat, stirring constantly, until mixture comes to a boil. Cook 3 minutes, stirring occasionally. Remove from heat. Stir in reserved cherries, almond extract and kirsch or water. Cool at room temperature, stirring occasionally. Cover and refrigerate until ready to use. May be refrigerated up to 1 week. Makes about 2-1/4 cups.

Variation
Sweet-Cherry Cheesecake Topping: Reduce cherry liquid to 1 cup. Refrigerate 1 hour or until cold before spooning over cheesecake.

Praline-Rum Sauce

Serve over ice cream, pound cake . . . even on pancakes! Or, omit nuts and use as a dip for fresh fruit.

1 cup packed brown sugar	1/2 teaspoon salt
1/2 cup light corn syrup	1/2 cup dark rum
1/4 cup butter	1/4 cup whipping cream
3/4 cup toasted finely chopped pecans	1/2 teaspoon vanilla extract

In a medium saucepan, combine brown sugar, corn syrup, butter, pecans, salt and 1/4 cup rum. Cook over high heat, stirring constantly, until mixture comes to a boil. Reduce heat to medium. Cover and cook 3 minutes. Remove cover; cook without stirring until syrup reaches 260F (125C) on a candy thermometer. Or, test by spooning a drop of sauce into chilled water; sauce should form a rigid but pliable ball. Pour sauce into a medium bowl; let stand 15 minutes. Gradually add cream, vanilla and remaining 1/4 cup rum; stir until blended. Cool to room temperature. Cover and refrigerate up to 2 weeks. Serve at room temperature or slightly warmed. Makes about 2 cups.

Hot Caramel Sauce

Velvety rich and gooey-good—definitely not for people wearing braces!

1-1/3 cups packed brown sugar	1/3 cup butter
3/4 cup whipping cream	1/8 teaspoon salt
3/4 cup light corn syrup	1-1/2 teaspoons vanilla extract

In a medium, heavy saucepan, combine all ingredients except vanilla. Cook over medium-high heat, stirring occasionally, until mixture reaches 230F (110C) on a candy thermometer or mixture forms a 2-inch thread when dropped from a spoon. Remove from heat; stir in vanilla. Cool 30 minutes. Stir before serving. Cover and refrigerate leftovers up to 1 week. To reheat, stir over low heat until desired consistency. Or, reheat in microwave at 50% power 2 to 4 minutes. Makes about 2 cups.

Brandy-Butter Sauce

A hearty dollop of butter gives this sensuous sauce a smooth and creamy finish.

1 cup sugar	1/3 cup firm cold butter, cut in 5 pieces
1/2 cup brandy	
1 (3-inch) cinnamon stick, broken in 4 pieces	

In a small saucepan, combine sugar, brandy and cinnamon. Cook, without stirring, over medium heat until mixture reaches 230F (110C) on a candy thermometer or mixture forms a 2-inch thread when dropped from a spoon. Remove from heat. Remove and discard cinnamon. Add butter; stir briskly until butter melts and sauce is smooth. Pour into a small pitcher. Serve warm or at room temperature. Sauce thickens as it cools. Cover and refrigerate leftover sauce up to 1 week. To reheat refrigerated sauce, stir over low heat until sugar crystals dissolve. Makes about 1 cup.

Variation
Hot-Buttered-Rum Sauce: Substitute 1/2 cup rum for 1/2 cup brandy.

Spirited Whipped Cream

The amount of sugar needed will depend on the sweetness of the liqueur you add.

1/2 pint whipping cream (1 cup)
1 to 3 tablespoons powdered sugar
1 to 3 tablespoons Grand Marnier,
 amaretto liqueur, Kahlúa, brandy,
 rum, or other liqueur or liquor

Place a small mixer bowl and beaters in freezer 15 minutes before preparing cream. Beat cream at high speed until the consistency of pudding. Add powdered sugar; beat until cream forms soft peaks. Gradually drizzle in liqueur or liquor, beating constantly until liquid is incorporated and cream is desired consistency. Makes about 2 cups.

Variations

To halve recipe, use 1/2 cup whipping cream, 1-1/2 teaspoons to 1-1/2 tablespoons powdered sugar, and 1-1/2 teaspoons to 1-1/2 tablespoons liqueur or liquor or 1/4 teaspoon extract of your choice.
Plain Whipped Cream: Substitute 1/2 teaspoon vanilla extract for liqueur or liquor.
Honey Whipped Cream: Substitute 1 to 2 tablespoons honey for liqueur or liquor.
Orange Whipped Cream: Substitute 2 tablespoons thawed frozen orange-juice concentrate for liqueur or liquor.
Chocolate Whipped Cream: In a small mixer bowl, stir together 2 tablespoons unsweetened cocoa and 2 tablespoons powdered sugar until blended. Slowly stir in whipping cream. Refrigerate 30 minutes before beating as directed above.

Crème Fraîche

A homemade version of the naturally thick and tangy French cream. The early American cousin to Crème Frâiche was called clabbered cream.

1/2 pint whipping cream (1 cup), preferably   **2 tablespoons buttermilk**
 not ultra-pasteurized

Combine cream and buttermilk in a glass jar with a screw top. Secure lid; shake 15 seconds. Set aside at room temperature 24 hours or until very thick. If using ultra-pasteurized cream, mixture may be less creamy when thickened. Stir once or twice during 24 hours. Cream will thicken faster if the room is very warm. Refrigerate at least 4 hours before using. May be refrigerated up to 2 weeks. Serve over fresh fruit, baked puddings or fruit pies. Makes about 1 cup.

Variations

Sweetened Crème Fraîche: Add 1 to 2 tablespoons powdered sugar to cream mixture before shaking.
Chocolate Crème Fraîche: In bottom of a glass jar, combine 2 tablespoons each unsweetened cocoa and sugar. Add 2 tablespoons buttermilk; stir until smooth. Add cream. Continue as directed above.
Honeyed Crème Fraîche: Stir 1 to 2 tablespoons honey into Crème Fraîche just before refrigerating.
Spiced Crème Fraîche: Add 1/4 teaspoon *each* ground cinnamon and ground nutmeg to cream mixture before shaking; continue as directed above. Or, stir 1 to 2 tablespoons finely chopped crystallized ginger into Crème Fraîche just before refrigerating.

INDEX

Index

Metric Chart

Comparison to Metric Measure

When You Know	Symbol	Multiply By	To Find	Symbol
teaspoons	tsp	5.0	milliliters	ml
tablespoons	tbsp	15.0	milliliters	ml
fluid ounces	fl. oz.	30.0	milliliters	ml
cups	c	0.24	liters	l
pints	pt.	0.47	liters	l
quarts	qt.	0.95	liters	l
ounces	oz.	28.0	grams	g
pounds	lb.	0.45	kilograms	kg
Fahrenheit	F	5/9 (after subtracting 32)	Celsius	C

Fahrenheit to Celsius

F	C
200—205	95
220—225	105
245—250	120
275	135
300—305	150
325—330	165
345—350	175
370—375	190
400—405	205
425—430	220
445—450	230
470—475	245
500	260

Liquid Measure to Liters

1/4 cup	=	0.06 liters
1/2 cup	=	0.12 liters
3/4 cup	=	0.18 liters
1 cup	=	0.24 liters
1-1/4 cups	=	0.3 liters
1-1/2 cups	=	0.36 liters
2 cups	=	0.48 liters
2-1/2 cups	=	0.6 liters
3 cups	=	0.72 liters
3-1/2 cups	=	0.84 liters
4 cups	=	0.96 liters
4-1/2 cups	=	1.08 liters
5 cups	=	1.2 liters
5-1/2 cups	=	1.32 liters

Liquid Measure to Milliliters

1/4 teaspoon	=	1.25 milliliters
1/2 teaspoon	=	2.5 milliliters
3/4 teaspoon	=	3.75 milliliters
1 teaspoon	=	5.0 milliliters
1-1/4 teaspoons	=	6.25 milliliters
1-1/2 teaspoons	=	7.5 milliliters
1-3/4 teaspoons	=	8.75 milliliters
2 teaspoons	=	10.0 milliliters
1 tablespoon	=	15.0 milliliters
2 tablespoons	=	30.0 milliliters